Palgrave Studies in International Relations

Series Editors:

Knud Erik Jørgensen, Department of Political Science, University of Aarhus, Denmark

Audie Klotz, Department of Political Science, Maxwell School of Citizenship and Public Affairs, Syracuse University, USA

Palgrave Studies in International Relations, produced in association with the ECPR Standing Group for International Relations, will provide students and scholars with the best theoretically-informed scholarship on the global issues of our time. Edited by Knud Erik Jørgensen and Audie Klotz, this new book series will comprise cutting-edge monographs and edited collections which bridge schools of thought and cross the boundaries of conventional fields of study.

Titles include:

Mathias Albert, Lars-Erik Cederman and Alexander Wendt (*editors*)
NEW SYSTEMS THEORIES OF WORLD POLITICS

Robert Ayson
HEDLEY BULL AND THE ACCOMODATION OF POWER

Gideon Baker (*editor*)
HOSPITALITY AND WORLD POLITICS

Joshua Baron
GREAT POWER PEACE AND AMERICAN PRIMACY
The Origins and Future of a New International Order

William Clapton
RISK AND HIERARCHY IN INTERNATIONAL SOCIETY
Liberal Interventionism in the Post-Cold War Era

Toni Erskine and Richard Ned Lebow (*editors*)
TRAGEDY AND INTERNATIONAL RELATIONS

Rebekka Friedman, Kevork Oskanian and Ramon Pachedo Pardo (*editors*)
AFTER LIBERALISM?
The Future of Liberalism in International Relations

Geir Hønneland
BORDERLAND RUSSIANS
Identity, Narrative and International Relations

Niv Horesh and Emilian Kavalski (*editors*)
ASIAN THOUGHT ON CHINA's CHANGING INTERNATIONAL RELATIONS

Beate Jahn
LIBERAL INTERNATIONALISM
Theory, History, Practice

Oliver Kessler, Rodney Bruce Hall, Cecelia Lynch and Nicholas G. Onuf (*editors*)
ON RULES, POLITICS AND KNOWLEDGE
Friedrich Kratochwil, International Relations, and Domestic Affairs

Patrick Mello
DEMOCRATIC PARTICIPATION IN ARMED CONFLICT
Military Involvement in Kosovo, Afghanistan, and Iraq

Palgrave Studies In International Relations Series
Series Standing Order ISBN 978–0–230–20063–0

You can receive future titles in this series as they are published by placing a standing order. Please contact your bookseller or, in case of difficulty, write to us at the address below with your name and address, the title of the series and the ISBN quoted above.

Customer Services Department, Macmillan Distribution Ltd, Houndmills, Basingstoke, Hampshire RG21 6XS, England

Power, Information Technology, and International Relations Theory

The Power and Politics of US Foreign Policy and the Internet

Daniel R. McCarthy
Lecturer in International Relations at the University of Melbourne, Australia

© Daniel R. McCarthy 2015

All rights reserved. No reproduction, copy or transmission of this publication may be made without written permission.

No portion of this publication may be reproduced, copied or transmitted save with written permission or in accordance with the provisions of the Copyright, Designs and Patents Act 1988, or under the terms of any licence permitting limited copying issued by the Copyright Licensing Agency, Saffron House, 6–10 Kirby Street, London EC1N 8TS.

Any person who does any unauthorized act in relation to this publication may be liable to criminal prosecution and civil claims for damages.

The author has asserted his right to be identified as the author of this work in accordance with the Copyright, Designs and Patents Act 1988.

First published 2015 by
PALGRAVE MACMILLAN

Palgrave Macmillan in the UK is an imprint of Macmillan Publishers Limited, registered in England, company number 785998, of Houndmills, Basingstoke, Hampshire RG21 6XS.

Palgrave Macmillan in the US is a division of St Martin's Press LLC,
175 Fifth Avenue, New York, NY 10010.

Palgrave Macmillan is the global academic imprint of the above companies and has companies and representatives throughout the world.

Palgrave® and Macmillan® are registered trademarks in the United States, the United Kingdom, Europe and other countries

ISBN: 978–1–137–30689–0

This book is printed on paper suitable for recycling and made from fully managed and sustained forest sources. Logging, pulping and manufacturing processes are expected to conform to the environmental regulations of the country of origin.

A catalogue record for this book is available from the British Library.

A catalog record for this book is available from the Library of Congress.

Contents

Acknowledgements	viii
List of Acronyms	x

1	**Introduction**	1
	The conceptual place of technology in International Relations	1
	Technology, facets of power and 'the International'	6
	American foreign policy and Internet politics	9
	Analysing policy rhetoric: discourse analysis and foreign policy narratives	12
	Plan of the book	15
2	**Power and Information Technology: Determinism, Agency, and Constructivism**	19
	Introduction	19
	Technological instrumentalism: emphasizing agency?	21
	Technological essentialism: the power of objects	28
	Techno-optimists: progress without power	29
	Techno-pessimists and structuralist determinism	30
	The social construction of information technology: between essentialism and instrumentalism	32
	Power, momentum, and the political economy of technology	35
	Conclusion	41
3	**A Historical Materialist Approach to Technological Power in International Relations**	43
	Introduction	43
	Marxist technological instrumentalism	44
	Evolving towards socialism: optimistic Marxist technological essentialism	45
	Degenerating into barbarism: pessimistic technological essentialism	47
	A critical theory of technology	50
	Power, information technology and 'the International'	55
	Structural power: rights and resources in technological design	56

v

Productive power: defining technological design 59
States and capitals in the international politics of
   technology 62
The institutional power of material culture 66
Conclusion 70

4 US Foreign Relations and the Institutional Power of the Internet 74
Introduction 74
The Open Door tradition 75
Bush and Obama: changes within a liberal constellation 80
Free markets, free societies, and the free flow of
   information 82
Pursuing net dividends: saturation and market expansion 86
Opening doors at a distance: the power of the Internet 88
Disconnection costs: rejecting Internet values 92
The Internet as a market and the uneven global economy 97
Conclusion: closure and the Open Door 99

5 Pursuing Technological Closure: Symbolic Politics, Legitimacy, and Internet Filtering 101
Introduction 101
Human rights and Internet openness 102
'21st century democracy promotion' 111
'With great code comes great responsibility' 117
Conclusion 120

6 The Narration of Innovation in US Internet Policy 122
Introduction 122
Property rights and models of software innovation 124
Linking property, the private sector, and innovation 127
Between politics and piracy: locating the identity of
   the private sector 131
The threat of Internet piracy 135
Not by narrative alone: technological closure and
   structural power 142
Conclusion 146

7 Conclusion 148
Historical materialism and the international politics
   of technology 151
The future of US power after Snowden 154
International Relations and technology: future directions 158

Appendix: Discourse Analysis Guide	162
Notes	164
Bibliography	175
Index	215

Acknowledgements

I have acquired many intellectual debts over the development of this project since this work began in the Department of International Politics, Aberystwyth University. I would like to thank the Economic and Social Research Council, the Department of International Politics Aberystwyth University, Caroline and Terry Adams, and the British International Studies Association for their financial support for this research, without which none of this could have been undertaken. Many thanks to Jeff Bridoux, Campbell Craig, Toni Erskine, Alastair Finlan, Richard Jackson, Luis Pedro, Roger Scully, Marie Breen Smyth, Richard Rathbone and Nick Wheeler for their helpful comments and advice. Michael Foley, James Vaughan, and Michael C. Williams provided excellent doctoral supervision, and I hope this book meets some measure of their own scholarly rigour. Ronald Deibert was kind enough to grant me his time, along with the opportunity to preview of some future arguments while I was a visiting doctoral fellow at the University of Toronto. Andrew Linklater and John Dumbrell's examination of the thesis was invaluable in addressing its gaps and shortcomings.

Parts of this book were written while I was an ESRC postdoctoral fellow in the Department of International Relations at the University of Sussex. The department was very welcoming, and I appreciated the opportunity to present facets of this current work to the PM Reading Group – thanks to Sam Knafo, Benno Teschke, and the PM group as a whole. Special thanks are due to Justin Rosenberg for allowing me to take up his busy time discussing some of the arguments in the book.

Thanks to Miles Townes and Matthew Fluck for reading parts of the manuscript and making excellent suggestions on how to improve it. John Dumbrell generously read and commented upon part of the manuscript after having read the entire thesis – many thanks for his continued interest in this project. A late conversation with Monroe Price and Ben Wagner proved very helpful. I would also like to thank the anonymous reviewers and the series editors, whose comments were very helpful in revising a baggy thesis into a tighter book and forced me to clarify some of my arguments. The remaining errors are, of course, my own. Thanks must also be extended to the editorial team at Palgrave Macmillan, with Harriet Barker being particularly patient.

My partner, Lisa Denney, read the book as a whole and brought her sharp intellect to bear on the work – it is much clearer as a result – and has been a constant source of support and encouragement. As we begin a new phase in our life, I look forward to many years of repaying this debt in particular.

Permission to reprint parts of 'Open Networks and the Open Door: American Foreign Policy and the Narration of the Internet' *Foreign Policy Analysis* 7, 89–111 and 'The Meaning of Materiality: reconsidering the materiality of Gramscian IR' *Review of International Studies* 37, 1215–1234, has been granted by Wiley and Cambridge University Press, respectively.

List of Acronyms

ANT	Actor Network Theory
ARPA	Advanced Research Projects Agency
BBG	Broadcasting Board of Governors
BSA	Business Software Alliance
CDA	Critical Discourse Analysis
DARPA	Defense Advanced Research Projects Agency
DFI	Digital Freedom Initiative
DMCA	Digital Millennium Copyright Act
DNS	Domain Name System
EEB	Bureau of Economic, Energy and Business Affairs
FOSS	Free and Open Source Software
GIFT	Global Internet Freedom Task Force
GNU-GPL	GNU's Not Unix-General Public License
GOFA	Global Online Freedom Act
HTML	Hypertext Mark-up Language
ICANN	Internet Corporation for Assigned Names and Numbers
ICT	Information Communications Technology
IETF	Internet Engineering Task Force
IIPA	International Intellectual Property Alliance
IPR	Intellectual Property Rights
IPv6	Internet Protocol version Six
ISP	Internet Service Provider
OECD	Organisation for Economic Cooperation and Development
ONR	Office of Naval Research
RFC	Request for Comments
SCOT	Social Construction of Technology
SIIA	Software & Information Industry Association
STS	Science and Technology Studies
TCP/IP	Transmission Control Protocol/ Internet Protocol
TRIPs	Trade Related Intellectual Property Rights
UDHR	Universal Declaration of Human Rights
USTR	United States Trade Representative
VoA	Voice of America
VOIP	Voice over Internet Protocol
WSIS	World Summit on the Information Society
WTO	World Trade Organization

1
Introduction

The conceptual place of technology in International Relations

Technology has been central to the discipline of International Relations (IR) throughout its history. The formal inception of the discipline emerged in the aftermath of the First World War, in which the horrific destructive potential of modern military weaponry had been amply illustrated. The industrialization of warfare and the utilization of the most advanced technological artefacts for the slaughter of a generation formed the background for the varied intellectual responses that the war engendered, ranging from institution building to reinforcement of the balance of power.[1] Alfred Zimmern, Leonard Woolf and Norman Angell, central figures in the early development of the field, emphasized industrialization as driving the process of international integration. It was this integration that made war both terribly destructive and pointless, as interdependence altered the material benefits bestowed by conquest. Zimmern – holder of the world's first chair in International Politics, created in Aberystwyth in 1919 – stressed the centrality of industrialization and modern communications technologies in the creation of the discipline of International Relations itself (Osiander 1998: 424). For Zimmern, international integration was a 'result of technological innovation, more specifically the increasing speed and ease and hence volume of global communications' (Osiander 1998: 417; Zimmern 1928: 154). Technological change formed a central conceptual and empirical referent point for interwar 'idealists'.

During the Second World War, and in its aftermath, the study of International Relations was similarly shaped by the discipline's reaction to technological developments, as Auschwitz and the atom bomb brought about a new realization of the destructive impact of human technological capabilities. Hans Morgenthau, perhaps the central figure in shaping the field of International Relations after the war, stressed that technological development was as destructive as it was productive (Morgenthau 1946). Reinhold Niebhur similarly noted that, while technological development had made a 'universal community imperative', it had in turn also provided the potential to destroy this nascent community (Niebhur 1944: 160, quoted in Craig 2003: 50). The intellectual trajectory of IR during the early Cold War was shaped by the encounter with humankind's newfound ability to destroy all life on earth through thermonuclear war (Craig 2003; Sylvest 2013). In the 1970s the transnationalization of production, enabled by shipping containerization and the continued spread of communications technologies, shifted the focus of the field from a concern with Armageddon towards a reconsideration of global politics and power in conditions of intense interdependence (Keohane and Nye 1989 [1977]). As the threat of nuclear exterminism allegedly receded in the post–Cold War era, the discipline engaged with the potential and impact of newly emerging information-communications technologies, from satellites to faxes to the Internet, a revolution in military affairs that seemed to alter the experience of warfare (at least for Western publics) and the potentially catastrophic environmental consequences of technological development and industrialization. The past decade has seen the re-emergence of weapons of mass destruction as a central fulcrum for the field, as threats of inter-state nuclear war and non-state nuclear violence appeared again as issues of concern. Biotechnology, robotics and big data look set to continue to shape both the discipline and its subject.

Yet, despite the centrality of technological growth in shaping IR's subject matter, conceptualization of technology within the discipline has been quite limited. While contestation over the meaning and practice of scientific knowledge has been at the centre of IR theory debates, the politics of technology are all too often treated as exogenous to the concerns of IR theorists – an environmental condition or set of instrumental possibilities rather than the product of political contestation in which the International itself is central. The politics of technological design, and thus the creation of the technological possibilities central to theoretical work throughout the history of the field, has largely remained on the sidelines.

Were the technological not central to various other concepts in International Relations Theory this gap may not matter: technology could be safely ignored, and a consideration of anarchy, sovereignty, power, institutions and systemic interactions could continue without harm. However, the technological is central both to these concepts and to the practices they attempt to grasp. As recent work in the field has noted, nuclear weapons may alter the historical condition of anarchy, pushing global politics towards the development of a world state (Deudney 2008; Craig 2003, 2009). Anarchy is thereby reconceptualized, not as a transhistorical condition, but as an historically limited form of interaction between political communities constituted by specific technological capabilities. Sovereignty, anarchy's attendant, is often viewed as undergoing processes of disaggregation due to the possibilities presented by information technology (Held et al. 1999; Scholte 2005). Sovereignty is, as a result, conceptualized as a condition exercised by multiple actors in territorially overlapping jurisdictions that are dependent on technological development occurring in directions that support these changes. Indices of power have often taken technological resources as central to the measurement of the 'effective power' of states, arguing that 'power is nothing more than specific assets or resources that are available to a state' (Mearsheimer 2001: 55). This stress on technology as one of the material resources that define power – the only shared characteristic across disparate Realist conceptions of power (Schmidt 2005: 528) – has, in many ways, defined our understanding of technology as a form of power in global politics, to the extent that scholars arguing for alternative perspectives effectively cede this ground to a Realist understanding (Guzzini 2005). Finally, the nature of various international societies is claimed to be constituted by the interaction present in the system, a function of the technological capacities present at any given time (Buzan and Little 2000). Approaches that seek to develop comparative historical sociologies of distinct international societies rely upon either an implicit or explicit understanding of how technology structures these societies. The place of technology is central, both to the conduct of international politics and to the manner in which we understand and analyse this conduct.

Consequently, excavating the discipline's treatment of technology presents itself as a necessary task. Absent this consideration, the precise nature of our concepts and the theories that encompass them remain incomplete. It is for this reason that, in conjunction with a wider reconsideration of the role that science has played in constituting IR – and the social sciences more broadly (Bell 2009) – over the past decade the field has engaged, sparingly but increasingly, with the politics of technological design and construction, drawing upon Science and Technology Studies (STS) and the philosophy of technology.[2] Alongside more general treatments of the technological (Fritsch 2011; Herrera 2006; McCarthy 2011b; McCarthy 2013; Sylvest 2013), and in an effort to deepen our understanding of how material objects are created and how they structure global political conduct, studies in IR have examined the politics of information technologies (Carr 2012; Herrera 2002, 2006; Hansen and Nissenbaum 2009; McCarthy 2011a; Townes 2012), nuclear weapons (Herrera 2006; Peoples 2009; Sylvest 2013; Wyn Jones 1999), technology and changing forms of warfare (Bousquet 2009; Holmqvist 2013; Sauer and Schornig 2012), border technologies (Salter 2004; Scheel 2013), and naval warfare (Mukunda 2010).[3] This present work stresses that technological development is not deterministic: it does not operate according to any intrinsic rationale and does not, as a result, follow any linear path. Instead, technological development is a deeply conflictual process with no predetermined outcomes. At a given moment of technological development, multiple potential design paths are present; the choice of any given path is the product of politics.

This book is part of the wider rethinking of technology in International Relations Theory and international relations practice. It seeks to contribute to this evolving body of work through a theoretical reconsideration of the relationship, in IR theory, between power and technology, arguing that technological artefacts must be considered as institutions with specific cultural norms and values embedded within their physical makeup. Technological objects share the characteristics of social institutions in general, in that they have formal 'routines, procedures, norms and conventions embedded' in their organizational structure (Hall and Taylor 1996: 938).[4] As institutions, they structure paths of historical development – the QWERTY keyboard is an oft-used example – and shape actors' interests and identities. Technologies are as social and political as any other human institution. For this reason, our understanding of the material aspects of power should be extended beyond a narrow concern with non-human objects as assets or resources. To this end, the book argues that technological artefacts are a form of institutional power – power at a spatio-temporal distance. This requires both rethinking how we understand technology and, as a result, how we think about technology as a form of social power. First, noting technology as socially constructed recognizes that social power relations are important in the making of design decisions. Levels of hierarchy or anarchy, democratic governance, legal institutionalization, and normative integration within an international system will thereby influence the types of technological institutions created at any given moment in time. In this manner, and to an extent largely unrecognized by Science and Technology Studies, international relations play a central role in the politics of technology, generating particular forms of technological development (including distinct national trajectories) and the manner in which these developments do or do not diffuse.[5] Second, technological objects are not merely resources in the manner in which bombs or bullets are normally understood as power resources. Rather, technological objects have a social content that structures forms of political organization and their attendant politics of identity, material reproduction, and geopolitical manifestations.

These theoretical arguments are given empirical bite through focusing upon the politics of information-communications technologies and the Internet within American foreign policy. The technological architecture of the Internet allows for the creation, conveyance and display of media content – allowing for representation to occur, or not, within the boundaries the technology sets. In this way the Internet is an end as much as a means – the medium does indeed express a message (McLuhan 1997 [1964]; Innis 1972; Deibert 1997).[6] Moreover, information technology is central to many of the core concerns of the discipline of IR, such as: the changing nature of global governance and transnational regulation; the transformation of the state; the extent, nature and possible limits of democracy; and the nature of hegemonic transitions within the international system. Far from being a narrow-issue area (contra Mueller 2010) the politics of information technology touch upon a broad terrain.[7] The contestation over the technological architecture of information networks determines how information and communications technologies (ICTs) contribute to these broader processes.

This focus is partially driven by a dissatisfaction with the dominant treatment of information technology as a form of power in IR, although, as noted, this situation is changing. Far too often, when investigating major changes occurring in the global system, scholars have attributed causal agency to information technology (Drezner 2007: 91). As discussed in greater detail in Chapter 2, such an approach casts technology in a deterministic mould. Barring the adoption of a radical ontology that attributes agency to inanimate objects – the stance taken by Actor-Network Theory, purposefully avoided here[8] – the formulation is unsatisfactory. Information technology does not possess intention. The attribution of agency to technology is an example of fetishism, a form of alienation that an historical materialist approach is well placed to examine. The drive behind this aspect of the book is, in some sense, a classic ideology critique of dominant approaches to technology in International Relations. If human agency and intentionality in crafting global politics are to be adequately acknowledged, the power of information technology should be examined as a human power, a product of historically specific social relations and created in historically specific ways, with temporally restricted (not universal) qualities and characteristics.

Of course, exposure of fetishism cannot be the sole task of an interrogation of information technology in international politics. While the socially constructed nature of information needs to be stressed within a discipline still prone to determinism, a critique of fetishism soon reaches its limits. IR theory needs to develop clear conceptual and analytical frameworks with which to investigate how information technology is developed and implemented, why it is developed and implemented in this manner, and the effects of these processes on the structure of global politics – to date, only the third of these has been of central interest to the field. Important steps have been taken in this direction within IR and in the amorphous field of Internet Studies (DeNardis 2009, 2012; Mueller 2010), but so far there have been fewer attempts to outline how the development of technology in international politics is related to one of the core categories of disciplinary work: power (Deudney 2008: 80–81). The resources for such a project are present within IR theory and social theory without having to invent neologisms such as 'network power' or 'smart power'. As institutions, technological artefacts can be analysed as the product of social power relations using concepts with which IR scholars are quite familiar: concepts such as structural, productive, institutional, and coercive power (Barnett and Duvall 2005). In this sense, the present study is not aiming to add to an already heavily burdened and complex conceptualization of power in the field. Instead, the aim is to rethink how technological objects fit within existing IR frameworks. As noted at the end of Chapter 2, one of the primary tasks in this project is embedding Internet scholarship in existing social theory with greater depth and clarity.

Technology, facets of power and 'the International'

The approach taken here is rooted in Marxist historical materialism, treating this literature in a catholic manner by drawing, in equal measure, upon neo-Trotskyism, Political Marxism and Gramscian scholarship (Wood 1981; Rosenberg 1994; Rupert 1995; Robinson 1996; Teschke 2003; Lacher 2006; Bieler and Morton 2008; Anievas 2011). This approach stresses the centrality of social property relations in generating specific strategies of reproduction for social actors – capitalists require certain profit rates to remain capitalists, and so forth – that shape the policies of state apparatus and, subsequently, the form of geopolitical relations in capitalist modernity (Teschke 2003; Lacher 2006). Examining the actions of the US state is more precisely comprehended as an examination of the actions of social forces that dominate the state apparatus (conceived of as an institution). Lest the pragmatic choice of statist language in the following obscure this point: for our purposes this is an examination of the policies and interests of American capitalism as narrated by its state managers, who articulate a holistic understanding of capitalism as a *political* economy, comprised of economic, political and ideological aspects.

While embedded within IR theory, however, the initial development of this approach in this book emerged not from IR theory but from a consideration of the literature within STS. Marxist IR theory has not outlined a clear theorization of the relationship between technology and power to a greater extent than any other approach in the discipline. Instead, the primary intellectual touchstone for the argument in this book is Andrew Feenberg's critical theory of technology (1991, 1999, 2002). Feenberg's work embeds the politics of technological development and design within a theory that emphasizes the importance of historical and structural aspects of social relations, in contrast to other scholarship within STS. As noted in Chapter 2, STS scholarship has a marked tendency towards the study of micro-political processes. The scholarship produced by such studies is empirically rich and methodologically rigorous. At the same time, however, there is a tendency in the field to neglect how social structures limit, and enable, some actors to undertake technological development – or the reasons why actors may push for some forms of development over others. With these thoughts in mind, this book argues that we should conceptualize the relationship between power, technology, and the International through a consideration of the interaction between structural, productive, and institutional power within an uneven and combined process of human social development. Again, technology is understood here as a form of institutional power. Technology as institutional power is created through struggles embedded within structural power relations – both necessary and contingent – and defined, given meaning, and ultimately closed off from further political contestation through the productive, symbolic power of discourse.

Historical social structures grant some actors significant social *power over* others. The historical materialist approach developed in the book outlines structural power as generated through structures of social property rights that grant some actors the right (and gives them the motivation) to develop technological artefacts, a right denied to others by virtue of property non-ownership. As a result, technological institutions reflect the aims and desires of actors empowered in this way, and will, in turn, express these values in their physical rules. The concept of structural power locates technological institutions within historical and social contexts. This study emphasizes the power of the American government to embed the values of a specific historical conjuncture within the Internet architecture.

Productive power is central to our analysis in order to grasp how technological institutions are given meaning and value in the international system. Actors draw upon cultural norms to create symbolic meanings that surround a given technology in order to give direction to its development, to argue that a technology should take one specific form rather than its possible alternatives. These symbolic politics also grant actors the ability to achieve 'technological closure', whereby the further development of technology becomes uncontroversial between social actors. This process – similar, in some respects, to the idea of 'securitization' in IR, which it may encompass (Buzan et al. 1998) – is central in securing the institutional power of technology for the long-term. Closure is necessary for technological objects to form part of our everyday background: it is central to technological reproduction. The meaning of the Internet in global politics does not currently meet this criterion. A variety of international actors, led by the United States, seek to achieve this consensus via their discursive power. Unless we attend to the centrality of symbolic politics, the achievement of technological path dependency often charted ably but incompletely by economic historians, will remain beyond our understanding. These two sets of power capacities allow some dominant actors to design and develop technological institutions. These institutions, in turn, play an important role in constraining (and enabling) social action by members of the institution: that is, by other actors employing the technology.

It is important that we locate these different facets of social power within a broader understanding of the international system that makes them possible. At times, treatments of the politics of Internet governance are disconnected from macro-processes. In this way, these approaches can mirror some of the limitations evident in the larger STS literature on which they draw (see Chapter 2). Underlying the consideration of technology and power in this book is an understanding of 'the International' – the presence of multiple political communities – as characterized by uneven and combined processes of social development (U&CD). The unevenness of social development across the international system means that certain political communities will develop more advanced forms of technology than other communities that exist with them contemporaneously. While technology transfer and recombination are focused upon in some economic history and economic sociology on national systems of innovation (Gerschenkron 1962; Nelson 1993; Freeman 1995) – with, possibly, shared roots in Trotsky's work (Selwyn 2011: 445) – and both deny a stagist, determinist conception of history, recent work in IR on U&CD integrates global politics as a *generative* aspect of explanation. The process of inter-societal interaction leads to the diffusion of advanced technologies to 'backward' states, either through the dynamics of geopolitical competition or through capital's requirement for new markets and new 'spatio-temporal fixes' (Harvey 2006 [1982]). As advanced technological objects are introduced into backward social contexts, they engender forms of combination shaped by the norms and biases of the objects themselves. This is the 'determinist moment' (McCarthy 2013) in the process of social development. Uneven and combined social development creates the possibility for technology to function as a form of institutional power. As we consider what generates American Internet policy, the diffusion of the network and its impact upon other states, these larger structural processes are present. The book thereby attempts to link up a macro-sociology of the International to specific policy practices.

American foreign policy and Internet politics

The theoretical discussion is applied here through an examination of the Internet as a form of institutional power that supports and furthers US foreign policy aims. The Internet is an essentially American invention (see Chapter 4). The values embedded within the network's hardware and software architectures reflect the context of its creation, expressing a liberal bias best encapsulated in the notion of a 'free flow of information'. Social actors who use the technology but seek to resist these values must pay a cost that the United States does not have to pay. Just as our concepts of power should take account of structural relations that are historically rooted and enduring, the analysis of American Internet policy presented here places it within a broader framework – that of the 'Open Door' tradition of American foreign policy. By locating US Internet policy discourse within a wider understanding of American grand strategy, a few aims are met. First, US policy becomes far more intelligible when located within the wider traditions of the American approach to foreign relations. Attempts to suggest that American policy is simply 'realpolitik' on the Internet (e.g., Manjikian 2010) cannot offer a clear account of why some policies are chosen over others. Realist approaches to Internet politics lack any social content, a criticism made of Realist IR Theory more generally (Rosenberg 1994, Teschke 2003, Ruggie 1983). Considering the social logic of American Internet policy makes it possible to comprehend, theoretically, US decisions and non-decisions.

Second, the divide between the American government and Western civil society organizations is recast once US policy is located as an expression of a drive for the 'Open Door'. The American government has promoted the growth and development of Western non-governmental organizations as part of its attempt to spread liberal democratic capitalist values internationally (Guilhot 2005; Robinson 1996; Sending and Neumann 2006). The United States does not control the actions of these actors – we are not in the realm of conspiracy theories here. Nevertheless, the United States promotes the growth and development of certain forms of global civil society in the belief that these groups will place pressure upon, and help to transform, authoritarian and non-democratic regimes. The project of creating liberal capitalist democracies – opening polities and opening markets – is advanced by US support for NGOs. As Inderjeet Parmar has noted, intellectuals within the American foreign policy establishment outline the development of transnational networks that intersect the international and the domestic as a central pillar in the spread of American power (Parmar 2009: 198; see, for example, Slaughter 2004). Internet governance is no different in this regard.

Third, understanding American foreign policy as the pursuit of a global 'Open Door' recasts the relationship between the US state and US capital. In the argument presented here, the state is not understood as an organization separate from and above domestic civil society (see Chapter 3). Instead, the state is depicted as an institution rooted in civil society, expressing the interests of dominant groups in that society while shaping the conduct of these groups in turn. This does not mean that the 'Open Door' is an 'economistic' policy. As this book makes clear, American Internet policy is designed to reproduce capitalist social relations in their economic *and* political aspects.

While illustrating the utility of the theoretical framework, this book is also intended as a contribution to the literature on the place of technology in American foreign policy. In the past 20 years, historians of American foreign policy have expanded their study of American power and global influence beyond the traditional domain of diplomacy and statecraft to examine how foreign policy interests have shaped – and are shaped by – anthropology, political science, social psychology, sociology, economics, the physical and natural sciences, and the non-human world (Adas 2006; Edwards 1996; Ekbladh 2010; Engerman 2007; Gilman 2003; Latham 2011; Guilhot 2005; Rotter 2011; Westad 2000). This literature has recast the traditional coordinates by which we have considered American power and its exercise. This current study contributes to the development of this literature, seeking to add to our understanding of the different forms of power possessed by the United States by theorizing the genesis of technological power with more clarity than the historical literature has to date. Historical studies of American power in relation to the politics of knowledge and the non-human world have, in general, produced interesting and detailed empirical accounts that still remain thin on conceptualizing how these processes are generated. The historical materialist theory of technological power presented here may help address this omission.

This attempt to develop a theoretical framework that grasps macro-social processes and locates US Internet policy within broader historical streams of American foreign policy requires abstraction. While the treatment of US foreign policy narratives is empirically detailed, at times specific policies in specific issue areas are necessarily glossed over. For example, the literature on cyberwar and cybersecurity is largely bypassed here, a choice made based on the general weakness of much work on the former topic (but this is changing – see Rid 2013; Stevens 2012) and on the integration of the latter into the 'why' of American policy. That is, cybersecurity scholarship should aim to tell us what actors are trying to secure and why, and the argument in the book outlines this in depth. Finally, our focus here is on power differentials in international relations; as Mueller notes, despite the dominant cybersecurity rhetoric regarding Chinese espionage and cyberwar capabilities, the United States possesses capabilities at least equal to China's in virtue of the strong links between industry, government and the military (Mueller 2012: 189). The decision is thus an analytical choice as well as a function of space constraints. This is not to suggest, however, that the current work attempts to produce a theory of global modernity derived from a passing familiarity with the Internet; as Mueller has noted, such sweeping accounts of the impact of information technology on global politics often claim too much. Rather, an empirically grounded method of abstraction has led to the middle-range theory outlined here (Sayer 2000; Ollman 1993). The development of mid-level theories of Internet governance are a pressing concern for both IR theory and Internet Studies.

Analysing policy rhetoric: discourse analysis and foreign policy narratives

The analysis of American foreign policy and Internet governance focuses upon US policy rhetoric in relation to the free flow of information and the creation of a liberal public sphere, and the move to secure intellectual property rights online. This focus was chosen partially through inductive methods: these aspects of Internet governance were repeatedly emphasized as central by US officials. These examples also have the benefit of adhering to a key methodological injunction of Science and Technology Studies (STS) by focusing upon controversial cases (Pinch and Bijker 1984: 407–410; Bijker 1995: 50). Conflict over the form of the Internet has become of staple of international relations. Examining this conflict illustrates the contested nature of the technology and the place of power in pursuit of a settled technological institution. Through these conflicts we see the values that the Internet expresses, the attempts to resist these values, and the centrality of symbolic politics in legitimizing or de-legitimizing these actions.

The empirical analysis undertaken was conducted using Critical Discourse Analysis (CDA) (Fairclough 1995, 2001, 2003; Milliken 1999; Hansen 2006). CDA was chosen as most appropriate method due to its focus on the power of rhetorical constructions and its utility in analysing these, particularly their intertextual aspects. Approximately 230 policy documents, press releases, and public statements by officials within the Bush and Obama administrations were examined to determine how they created a system of signification. The analysis of the Obama administration ends at the close of his first term. It should be noted that the volume of policy documents and press statements exploded during the Obama administration; while the analysis presented covers its specific issues areas in some depth, it is not a complete or comprehensive picture of all aspects of Obama's Internet policies. Interviews were conducted with seven officials in the Bush administration: in the Department of State (3), the Department of Commerce (1), the Federal Communications Commission (1), the Broadcasting Board of Governors (BBG) (1) and the White House (1). Please note that, in keeping with US government practice, all civil servants are identified as speaking on behalf of their respective departments and never as individuals on their own.

The analysis proceeded as follows. First, a general survey of the primary source documentation was conducted in order to grasp the main themes and narratives of the official discourse (Hansen 2006: 52–53, 58–60). After conducting this broad reading, the most important tropes used by US officials were identified, as were the primary institutional actors responsible for crafting US policy, a process greatly aided by the semi-structured interviews with American officials. The result was a focus on the discourse of Internet freedom produced during the Bush administration by the US Department of State and the Bureau of Economic, Energy, and Business Affairs (EEB). In the analysis that follows, Ambassador David Gross has a high profile as a result of this focus; Gross was the lead official for US international information policy within the EEB at this time. During the Obama administration the greater importance granted to the politics of the Internet sees this focus shift slightly; while the State Department remained central to the discourse of Internet freedom, other actors and agencies began to articulate Internet policy with greater frequency – the White House and the Department of Commerce both being significant in this regard. In both administrations, the rhetoric surrounding intellectual property rights emerged from both the State Department and the Department of Commerce, with Commerce placing greater emphasis on property rights and innovation. 'Following the actors' was central to the recognition that US policymakers did not regard the Internet Corporation for Assigned Names and Numbers (ICANN) as the central aspect of Internet governance – indeed, the scope of governance was viewed as significantly wider than anticipated when this project began. Moreover – and more relevant for our purposes here – the interviews were central for providing an insight into the assumptions and political culture surrounding the creation of Internet policy, which was significantly more cohesive than anticipated. This is evident in the repetition of US officials' arguments across diverse issue areas and across administrations.

Using a content-analysis guide – open to revision over time – the policy documents were scrutinised to see how American policymakers constructed the major themes creating the overarching discourse, and which symbolic resources they drew upon to make their arguments. The first step was to contextualize the document, looking at who was speaking, to whom they were speaking, what type of document was being analysed, and whether the document was consistent with the overall discourse. This allowed control for the potentially different forms of speech that US policymakers used to address different audiences: domestic, international, business, nongovernmental, and so forth. In the end, no difference was found – the US message was consistent, if slightly more forceful or less forceful, across the board and in relation to different actors, friend and foe. The second step was to outline the overall narrative of the individual article, the macro-reading of the micro analysis.

Following this, a closer breakdown of articles was undertaken, looking at the different discursive elements with which the overall narrative was constructed. This involved asking questions such as: What are the binary oppositions that take place within the document? What are the verbs/adjectives attached to the Internet? Is the Internet an actor/agent, does it cause things, or is it granted a particular state of being? (Fairclough 1995: 104–105; Milliken 1999: 231–237). Using these questions as a guide made possible the detailed tracing of rhetorical devices that US officials repeatedly employed in constructing their narrative, assigning certain predicates, certain actions or events, and certain actors within a series of constructions that lent value to the Internet as one type of technology as opposed to alternative meanings and network configurations. Emerging from these analyses were both the value that the United States attached to the Internet (its discursive construction of the Internet as a particular kind of technology) and, in turn, the construction of political identities for other actors in relation to their own policies toward this American vision of the technology. Finally, putting all of the pieces back together again required reconstructing the overall narrative of US discourse from its basic building blocks. This methodology emphasizes the significant scope for the agency of policy officials, recognizing that while these officials draw upon pre-existing symbolic resources – those norms and values which resonate with target audiences – the construction of a discourse is not predetermined.

Perhaps the most interesting finding of the empirical research was the sheer consistency of the fundamental US foreign policy message across the Bush and Obama administrations (and, indeed, extending in many ways back to the Clinton administration as well). There were changes in US rhetoric, without doubt. First, the Obama administration stressed, in far more comprehensive terms, the centrality of 'cybersecurity' to national security. Bush officials began to note the central role of cybersecurity as a policy driver, but only during the Obama administration does this process take off to the extent that one could claim some element of 'securitization' (Buzan et al. 1998) may be under way. Second, the Obama administration illustrated greater consistency of message across diverse agencies and issue areas; Obama officials used shared turns of phrase and rhetorical constructions more often than did Bush administration officials – the formulation that 'there is only one Internet' being a notable example –perhaps reflecting greater leadership from the administration on this issue overall. Finally, the Obama administration placed a greater emphasis on the central role of 'trust' to the functioning of the Internet. The idea of 'trust' did not feature in

Bush administration documents – if it was mentioned at all it was never emphasized in any respect. Obama administration officials, on the other hand, noted the centrality of trust on numerous occasions. As a form of rhetorical coercion, the shift to notions of trust is interesting in its attempts to suggest shared normative ground. As noted in this book's conclusion, however, the attempt to draw upon norms of trust has been undermined by revelations leaked by Edward Snowden regarding the conduct of the National Security Agency (NSA).

The discourse analysis effectively outlines how American officials relied on their productive power in the attempt to legitimize their vision of the Internet and, subsequently, the shape of the network's architecture. The policy narrative draws upon norms institutionalized within international society, an example of the 'intertextual' linkages; in this manner, American officials' political vision for the Internet possess a greater rhetorical 'fit' (Bernstein 2002) with existing norms. The method of analysis thereby frames both the understanding of Internet governance held by the United States government – what US officials want and why – and, in addition, considers these narratives as central in crafting the very political outcomes the United States would like to see occur. While CDA approaches trace micro-discourses, they also emphazise the necessity of placing rhetoric within a wider historical context, outlining how narratives are produced and how they reinforce or undermine existing power structures. Meeting this central aim of the book is a further reason for employing this approach.

Plan of the book

Chapter 2 outlines the main shortcomings of the theorization of information technology within IR theory. This discussion does not focus upon different 'schools' of IR theory – the treatment of technology is as dissimilar within schools as between them. Rather, the chapter argues that the dominant approaches to information technologies have been technological instrumentalism, optimistic technological determinism, and pessimistic technological determinism. All three variants have relied on separating the technological from the social, with the result that it becomes impossible to explain technological development as the product of human action. As a result, the interrelationship between technology and social power within these theories is seriously weakened. Turning to recent work in IR and Internet Studies that draws upon the Social Construction of Technology (SCOT) approach, the chapter outlines the significant advance that such work has made in breaking down the boundary between the social and the technical, allowing us to grasp the politics of information technology design and development as central to the conduct of global politics. At the same time, while the present work builds upon these approaches, it is also necessary to acknowledge some of their limitations. These are primarily the limited attempts to pinpoint the politics of Internet design within larger historical processes and wider traditions of social theory.

In Chapter 3 an alternative historical-materialist understanding of technology is presented in an effort to meet these shortcomings. Reviewing the heritage of Marxism finds that it replicates many of the theoretical errors found in the approaches reviewed in Chapter 2. The chapter sketches how Andrew Feenberg's critical theory of technology presents the necessary resources for a non-determinist theorization of technology from a critical IR perspective. Feenberg outlines technology as 'biased but ambivalent'. Its bias is the product of the particular social and historical context in which it was created, causing the physical structure of the technology to express the values of this context. However, this bias is not completely determining. Within a technological artefact there remains scope for change, the 'ambivalence' of the object opening space for agency and for resistance to technologically expressed norms. With this insight in hand, the chapter proceeds to outline the concept of technology as a form of institutional power in international politics, institutional power embedded within structural power relations and supported by the productive power of symbolic politics.

Chapter 4 is the beginning of the empirical illustration. The chapter first describes American foreign policy as driven by the pursuit of the 'Open Door' policy, an approach to foreign affairs shared by both the Bush and Obama administrations. The US government has traditionally asserted a drive to open up foreign governments to the free flow of information in order to open polities to political liberalization and to open markets for American goods. The chapter proceeds to note how, as a historical product created by the United States, the Internet functions to advance these goals, illustrating how the hardware and software architectures of the technology function as a form of institutional power in global politics. This chapter argues that states have a particular foreign policy of technology, and actively work to construct technological institutions to meet that policy's aims.

From this discussion, Chapter 5 and Chapter 6 outline the attempt of US policymakers to secure a technological closure of the Internet. In Chapter 5 the discussion outlines how US policymakers are utilizing powerful, internationally legitimate norms, such as those of human rights and democracy, to argue for the Internet as a specific kind of technology that meets these aims. Alternative understandings, such as those held by content-filtering states that stress national sovereignty, are subsequently portrayed as illegitimate. The discourse legitimizes American practises which work to circumvent censorship techniques, counteracting the ambivalence of the institution which other actors in the international system have hitherto exploited. Productive and structural power are thereby analytically illustrated as central to securing the ongoing bias of the Internet's institutional power.

Finally, Chapter 6 outlines the symbolic politics at play in the international debates over intellectual property rights and the Internet. US government officials, encountering various forms of resistance to property rights on the Internet, outline a model of technological innovation which can only occur with these rights in place. In the process, they cast actors who ignore these rights and this model of innovation as backwards and unproductive. The attempt to secure intellectual property rights on the Internet is an attempt to ensure that the essentially liberal bias of the technology – which affords the *equal opportunity* to access information but not the *equal ability* to access information – remains in place. It is only in this manner that American capital can profitably realize its investments on the Internet. In this chapter the role of productive power in securing the continued reproduction of structural power relations surrounding the Internet is central.

The final chapter recaps and summarizes the preceding argument. It also outlines – briefly – how US Internet policy may be altered and undermined by the NSA scandal. This analysis suggests that the conduct of the NSA is not historically novel, and that the surveillance of foreign leaders, friends and potential enemies is not terribly shocking, at least not to an informed student of international politics. Yet, this does not mean that the NSA scandal will not impact upon the capacity – the power – of the United States government to achieve its Internet foreign policy aims. US policy aims will not change, nor will the policy aims of its most strident opponents in the field of Internet governance. However, the leaks may serve to undermine the credibility and legitimacy of the American narrative; the 'free flow of information' may now strike foreign and domestic audiences as disingenuous.

With these final considerations of current and future US policy, the conclusion ultimately points towards the theoretical and conceptual impacts this argument has on fundamental categories of International Relations theory. Emerging scholarship seeking to integrate Science and Technology Studies and International Relations theory is not simply additive – this is not just an exercise in bolting on external sociological concepts to IR theory traditions. Instead, the entire project suggests a rethinking of many of the key concepts of IR theory in order to draw out the implicit understanding of technology and materiality that they disclose.

The book thereby establishes a framework for reconceptualizing information technology as a form of institutional power in international relations. It illustrates the utility of this exercise through the empirical illustration of the Internet as a form of power for an American 'Open Door' foreign policy. These preliminary insights open up the problem of information technology which has largely remained closed within IR theory. They provide space for reconsidering the creation of information technology as always already embedded within the international, while suggesting promising lines for further detailed empirical study on the nature and conduct of conflicts over the form of information technology within international society. Given the centrality of ICTs to the current problems of global politics, these issues could not be more pressing. Moreover, as noted in the book's conclusion, this study of the relationship between concepts of power and information technology raises as many productive research topics as it may resolve. Open flows of information are a dominant trope explored in these pages; if this work can open up some conceptual terrain for further debate on the place of technology in global politics it will have achieved its aim.

2
Power and Information Technology: Determinism, Agency, and Constructivism

Introduction

Information communications technologies (ICTs) have occupied a curious place within International Relations Theory. ICTs have often been accorded a central role in changing the international system, with new media altering interaction capacity, posing problems of political control for established actors, and opening up new spaces and new possibilities for different political actors to emerge and exercise influence (Buzan and Little 2000; Buzan and Albert 2010; Keohane and Nye 1998; Deibert 1997; Krasner 1991; Rosenau 1990, Scholte 2005). Implicitly, ICTs affect international power dynamics, enhancing, eroding, or altering the distribution of power and the context in which power is exercised. Yet, for all the apparent weight that ICTs carry in such analyses, the design, development and diffusion of these technological artefacts – the actual physical development of these technologies – has remained relatively understudied within the discipline. Instead of inquiries into the construction of technological objects, IR Theory has tended to treat non-human artefacts as given.[1] Whether technological objects are viewed as neutral tools or as having inherent properties that cause social change, a deterministic technological rationale has been prominent in the field (Herrera 2006: 27–30; McCarthy 2011a, 2013; Peoples 2009).[2] As a result, a precise conceptualization of the relationship between forms of social power and the creation of biased technologies has been foreclosed.[3]

This chapter will proceed by discussing the two dominant approaches to ICTs in IR, technological instrumentalism and technological essentialism, in order to detail the problems with these – ultimately untenable – determinist accounts. First, we will clarify how instrumentalist and essentialist arguments exclude consideration of technology as a specific form of social power. This discussion will begin by looking at the instrumentalist perspective. This view, which subscribes to an understanding of technology as a neutral tool, outlines power as event-based, discrete, and observable. While this view of power is certainly appropriate for some contexts and issues (Haugaard 2010), it is unable to fully grasp the complex power dynamics that surround ICTs.

We will then examine the technological essentialist perspective and its central claim – often implicit – that technology causes social change. Essentialists view technological objects as possessing inherent characteristics. The essence of technological objects causes social and political change. Neither those who view this process optimistically or pessimistically explicitly analyze technology as a form of social power, yet their arguments suggest that ICTs have powerful causal effects. However, excising human agency from their accounts, these viewpoints are difficult to defend, even as they present an often appealing grasp of the centrality of the material world to our social lives. Ultimately, both instrumentalism and essentialism are forms of technological determinism, attributing to technological design and development a rationale beyond human sociality and historical processes.

Finally, with the weaknesses of technological determinism in mind, the chapter will engage with recent attempts to integrate Science and Technology Studies (STS) and, in particular, the Social Construction of Technology perspective, with International Relations Theory (Carr 2012; Herrera 2003, 2006; Fritsch 2011; DeNardis 2009; Sylvest 2013; cf. Bijker, Hughes, and Pinch 1987; Bijker 1995). These attempts are valuable correctives to determinist approaches. In opening up the black box of technology they point towards the central role of materiality in structuring global politics. What is missing from these accounts, however, is a clear theorization of how different forms of social power interact to create and maintain technological institutions, and how these institutions, in turn, function as a distinct form of social power.[4] This discussion will highlight the limits of these approaches in three aspects. First, examining the concept of 'technological momentum' (Hughes 1983), we will note that, at times, these approaches still endorse a form of soft essentialism. Second, we will note that the understanding of power discussed within this literature is often based – implicitly or explicitly – on a highly contested liberal understanding of politics and the relationship between states and markets. This points, in turn, to a third limitation: the absence of an explicit grounding in social theory, with the concomitant exclusion of central concepts of social and political thought, including the concepts of capitalism and the state. This sympathetic critique thereby points the way towards construction of an alternative historical materialist understanding of power, information technology, and International Relations Theory undertaken in Chapter 3.

Technological instrumentalism: emphasizing agency?

Technological instrumentalism is a prominent approach to the conceptualization of technology in International Relations. This understanding of technology is premised on the argument that, in and of themselves, technological objects do not affect political outcomes or cause social change. This is not to suggest that instrumentalists view technological objects as unimportant – the fact that one set of actors possess gunpowder while another does not is of course relevant to social outcomes. Instead, it is the use to which a technological object is put that affords technology a causal role in human affairs, a use which is not determined by the characteristics of the technological object itself. To use a prominent example from IR: in the instrumentalist understanding, weapons are not biased towards offensive or defensive purposes (Jervis 1978; Lieber 2000). Weapons only achieve this orientation when used either offensively or defensively, thereby introducing the tension and uncertainty surrounding actors' intentions characteristic of the security dilemma. This viewpoint is in direct opposition to essentialist understandings of technology in which the inherent properties of technology cause social change absent human intention.

Instrumentalist understandings are often implicitly held. Much of the debate surrounding whether the Internet promotes autocracy or democracy is conducted along these lines, with instrumentalists asserting it does neither inherently. Perhaps the most prominent and thoroughly articulated instrumentalist position centred upon ICTs is found in the work of James Rosenau, although this position is evident more broadly (Bremmer 2010; Biden 2011; Diamond 2010: 71; Fukuyama 1992: 7; Kalathil and Boas 2003; Taylor 1997: 8; cf. Morozov 2011: 295–299). For Rosenau, authority is undergoing a process of disaggregation, undermining hierarchical politics through the growth of governance networks (Rosenau 1992a: 3–5; 1992b; 1995: 13–15). Information technologies are front and centre, driving and facilitating this process. He states that

> the various electronic technologies that continue to proliferate in the global market – most notable perhaps are the mobile phone and global television as well as the internet – are central to developments

at every level of aggregation. Among their many consequences, they have facilitated an explosive growth in networks, in horizontal links among people and groups that have served to diminish the extent to which hierarchy marks the life of organizations and communities. Such consequences are so extensive that it is tempting to yield to a form of determinism in which humans and their societies are deprived of choice and are posited as conducting themselves in response to the imperatives implicit in the technologies. (Rosenau 2005: 78; see also Rosenau 1990: 4, 17, 315, 321)

The spectre of technological determinism raised is quickly rejected. Rosenau asserts that the adoption of a determinist perspective obscures the functioning of human agency, and for this reason is inappropriate: all technologies are 'profoundly neutral' (Rosenau 2005: 78).[5] In a clear statement of technological instrumentalism, he argues:

> It is more permissive than dismissive to argue that information technologies are essentially neutral. They do not in themselves tilt in the direction of any particular values – neither good or bad, nor left or right, nor open or closed systems. They are, rather, neutral, in the sense that their tilt is provided by people. It is people and their collectivities that infuse values into information. For better or worse, it is individuals and organizations that introduce information into political arenas and thereby render it good or bad. Accordingly, the neutrality of information technologies is permissive because it enables the democrat as well as the authoritarian to use information in whatever way he or she sees fit.
>
> There is, in other words, some utility in starting with the premise that information and the technologies that generate and circulate it are neutral. It enables us to avoid deterministic modes of thought in which people are seen as being deprived of choice by the dictates of information technologies. Put more positively, the neutrality premise compels us to focus on human agency and how it does or does not make use of information technologies. (Rosenau 2002a: 275; see also Rosenau 1990: 15–17, 315–322; 2003: 256–272; Herrera 2006: 29–30)

Clearly, for Rosenau, information communications technologies do not exercise any power independent of human agency.[6] Similarly, Robert Keohane and Joseph Nye assert that information technology has been central to changing the nature of the international system while maintaining an instrumentalist position (Keohane and Nye 1998; Nye 2010c: 4).[7] Their project – outlined with greater consistency than Rosenau's – has been the attempt to chart the nature of complex interdependence in the international system. Complex interdependence is not leading to a fundamental reconfiguration of authority in global politics – the state and power politics remain central. Instead, they argue, the task is to chart how governments shape, and are shaped by, the growth of transnational politics (Keohane and Nye 1989 [1977]: 4–6; 1998: 81–94; Nye 2004; Nye 2010c).

Information technologies are central to this process. They are important in two ways. First, ICTs create increased information flows and thus increased transparency, pushing state interactions towards more cooperative forms (Keohane 2002: 10, 51–59, 245–259). The greater the amount of information available to actors the easier it is to make decisions that are mutually beneficial and meet common interests (Keohane 1984: 12–13; Keohane and Nye 1989 [1977]: 32–33; Keohane 1989: 64). Transparency allows actors to gauge the intentions of others with increased precision, mitigating the uncertainty that surrounds the security dilemma (Keohane 1984; see Booth and Wheeler 2007). In contrast to Realist claims that security competition is endemic to the international system, Keohane and Nye point towards forces that may help reduce conflict, with information flows central.

Second, as a result of increased transparency, ICTs are changing the nature of power in the international system, degrading the importance of 'hard power' – military resources – increasing the role of 'soft power', and diffusing power to a larger number of actors in the international system (Nye 2010c). Keohane and Nye assert that information communications technologies make transparency and the attractiveness of one's culture the most important elements of power internationally. Thus, 'soft power', Nye's theoretical project of the past 25 years, has become the most important form of power within the changed context provided by information technologies. Nye defines soft power as follows:

> A country may achieve the outcomes it prefers in world politics because other countries want to follow it or have agreed to a system that produces such effects. In this sense, it is just as important to set the agenda and structure the situations in world politics as it is to get others to change in particular situations. This aspect of power – that is, getting others to want what you want – might be called indirect or co-optive power behavior. It is in contrast to the active command power behavior of getting others to do what you want. Co-optive

power can rest on the attraction of one's ideas or on the ability to set the political agenda in a way that shapes the preferences that others express. ... The ability to establish preferences tends to be associated with intangible power resources such as culture, ideology, and institutions. This dimension can be thought of as soft power, in contrast to the hard command power usually associated with tangible resources like military and economic strength. (Nye 1990: 32; Keohane and Nye 1998: 94; see also Rosenau 1990: 93; 2003: 260)[8]

Information communications technologies have altered the nature of power by making soft power more important than coercive hard power. Within an international system characterized by rapid movement of information, the ability to use the 'attractiveness' of soft power to get others to want what you want becomes a key attribute for achieving one's aims. Soft power rests on the credibility of one's claims, with those likely to gain in soft power defined by:

(1) those whose dominant culture and ideas are closer to prevailing global norms (liberalism/pluralism/autonomy); (2) those with the most access to multiple channels of communication and thus more influence over how issues are framed, and (3) those whose credibility is enhanced by their domestic and international performance. (Nye 2002: 69; 2008: 44; 2010; Rosenau 1990: 101)

Despite the amorphous nature of this concept, for which Nye has been rightly criticized (Bially Mattern 2005: 587–591; Adler and Bernstein 2005: 298; on 'influence' more generally see Morriss 2002: 8–13), the conceptualization of the relationship between power and technology in international politics is relatively clear in Nye and Keohane's work. The ability to shape agendas is, for Keohane and Nye, the most important form of power in world politics.[9] This ability is not created by ICTs – again, Keohane and Nye reject technological essentialist positions (Keohane and Nye 1998; but see Nye 2008: 47, 133, 144–145). Rather, ICTs set a context within which soft power is increasingly important. Within this context actors may (but do not have to) use their soft power.

ICTs do not create the 'attractiveness' that constitutes soft power. There is no sense in the work of Keohane and Nye that the context created by new ICTs – the ability to structure actors' actions – is the focus of their account. For example, in Nye's discussion of 'intra cyberspace' and 'extra cyberspace' forms of power the analysis never extends to the power of the rules and norms of the technology itself (Nye 2010c: 5, passim). Nye illustrates the 'hard' and 'soft' dimensions of these internal and external dimensions of cyberspace power – DDOS attacks and information-shaping norms in the former case, critical infrastructure attacks and naming and shaming campaigns in the latter (Nye 2010c: 5). Nye discusses the use of filtering technologies as an exercise of state power but does not extend this example of how code functions as a set of norms and rules at the heart of the network itself, in its hardware and software infrastructure. Agenda control happens, for Nye, only when the free flow of information is prevented (2010c: 8). This account of information technology thereby remains instrumentalist by asserting that technology does not cause social change. Information technology alters the context in which – to use the classical denotation of behaviouralist power analyses – 'A has power over B to the extent that he [sic] can get B to do something B would not otherwise do' (Dahl 1957: 202–203). Information technology does not cause any specific outcome to arise. Instead, information technology can be used by actors to realize their capacity to change other actors' preferences.

This understanding of the relationship between technology and power finds its roots within American social science and the 'faces of power' debates of the 1960s and 1970s (Dahl 1957; Bachrach and Baratz 1962; Lukes 1974).[10] Within this framework power is exercised in discrete instances of decision-making as 'power over' (Nye 2002: 2). These debates, conducted along behaviouralist and positivist lines, emphasize power as the ability to create discrete outcomes in specific issue areas, a concept of power Haugaard has deemed 'episodic' (Haugaard 2010; Lukes 2005: 5, passim). In this 'power-as-outcomes' approach, power is not fungible between different issue areas, making it essential to specify the context of each individual decision-making event (Nye 2002: 3; Keohane and Nye 1989 [1977]: 50). Context discloses the options that are or are not available to actors, allowing the analyst to outline the preferences of actors prior to the act of decision itself, ensuring that attributions of power are rooted in an observable exercise (Isaac 1987). As Nye notes, 'Power always depends on the context of the relationship' (Nye 2008: 28; 2010a; 2010c: 2–3). Asymmetrical power relations are only important for bargaining on a specific issue at a specific time, not before or after this event; this claim is necessarily entailed by Keohane and Nye's epistemological commitments to positivism and Humean accounts of causation (Keohane 1989; King, Keohane and Verba 1994; Kurki 2008: 100–115). For this reason concepts of structural power, implying a long-term historical relationship, are foreclosed. Keohane and Nye also reject the equation of power with resources (Nye 2010a: 4;

2010b: 4). The concept of power employed by instrumentalists thereby attempts to avoid the 'vehicle fallacy' whereby power is attributed to the vehicles with which it is exercised rather than to human agents (Morriss 2002: xxvii-xxxii; Dowding 2008). Nye stresses that the technologies of the information revolution are changing the nature of power rather than being power themselves (Nye 2010a: 1; 2010c: passim). In stressing power as a relation between human actors, the instrumentalist approach effectively distinguishes power from the means by which it is exercised. While this desire to stress agency against potential determinisms is appealing, we need to ask whether this conceptualization actually achieves these aims. There are two primary problems with the instrumentalist understanding of technology and related conceptualization of power.

First, instrumentalist treatments of technology obscure the role of human agency in developing technological objects to meet specific social aims, an intentional exercise of power capacities. Missing in this account is the process by which technologies are created and developed. Agency is not applied to the human ability to create technological artefacts to meet our social purposes. The emphasis on technological neutrality suggests that whether or not we are trying to create swords or plowshares neither object will be biased towards the ends of fighting or farming. Struggles over the design of technological objects are, for instrumentalists, ultimately irrelevant: they have no role in structuring social outcomes and are the same in any social context (McCarthy 2013: 474). Instrumentalist accounts are based upon an understanding of technological development as external to human social relations, a variant of determinism that suggests that 'technical' developments are not the product of historically located actors, an empirically suspect claim, as countless historical studies of technological development have illustrated. Creating technological objects with a bias towards particular social or political outcomes is an inevitable part of human social relations and their metabolism with nature – we could not avoid doing this even if we tried. By suggesting that means do not affect ends, instrumentalist accounts stress agency in the use of technologies but not in their design and creation.

Second, this theoretical gap is quiet on how soft power is generated. Keohane and Nye are not engaged in a project of developing a full account of social reality, and the drive for parsimony and policy relevance undoubtedly informs some of their analytical choices.[11] Even within a set of 'problem-solving' coordinates, however, the inability to account for the creation of technological institutions limits their account of soft power and their subsequent understanding of power distribution in the international system. The conception of power outlined by Keohane and Nye – shared by all the main participants in the classical social power debate, including Lukes (Isaac 1987: 17–40) – does not allow us to grasp the different abilities actors have to create contexts in which 'soft power' is, or is not, important – in contrast to the dominant understanding of 'power as capacity' in philosophy and the social sciences (Isaac 1987; Morriss 2002; Dowding 1996: 4–7, 2008). This is not due to a simple empirical omission, but is in some sense entailed by the concept of power as 'power over' allied to Humean concepts of causation. If, in Dahl's classic formulation, power is A causing B to change course, technology cannot be a form of power. An attribution of power to technology must conceptualize technology as an actor and as causing outcomes in a Humean sense. Technology is not, of course, an actor for Keohane and Nye (cf. Latour 2005). Within this conceptual framework, attributing power to technology is *necessarily* determinist. The conceptual foundations of this concept of power cannot grasp technology as institutional power.

Focusing upon power as a form of causation, in which powerful actors cause others to change their behavior rests upon a quite specific understanding of both power and of concepts of determination and causation. It involves claims that actors are constituted prior to their interactions, in contrast to concepts of structural power relations in which actors are internally related (Singh 2013: 25; Isaac 1987; Sayer 2000); and that causation or determination is conceived in terms of constant conjunctions, rather than the setting of limits (Williams 1977; 2005 [1980]; Thompson 1978; Isaac 1987: 56; Kurki 2008). Moving beyond cause as 'constant conjunction' is necessary if we are to understand technology as a form of institutional power. The capacity to set limits via technological development and design, and the structuring qualities of technological institutions themselves, may not lead to the observable exercise of power – as Raymond Williams noted in another context, 'We have to revalue "determination" towards the setting of limits and the exertion of pressure, and away from a predicted, prefigured and controlled content' (Williams 2005 [1980]: 34).[12] Similarly, while attending to forms 'power over' remains of central importance in this analysis, it is similarly important to grasp the centrality of 'power to' for analyses of the role of information technology in global politics. The 'power to' create technological institutions grants certain actors significant 'power over' others by determining the context of their actions. This shift requires, of course, integrating the concept of institutional power into our consideration of information technology in global politics. This move is uncontroversial for institutions conventionally understood as social – the rules of the WTO or international regimes in general – and becomes similarly uncontroversial for technology, as the historical design process is considered (see below and Chapter 3).

Our ability to analyze the social world is truncated by the instrumentalist and behaviouralist understandings of technology and power. If we are to account for the deeply contested 'protocol politics' (DeNardis 2009) that surround Internet governance, it is necessary to understand this as a fight over the bias that technological objects will express. The instrumentalist alternative is rather unsatisfactory, suggesting political conflicts over technical standards are somehow irrelevant in structuring future political conduct. This suggests, in turn, a deep misunderstanding on the part of participants in these conflicts, struggling over technological alternatives to no discernible end. This approach to technology is both theoretically implausible and empirically disabling. When technological development is historicized, the ability to shape these norms and 'set the rules of the game' for other actors emerges as a theorizable form of social power. Changing the social context within which action takes place and setting institutional rules and norms are recognized as key facets of power across quite varied theoretical perspectives in International Relations (Hurrell 2005; Gruber 2005; Rupert 2005). A problem-solving perspective cannot investigate the historical development and reproduction of technology as a context that structures others' choices.[13] Treating technology as a context without inquiring into its creation and maintenance typically accepts the dominant understanding of a technological institution as natural or valid, closing off alternative constructions in theory that remain open in practice. In turn, this limits a full grasp of the nature of power in global politics. Technological institutions are the product of historical processes, not merely discrete interactions (Bijker, Hughes, and Pinch 1987; Bijker 1995: 261, 269), and we must investigate these processes to adequately account for the power capacities of actors in world politics.

Technological essentialism: the power of objects

Although instrumentalists' perspectives are evident in International Relations, technological essentialist viewpoints have been more prevalent overall, although this situation may be changing (Milner 2006; Choucri 2000; Der Derian 2001, 2003; Held 1999; Matthews 1997: 57–66; Mingst 1999; Scholte 2005: 189, passim, 2008: 1482; cf. Dunn-Cavelty and Brunner 2007: 3–6; Sylvest 2013). If instrumentalists stress agent-focused explanations, essentialists propose a structuralist explanation of social action. Essentialist approaches characterize technology as inherently biased towards specific social and political outcomes: technology causes social change. Social actors are not free to use technology as they please. Instead, non-human objects have particular ends embedded within them that lead to definite outcomes; for example, 'Globalization Theory' has been especially prominent in forwarding the view that the increased information flows fostered by ICTs are undermining sovereign state power (Scholte 2005; M. Mueller 2010: 4). Essentialist work is quite diverse, and the purported effects of ICTs are similarly diverse, but they can be divided, roughly, into optimistic and pessimistic camps, although essentialist positions need not stress any specific value judgements. Techno-optimists stress that information communications technologies cause greater democracy and freedom in international relations. Techno-pessimists, by contrast, argue that the 'information revolution' – and often technology itself – is causing new forms of oppression. We will briefly review the optimist perspective before turning to the more substantive arguments of technological pessimists.

Techno-optimists: progress without power

Techno-optimism has deep roots in social and political thought. From Francis Bacon to Pierre Teilhard de Chardin to Second International Marxism and Modernization theory, technology has often been conceived as a means by which humans can realize perfection on earth (Winner 1977: 21–23; Smith 1990 [1984]: 1–5; Barbour 1992: 8). Techno-optimist approaches to the Internet emerged in public discourse during the 1990s. In the first flush of the Internet's diffusion and adoption by the general public, the hype that typically accompanies new technological innovations was prominent. Walter Writson, former head of IBM and a former official in the US State Department, encapsulated this mood:

> Today, the marriage of computer and telecommunications has ushered in the Information Age, which is as different from the Industrial Age as that period was from the Agricultural Age. Information technology has demolished time and distance. Instead of validating Orwell's vision of Big Brother watching the citizen, the third revolution enables the citizen to watch Big Brother. And so the virus of freedom, for which there is no antidote, is spread by electronic networks to the four corners of the earth. (Writson 1997: 172)

The hyperbole of this passage is evident. However, it is effective in illustrating the central features of techno-optimist essentialism. Democratic freedoms are spread by the technology itself, not by the use of the technology in particular ways, as instrumentalism asserts. Technological development contains an internal dynamic that individuals cannot alter. Implicitly, agency is ascribed to the technology objects.

The picture is quite seductive, and it is reassuring to think that technological development will promote human freedom. The power that techno-optimists attribute to technology may be a constraint on human agency, but it is a constraint that we should gladly accept.[14] In any case, these ideas remain prevalent, even when determinism is explicitly denied (Allinson 2000: 76; Choucri 2000: 244; Friedman 2005: 459–460; Deibel 2007: 60–62, 65). There are no real politics in this vision, and certainly no social power, which ultimately means that there is no responsibility for political outcomes (Guzzini 2005: 508–511; Connolly 1983; Lukes 2005; Morriss 2002). Always questionable on theoretical grounds, empirically a techno-optimist perspective towards ICTs has been severely complicated by the prevalence of Internet filtering and the rise of state surveillance regimes (Deibert et al 2008, 2010, 2012; Morozov 2011: passim). The ideological function of these arguments remains fascinating, but we can safely leave techno-optimist views aside as we consider the core features of technological essentialism through pessimistic accounts of ICTs in IR.

Techno-pessimists and structuralist determinism

Unlike the techno-optimist perspective, power as domination – 'power over' – is repeatedly emphasized within techno-pessimist viewpoints.[15] As with techno-optimists, pessimistic accounts of technological essentialism are quite diverse (including the Romantics, Heidegger, the Frankfurt School, and Foucault, among others). Techno-pessimist perspectives in contemporary social theory are perhaps most-often associated with scholars drawing upon French postmodernist and poststructuralist thought, but sources of inspiration vary considerably. Pessimist essentialism has a broad issue-based focus, with the politics of speed (Der Derian 1990, 1992, 2001, 2003; Glezos 2011, 2013; Scheuerman 2001) or dissections of surveillance and the panopticon created by information technologies (Howarth 2006, Lyon 2010) most prominent.

A concern with the politics of speed and acceleration created by new technologies has been an enduring focus of IR scholarship (Herz 1950; Deibert 2000; Scheuerman 2009; cf. Connolly 2000; Scheuerman and Rosa 2009). The most sustained recent engagement is found in the work of James Der Derian. Der Derian has extended the general concern with the role of social acceleration to a specific focus upon speed and the role of information technologies in altering the conduct of global politics. For Der Derian, the speed, virtuality and simulation fostered by ICTs have overcome our ability to interpret events. As a result, we are forced to rely on scenarios pre-wrapped and produced by the Military-Industrial-Media-Entertainment network (MIME), the acronym suggesting the centrality of mimesis to the current politics of international relations. Simulation and the 'hyper-real' are replacing politics by removing the difference between the true and the false (Der Derian 2001: xxxiv, 214; cf. Carruthers 2001). ICTs have raised the quality of virtualization, so that the representation of the real (its simulation) has taken on a new character, in which the two are increasingly difficult to distinguish. Whereas communication technologies were once central to mediating inter-state relations and managing the alienation that exists between political communities (Der Derian 2003: 450; Der Derian 1988; M.S. Anderson 1993; de Callierers 1919 [1713]: 25–28, 65) simulation alters the political process by which we encounter others. Der Derian, developing a Hegelian ethical framework, argues that 'the closer technology and scientific discourse bring us to the "other" – that is, the more that the model is congruent with reality, the image resembles the object, the medium becomes the message – the less we see of ourselves in the other'. (Der Derian 1990: 298; see also Lyon 2010: 333–334). Speed reduces differences, creating an identity between recognition and reaction, here and there, self and other. Diplomacy, as the mediation between estranged communities, is slowly giving way to 'anti-diplomacy', which has as its goal the transcendence of difference.

This account stresses that ICTs are not a neutral tool of human agents. They structure subjectivity, agency, and our very ways of being in the world. ICTs pose significant problems of knowledge (Der Derian 2003: 445–446). Moreover, these effects are beyond human control. Der Derian thereby suggests that 'The global networking of multi-media has become unstoppable, and I believe that its effects may have well accelerated beyond our political as well as our theoretical grasp', (Der Derian 2003: 445). Information technology is written into this work as an agent: 'technology has taken us into grave new worlds where the other is virtually disappeared'; 'the Internet produced the world wide web' (Der Derian 1992: 2; 2003: 442). The effect of these proclamations is to suggest that it is technology, and not human action, that causes social outcomes.[16] Here the central tropes of technological essentialism are clearest.

This account is open to question on empirical grounds. Certainly the role of 'speed' and the concomitant fear of its effects on social order are not unique to contemporary political life. Marshall Berman's fascinating account of the dialectics of modernity effectively documented perceptions of temporal acceleration – long-before information technology emerged, one of many similar accounts charting the course of modernity (Berman 1982: 15–36; Habermas 1992: 1–22; Thompson 1967; Winner 1977: 48–52). Arguments that state sovereignty is under threat from increasing and uncontrollable information flows similarly represent classical 'Westphalian' sovereignty as far more complete than even the most powerful state ever managed to achieve historically. Indeed, the ease with which intense censorship was evaded in, say, Tsarist Russia, Mussolini's Italy, or the Shah's Iran suggest that this historical point is, at the very least, highly contestable.

Essentialist perspectives tend towards a structuralist emphasis, to the exclusion of human agency, and are more clearly determinist than instrumentalist accounts. In addition to empirical limitations, essentialism excises human agency in the historical process, tending towards fetishism of the technological. Even when essentialist work notes that technological objects are the product of human practices, this point is extended to argue that technology is 'unstoppable'. Similar to the concept of momentum discussed below, such an approach discounts the reproduction of technological bias – those practices that ensure that information technologies continue to produce specific effects. Human agents are the bearers of technological structures but lack the ability to alter these structures. Power, inextricably tied to concepts of agency (Lukes 2005; Morriss 202), is sidelined as a result. Information technology requires continual maintenance and repair; social structures do not reproduce themselves.[17] Despite these limitations, the essentialist perspective does capture something important about technological objects, particularly for complex technological objects: while simple objects may not cause social outcomes in any specific direction – we can use screwdrivers, hammers, or scissors for a wide variety of purposes – complex objects do structure social relations in specific directions. In order to grasp this central point, however, we must move beyond determinism – in both its instrumentalist and essentialist variants – to consider Social Construction of Technology (SCOT) perspectives.

The social construction of information technology: between essentialism and instrumentalism

Within International Relations there is a limited but expanding body of research that takes the social construction of information communications technology seriously, integrating insights from Science and Technology Studies with IR theory to produce novel understandings of the relationship between global politics and technological development (Carr 2012; Hansen and Nissenbaum 2009; Herrera 2002, 2003, 2006; Marlin-Bennett 2013; McCarthy 2011b, 2013; DeNardis 2009, 2012; Townes 2012). This work, drawing on the Social Construction of Technology (SCOT) approach in STS, charts a middle-course between instrumentalist and essentialist perspectives on technology, recognizing aspects of technological path-dependency alongside an emphasis on human agency in the design and development of ICTs. The following section outlines the core claims of this work, noting its significance for understanding the role of technology in IR. Particular attention is paid to two aspects of this scholarship. First, the concept of 'momentum', borrowed from historian of technology, Thomas Hughes' and employed by various authors (Hughes 1983, 1994; Herrera 2006: 27–30; DeNardis 2009: 54; Fritsch 2011), is outlined in order to grasp how the ability to design technological objects is understood as a unique form of power in global politics. Second, we examine more closely how power is conceptualized in these approaches. Highlighting the lack of an explicit theory of social power, we suggest the need to advance these approaches through a deeper conceptualization of social structure, political economy and the state. This points towards the historical materialist theory of technology as a form of power in chapter three.

The starting point for SCOT perspectives in IR is the recognition that technology must be conceptualized as part of the international political system. SCOT stresses that technology does not develop in a linear, socially exogenous manner. Technological development does not follow a rationale of its own, with successive objects realizing a movement towards greater technical perfection. This teleology is central to both forms of determinism discussed above. Instead, SCOT approaches argue that our understanding of technological development should recognize that this process takes places in particular social and historical contexts. The result is that technological development is understood as a non-linear process. In the development of technological artefacts, multiple forks in the road are created, and the choice of which path is taken – VHS or Beta, as it were – is not the product of an inherent technical rationale. Instead, it is the outcome of political decisions and struggles over the form of the object and, subsequently, the shape of the social world.

Technology is thereby understood as a factor endogenous to the international system and a key facet of systemic change (Herrera 2003: 562, 576; M. Mueller 2010: 12). Actors struggle over the creation of technological objects; as Herrera notes, the result is that technological objects 'close off certain kinds of social and political action and make other kinds possible' (Herrera 2006: 32), an understanding of causal determination similar to that of Williams, outlined above. In relation to the Internet, and information communication technologies generally, these authors stress the crucial point that the structure of the technology itself is of central importance in enabling or constraining specific types of social action. This shifts our focus beyond the level of content – beyond examining the impact of Facebook or Twitter on political events – towards the underlying technological conditions that allow these applications to have an impact at all (McCarthy 2011a). SCOT approaches to ICTs in IR and political science thus build upon and extend the insights of Lessig (1999) that 'Code is Law'. The clearest statement of this viewpoint is provided by DeNardis:

> Although this architecture lies well beneath the level of content, it is not at all external to politics and culture. Infrastructure design and administration internalize the political and economic values that ultimately influence the extent of online freedom and innovation. (DeNardis 2012: 721)

Work in IR and Internet Studies effectively stress both the constructedness of technology and the subsequent impact that these objects have upon users, an important extension of SCOT work in STS that had, in its initial incarnations, often neglected this (Herrera 2006: 32–34). SCOT perspectives have thereby significantly deepened our consideration of how technological objects shape social action, conceptualizing technology as akin to social institutions as they are conventionally understood, with Herrera's work being particularly notable in this regard. (Herrera 2006: 36, passim; Hughes 1994).

Despite these strengths, however, SCOT-influenced approaches in IR and Internet studies have at times denied the entirely social nature of technological objects and their development and reproduction. There is a tendency in such accounts to try and chart a 'middle ground' between technologically determinist accounts and social constructivist arguments (Fritsch 2011; Mueller and Bendrath 2011; Townes 2012; cf. McCarthy 2013). For example, Herrera argues:

> No technology is truly autonomous; they are all partly social. Yet neither are the political meanings of technology infinitely malleable. The two do, however, complement each other nicely. Technology as

used here is simultaneously a social and a technical product. (Herrera 2006: 34, 220ff. 76)

This approach suggests that a social constructivist perspective on technology fails to recognize material limits and the centrality of materiality. The middle ground allows us to consider – in these viewpoints – technology as constituting the social, while being constituted by the social in turn, allowing us to avoid the twin determinisms of technology and social constructivist approaches (Fritsch 2011; Hanson 2008). The reason may be a desire to hold onto a Realist ontology of social life, but a recognition of the constructed nature of technological objects and scientific facts does not entail a rejection of Realism.

While this seems like a promising line of argument, it ends up re-establishing the division between technology and society and reconstituting an understanding of an inherent rationality to technology. This is evident in repeated attempts to assert the presence of distinct 'technical' choices in the design of technological objects, as suggested in Herrera's quote above. Thus, Mueller and Bendrath argue that the design of the Internet reflected a drive for political openness, for economic freedom, and for 'technical flexibility' as the optimal network design. The problems with these arguments are precisely those noted above: this move suggests that, beyond human sociality lies the technical. Technical choices are made – and evaluated – via criteria not already shaped by a given historical context and set of cultural norms and material interests. Again, this treats technology and society as distinct and seemingly reintroduces an ahistorical determinism into these accounts. A great tranche of detailed historical and sociological study suggests – and, indeed, the very foundations of the disciplines of the Sociology of Scientific Knowledge and Science and Technology Studies suggest – that this distinction cannot be sustained (Bloor 1976; Latour and Woolgar 1987). That is, there are no 'technical choices' as such, even as the structure of the world limits what can and cannot be created.[18] The most sophisticated attempts to solve this dilemma, such as Herrera's, argue that temporality introduces the moment of determinism by altering the social context for actors in the future (Herrera 2006: 34). We will now assess the strength of this claim via the concept of 'momentum'.

Power, momentum, and the political economy of technology

The concept of momentum, as developed by Hughes and used by Herrera and DeNardis, is important in drawing attention to the path-dependent dynamics of information technology. Herrera and DeNardis very effectively demonstrate the process by which technical decisions, influenced by political and social interests, endure over time, structuring the course of technological and social development. They stress that the use of information technology is shaped by the prior process of technological development: the instrumentalists' social context, or the essentialists' intrinsic properties are products of human agency (Herrera 2006: 34–36). Their work represents an important advance over previous scholarship in IR and Internet Studies, and should form a central reference point for any discussion of ICTs in the field of International Relations. Despite the merits of these approaches, there is significant space for further theoretical development. Two elements stand out as underdeveloped: the concept of 'momentum' and its relationship to capitalism, and the conceptualization of the state and politics more generally.

'Momentum', as an explanatory device in Science and Technology Studies, was developed initially in the work of Thomas P. Hughes.[19] Hughes, a historian of technology, employed an understanding of momentum to explain why technological design decisions, once taken, tend to endure over time. For Hughes, a technological system with momentum has mass, velocity, and direction. Hughes writes: 'In the case of technological systems...the mass consists of machines, devices, structures and other physical artefacts in which considerable capital has been invested'. (Hughes 1983: 15, passim; Herrera 2006: 34–37; DeNardis 2009: 54, 188). For Hughes, technologies endure when they attract significant investment, both material and reputational, leading groups to promote and sustain technological institutions over time. Path-dependency results, with future technological development structured by these decisions.

What is striking about this passage, however, is the nature of the explanation that is promoted. Hughes's central explanatory concept – momentum – is primarily descriptive. It describes how technologies endure over time but does not explain why technologies endure over time. That is, Hughes does not outline why sunk costs or reputation matter to individuals or groups, or what generates these social dynamics. Similarly, Herrera notes the pursuit of profit as an important driving factor in the development of railways, but never *why* the cost savings introduced by the railway are important. Capitalist social relations are never theoretically integrated into the concept of momentum, even as capitalism is empirically central to his (and Hughes') narrative (Herrera 2006: 47–54, 198; Hughes 1983; DeNardis 2009: 188). The unstated assumption of momentum is the development of technology within a capitalist political economy, with the need for an acceptable rate of return due to market competition ever present for the owners of capital, an assumption based upon a general utilitarian conception of path dependency (Mahoney 2000: 508, 516–519). The process by which capitalists with sunk capital seek to retard innovation and realize the value of previous investments is a familiar one and generates the temporal endurance that the concept of momentum suggests (Brenner 2006: passim; Mowrey and Rosenberg 1999). The logic that drives this process is structured by capitalist social property relations. Capitalists who have invested in technological innovation must recoup the costs of their investments through the market, generating profits in the process. Increasingly, innovation itself creates profits via intellectual property rights and the rents they generate. The interest in perpetuating specific technological objects is driven by the needs of material reproduction. Momentum – and its close cousin, the 'S' curve – describe these social mechanisms, but do not explain them. In order to explain these processes it is necessary to outline why actors would seek to reproduce institutions. Attending to this element of reproduction ensures that claims for a separation between the social and the technological are forestalled. Multiple sources of explanation for 'momentum' are available, explanations that stress, respectively, the centrality of power, cultural norms, belief systems and legitimacy, the functional requirements of social systems, and policy feedback (Mahoney 2000: 517; Djelic and Quack 2007: 165). Absent the specification of some generative and reproductive mechanisms, however, momentum remains descriptive rather than analytical.

Momentum clearly, if incompletely, identifies the course of capitalist technological development and reproduction. Concepts of power within SCOT approaches, however, require significant clarification. It is not that SCOT theorists do not propose an understanding of social power. Often theorists drawing on SCOT work explicitly to identify both the centrality of power in creating technological objects and the subsequent power embedded in the technology itself (Carr 2012, DeNardis 2009, 2012). On this latter point SCOT approaches are strong, and this book builds upon these approaches in clarifying this as a claim for the *institutional* power of technology (see Chapter 3). Herrera's work is particularly valuable in this regard, noting not only the institutional character of technology (2006: 193) but also the central role of diffusion in the operation of that power. Elaborating this point in Chapter 3, we will note that it is the nature of the International itself – the product of Uneven and Combined (social) development (U&CD) – that makes this possible.

However, as with the SCOT approach in STS, scholarship in IR that builds upon this approach tends to emphasize a pluralist understanding of power.[20] Pluralists focus upon actors who are immediately involved in the process of technological construction. Herrera provides a succinct elaboration of this approach when discussing what is required for SCOT analysis. He notes:

> To do this, we needed answers to several questions: In what institutional context is the [technological] system developing, who are the important players, what are their interests and objectives, and what is the physically possible (and impossible) – in other words, what are the politics of the emerging system? (Herrera 2006: 200; see also DeNardis 2009: 10–12)

This focus upon institutional context is an important step in any analysis – we could not proceed without locating actors involved in the design process within a specific institutional context. And locating actors within this context also provides an avenue to understand their interests and goals. However, the analyses produced tend to neglect any elaboration of the distinct power capacities of actors to shape the design process. While the state, engineers, and owners of capital are discussed as the various relevant interest groups, we never have a sense of a political conflict in which the outcome is the product of different capabilities. This neglects the overarching social structure that allows these actors, as opposed to others, to occupy the role of technological decision-makers. For this reason, network-centred approaches have been increasingly criticized within STS and sociology more broadly (Elder Vass 2008; Klein and Kleinmann 2002; Sismondi 2008: 13–31; Thorpe 2008: 63–82; Vandenberghe 2002: 59–62). That certain actors are important players in technological design is the product of wider social relationships and of the structural power they endow. Approaches that emphasize the centrality of multi-stakeholder participation within the context of Internet governance institutions may not fully account for the nature of social power surrounding this technology due to a neglect of structural power, a tendency present in forms of network analysis more generally (Joseph 2010).

Actors bring different capabilities to the table of formally egalitarian discussions. These capabilities are the product, at least in part, of the role different actors occupy within a given social structure. The possession of different capabilities means that actors will prepare for discussions differently, will have different resources available to them in contributing to discussions, and will thereby make contributions of an uneven nature. A striking example is the US Department of Commerce request for comments on its Internet Task Force Cybersecurity Green Paper of 2011. Formal equality ensures that anyone can contribute to the request for comments and, indeed, some private individuals did contribute. The contributions from sole members of the public, however, are vastly different in quality and scope from those of industry associations and technology corporations (NIST 2011). Legal and technical expertise are not equally distributed internationally, and this is due to the different structural roles that various actors – collective and individual – occupy within this structure. Formal equality does not equal substantive equality.

The domestic American differences in the capacity to contribute are present in the international governance of the Internet. Ongoing debates over freedom of expression and the free flow of information online in the Internet Governance Forum include the active participation of global civil society groups, a process that suggests consensual norms are being promoted. Muller (2010, 2013) emphasizes the broadening of Internet governance to include civil society organizations as an important extension and example of democratic forms of global governance. Nonetheless, these organizations are not democratically elected, not representative of all shades of political opinion, nor globally representative. Of the NGOs present in the IGF Freedom of Expression coalition, most are Western-based NGOs promoting Western norms and values. While these groups may or may not have ties to Western states – they are often, but not always, funded through government contributions – they certainly share the norms of Western governments towards the Internet in general.[21] Civil society organizations that promote freedom of expression are heavily represented at the Internet Governance Forum, while organizations that may oppose freedom of expression – and there are groups in global civil society who would object to freedom of expression along religious, political, or social lines – do not participate. Ignoring the agenda-setting power involved in this process unnecessarily limits our analyses to the visible exercise of power, an understanding derived from Dahl that, as noted, has been heavily criticized (Bachrach and Baratz 1962; Lukes 1974; Hay 1997; Hayward 2000: 11–18; Morriss 2002).

Globally, then, Internet governance is not free of power dynamics even if, in a given institutional forum, it appears that it is due to formally equal rules and procedures. Even when states do not directly intervene in the governance process to secure their interests – a phenomenon which cannot be discounted (Drezner 2009; Goldsmith and Wu

2006) – social power is not absent. As Krasner notes – as part of a critique of 'Globalization Theory' – 'Even decisions that have been entirely taken by private actors, such as the technical protocols for the Internet, are contingent upon the willingness of public authorities to refrain from intervention' (Krasner 2004: 67). This requires moving beyond episodic or positivist models of power, drawing instead upon concepts of power-as-capacity that stress its unobservable aspects (Isaac 1987). Powerful actors are those that have the capacity to intervene in the process of technological design and development. Establishing why they do not intervene – whether due to ignorance, disinterest, tacit support or acquiescence – thereby becomes a crucial aspect of our analyses.

These criticisms point towards perhaps the most significant lacunae in the literature on Internet governance: the lack of an explicit grounding in social or political theory, a point Farrell has stressed (Farrell 2012: 38). While many accounts of Internet politics are impressive, they are often (with the exception of Herrera's stress upon anarchy and security competition) not articulated within an identifiable theoretical framework that stresses why actors undertake specific actions or how they are able to undertake these actions. Across a range of work, impressive accounts of the various technical levels at which Internet governance occurs clearly outline the relationship between these levels and various political and social projects (Deibert et al. 2008, 2010, 2013; DeNardis 2009, 2012). Van Eeten and Mueller outline the need to consider a wider range of actors and a broader range of issues in an attempt to grasp the politics of Internet governance in their various manifestations, pushing beyond a narrow focus upon ICANN and the IGF, an analysis endorsed here (van Eeten and Mueller 2013). Nevertheless, their argument consists in elaborating and categorizing the different actors involved in Internet governance, not explaining how the actors relate to each other, how they are constituted, or why actors are pursuing specific aims. For example, the assumption that states pursue hierarchical governance in contradistinction to networked governance needs greater theoretical explanation if this analytical choice is to be justified; similarly, the treatment of markets as the interactions of 'autonomous actors' (van Eeten and Mueller 2013: 732) needs deeper conceptualization. Constructing a clearer model of Internet governance requires all that van Eeten and Mueller suggest, but also attentiveness to the broader conditions of possibility that make 'networked governance' possible. Embedding such studies within a social theory can explain the actions that are taking place – the structural field within which certain actors are enabled to pursue these projects and the generation of these projects by specific social relations. The following chapters will offer a historical materialist account of social power dynamics surrounding Internet governance. However, while in my view this approach is the most convincing, in order to move the field of Internet governance studies forward there should be greater articulation of the relationship between Internet governance studies and existing social and political theory across a variety of perspectives. In this way we can move further beyond the need to stress the constructedness and power of technological objects to substantive discussion of how this process of construction should be understood. That the Internet is socially constructed is clear. How it is socially constructed requires far more extensive elaboration.

Conclusion

This chapter has outlined the limitations of technological determinist perspectives through a discussion of both instrumentalist and essentialist perspectives. Neither approach to technology is able to grasp it adequately as a form of social power. Instrumentalists, in denying any determining bias to technological objects, cannot grasp why actors would fight over the design of a given object, or the manner in which the structuring power of objects is a distinct form of social power. Determinists, by contrast, entirely excise human agency from the process of technological development. They claim far too much power for objects, failing to account for their construction and maintenance by specific social practices.

Instead, we have noted the need to push towards an alternative – discussed in the next chapter via Feenberg's understanding of technology as 'biased but ambivalent' – that points towards the structuring power of technological objects while also accounting for their reproduction by specific social relations. The brief survey of SCOT approaches has outlined how previous approaches in IR have moved towards this position. However, it has also pointed to some of the limitations of this work. While SCOT approaches in IR have been very valuable correctives to the dominant consideration – or inconsideration – of technology within the discipline, they require further elaboration. First, we need to account for the everyday reproduction of technological objects in a manner that the concept of 'momentum' cannot achieve. Second, and linked to this, it is vital to ground our accounts in some concept of social structure if we are to analyze the different conditions that enable or constrain actors in their pursuit of particular technological biases. Third, this points towards a political economy of technological development that can grasp the centrality of the state. And, finally, it requires a more developed and explicit grounding of SCOT work within existing traditions of social theory if these prior criticisms are to be met. It is the aim of the next chapter to development a preliminary account along these lines, drawing upon Marxist historical materialism.

3
A Historical Materialist Approach to Technological Power in International Relations

Introduction

The discussion in the previous chapter highlighted some of the problems in current International Relations (IR) approaches to technology as a form of power in global politics. Technological instrumentalists and essentialists bracket the social construction of technology and the power relations that surround its creation and maintenance, reifying a relatively contingent order as natural. They share an underlying determinist conception of technology and, as a result, do not adequately conceptualize how technology functions as a form of power in global politics. Theories influenced by Social Construction of Technology approaches overcome the limitations of determinist work and represent a significant advance for IR Theory; this chapter will elaborate their implicit conception of technology as a form of institutional power. However, SCOT approaches neglect the centrality of structural power relations and wider forms of social power in shaping technological design. Moreover, these approaches do not theoretically account for the significance of 'the International' in creating the conditions necessary for this form of institutional power to operate. This chapter will develop an alternative theoretical perspective to address these issues.

It is not without some measure of irony that the theoretical resources for this attempt are to be found within Marxist historical materialism, given its often broad characterization as a structurally determinist theory of social life.[1] Picking up the themes of the previous chapter, I will outline the construction of technology as a historical process in which structural power relations – *power over* – are central to endowing certain agents with the ability – *power to* – to embed their values within technological artefacts. This chapter will thereby move beyond SCOT approaches to account for the enduring unequal social power relations central to embedding specific norms within technological objects.

The chapter will proceed as follows. First, the main conceptions of technology in historical materialism will be outlined, highlighting weaknesses of instrumentalism and essentialism that mirror those found in International Relations. This is a necessary ground-clearing exercise given the heavy theoretical baggage and misunderstandings that the adoption of an historical materialist approach to technology can generate.[2] Second, an engagement with Andrew Feenberg's critical theory of technology opens the space for a historical understanding of technological development that, like SCOT approaches, acknowledges the path dependency of technology and its potential for change, but locates this process within wider social relations. Third, the chapter will seek to make Feenberg's insights more concrete, providing a clearer analytical framework for the examination of the international politics of technology. This discussion will highlight the centrality of structural and productive power in the creation of the institutional power of technology. Unless we attend to both forms of power we will miss how technology comes to reflect the dominant values of a specific social order and, in turn, how the path dependency of technology is practically secured. Embedding these concepts of power within an understanding of the international system as structured by uneven and combined (U&CD) processes of social development provides greater analytical purchase on the precise character of technological institutions as a specific form of power in global politics.

Marxist technological instrumentalism

Technological instrumentalism has had a relatively limited impact within Marxism, with materialist analyses not lending themselves to this perspective. Essentially, instrumentalist Marxist approaches tend towards idealism via an inability to link material conditions to social organization and ideology. Feenberg divides instrumentalist perspectives into 'process' or 'product' critiques of the relationship between capitalism and technology (Feenberg 1991). He summaries the 'product critique' as follows: 'Although the advance of technology has the potential to serve the human race as a whole, under capitalism its contribution to human welfare is largely squandered on the production of luxuries and war' (Feenberg 1991: 32). The 'process critique' of technology – contradictory and ambiguous – emphasizes the destructiveness of technology as applied by capital:

> Under capitalism technology is *applied* destructively because the pursuit of maximum profit and the maintenance of capitalist power on the workplace conflicts with the protection of the workers and the environment from the hazards of production. (Feenberg 1991: 33)

Such arguments assert that technological artefacts and institutions, in and of themselves, do not determine social outcomes. Instead, technology – conceived as the machinery of industrial capitalism – is an instrument that can be put towards any particular ends, including the use of technology built by capitalists to create socialism (Nyland 1987; cf. Kossler and Muchie 1990). Karl Kautsky, leading light of the Second International, argued that the transition to socialism will result in a reduction in working hours, but no change in the labour process itself (Feenberg 1991: 33; Kautsky 1964 [1918]: 5–7, 122). While capitalist social relations use technological objects to meet the goals and desires of capital by increasing control over labour and the production of surplus value, socialism will use technology to increase human development.

This line of reasoning, as with that of instrumentalists outlined in the second chapter, seems at one level to emphasize human agency. Technology does not create any specific outcomes and therefore can be used towards any ends. Theoretically untenable, as illustrated in the previous chapter, this understanding proved to be politically disastrous for the project of building socialism in the Soviet Union (Bailes 1981; Dyer-Whitherford 2000: 6–7; Josephson 1995; Kossler and Muchie 1990; Rupert 1995: 77). An instrumentalist perspective is not historical in its claims regarding the development of technological artefacts, and it is not materialist, as it fails to emphasize the central place of material structures in limiting possible forms of social organization. This perspective suggests that any form of social relations can exist alongside any technological configuration – a step too far in its rejection of the determining qualities of technology.

Evolving towards socialism: optimistic Marxist technological essentialism

An optimistic technological essentialist perspective characterizes the tradition of Marxism most often labelled orthodox or classical. Optimistic essentialism has deep roots in Marxist thought, exemplified in the work of Plekhanov, Bukharin, and Soviet Marxism in general, and retaining adherents to the present (Callinicos 1990: 110–115; Callinicos 2004: xxxii–xxxix; Callinicos 2006: 269–270; Davidson 2005: 32–39; Harman 2004).[3] I will discuss this approach with reference to the work of G.A. Cohen, the foremost representative of this position. The focus of this discussion is Cohen's conception of technology, rather than his larger defence of a deterministic theory of history, given its centrality to his self-professed 'technological' Marxism. In any case, Cohen's work represents the strongest and most detailed defence of Marxist technological essentialism.

Relying on a reading of Marx that draws centrally upon the famous 'Preface to a Critique of Political Economy', Cohen emphasizes the manner in which the economic base of society – the combination of the forces and relations of production – determines social organization, reproduction, and change in the 'last instance' (Cohen 1978: vii–viii, 29; Shaw 1978).[4] In the 1859 'Preface', Marx states:

> In the social production of their life, men enter into definite relations that are indispensable and independent of their will, relations of production which correspond to a definite stage of development of their material productive forces. The sum total of these relations of production constitutes the economic structure of society, the real basis on which rises a legal and political superstructure, and to which correspond definite forms of social consciousness. (Cohen 1978: vii)

This passage outlines a base-superstructure metaphor of society in which the economic-base determines the superstructure of law, politics, and culture. For Cohen, the productive forces are *not* part of the economic base. Rather, they stand below the economic foundation, strongly determining the economic structure while forming no part of this structure. The productive forces are comprised of instruments of production and raw material, which are the 'means of production' and labour power – 'that is, the productive faculties of producing agents: strength, skill, knowledge, inventiveness, etc.' (Cohen 1978: 32, 55). These productive forces are quite literally those things used to produce. In determining the relations of production, the forces of production cause the economic base to take a particular form, in that they shape the scope and extent of productive activity.

As the productive forces develop (exogenously) and make possible different forms of social organization, relations of production become a fetter on the productive potential of new technologies. Alex Callinicos sums up this approach:

> Historical materialism explains the outcome of social transformations as the outcome of two mechanisms: first, the structural contradictions that arise between the development of the productive forces and the prevailing productive relations; and, secondly, and only in the context of the socio-economic crises generated by these contradictions, the class struggle. (Callinicos 1990: 112–113)

It should strike the reader that no account of technological development is actually offered in this model. Technology is the unmoved mover, the *deus ex machina* causing social change. There is little-to-no theorization of how technology is created, why it takes specific shapes, or why some technological objects rather than others emerge and take on qualities of path dependency – no social grasp of technological development is present. Cohen's functionalist argument – that success in market competition selects successful from unsuccessful innovations – is, in this respect, question begging (Cohen 1978; cf. Elster 1982, 1989; McLaughlin 2001).

The absence of a sociology of scientific knowledge is central to these limitations. Cohen concedes that super-structural and ideological phenomena influence scientific development and, therefore, influence the productive forces, arguing that science and the development of knowledge is 'the centre of the development of the productive forces' (Cohen 1978: 45–46). Science is not super-structural, however, because it is neither an institution nor an ideology, 'since a defining property of ideology is that it is unscientific' (Cohen 1978: 45–46). This understanding of science is quite limited and takes little note of theoretical and empirical developments that have emerged to challenge this account, from Kuhn to the present – something Cohen has noted but not adequately defended (Cohen 2000: 46). Science is a historical practice and, as such, must be contextualized as the outcome of historically specific social relations. Any productive forces that result from the application of this historically embedded scientific practice will necessarily reflect these roots.

Degenerating into barbarism: pessimistic technological essentialism

While orthodox Marxism has tended to stress the beneficial role of technological development for emancipatory social change, significant strands of Marxist thought reject this optimism. Foremost among these is Frankfurt School Critical Theory, which has been particularly influential among critical International Relations theorists.[5] The Frankfurt School consisted of a group of Marxist and Marxist-influenced scholars clustered around the Institute for Social Research in Frankfurt and included, among others, Max Horkheimer, Theodor Adorno, and Herbert Marcuse (Jay 1973; Kellner 1975; Wiggershaus 1995). The work of the early Frankfurt School in the 1920s and 1930s adhered to a fairly conventional orthodox Marxist conception of the forces and relations of production in which the latter become a fetter upon the former. The forces of production under capitalism had reached an advanced stage: it was now possible for the first time to provide material goods for all people equally, labour and capitalist alike. Horkheimer's initial conception of technology was thus quite optimistic (Horkheimer 1992; Kellner 1975: 134; Wiggershaus 1995: 3–39). In a critique of Malthusian reasoning, he argued that 'the idea that we may have already passed the optimum level of technological productivity' was inaccurate: 'Such ideas and images interpret the dilemmas inherent in a form of society which inhibits human power as a weakness of mankind' (Horkheimer 1992: 27; Wiggershaus 1995: 48–49). Domination was the product of social relations that fettered the potential of the productive forces that had developed. Horkheimer's early critique was of a piece with orthodox Marxist approaches: 'Society in its present form is unable to make effective use of the power it has developed and the wealth it has amassed...its application is sharply disproportionate to its high level of development and to the real needs of mankind' (Horkheimer 1992: 4, 196, 212–213). This perspective was shared amongst the other members of the Institute for Social Research, with Adorno, Erich Fromm and Leo Lowenthal all elaborating some version of this thesis in their early work (Wiggershaus 1995: 118–122).

The fruitfulness of science was not the product of a particular scientific practice, but rather adhered to science in and of itself. The misuse of science by capitalism led to capitalist domination over labour, with domination conceived largely in distributive terms. Horkheimer's famous critique of 'traditional theory' did not encompass a critique of scientific rationality. Instead, it is directed towards the application of scientific rationality – its forms of thought, it categorizations, and its conception of the separation between theory and practice – to social scientific study (Horkheimer 1992 [1937]). Scientific thought thereby remains a realm of knowledge separate from political thought. Thus, while Frankfurt School Critical Theory pushed Marxist scholarship in new directions, its basis remained orthodox in orientation.

This situation changed significantly in response to the rise of fascism, Stalinism, and the horrors of the Holocaust, as Frankfurt School critique shifted into pessimistic and esoteric territory, epitomized in Horkheimer and Adorno's *Dialectic of Enlightenment* (1997 [1944]). Enlightenment thought, they asserted, was no longer reflexive and no longer capable of its own critique. Reason, which began the Enlightenment as an attack on mythology and religion, instead became its own mythology: its rationality took the place of the transcendent, its goal – the domination of nature – entailing man's domination of himself as part of nature (Horkheimer and Adorno 1997 [1944]: 22–30, 120–121; see also Horkheimer 1974 [1947]: 92–104; Marcuse 1964; Feenberg 1994: 85; Wyn Jones 1999: 83–84).[6] Alienation, the central ethical concept in Marx's critique of capitalism, was created not by capitalist social relations and their fetishism but by the process of technological development (Adorno and Horkheimer 1997 [1944]: 28). Far from serving as the foundation for socialism, technology created the conditions for ever-deeper forms of oppression. One sees here the increasing influence of Weberian thought on Horkheimer and Adorno. As Peoples notes, 'At the risk of oversimplification, the School essentially fused Weber's "Iron Cage" of bureaucratic rationality with the instrumental rationality they perceived as inherent in modern technology' (Peoples 2009: 32; Feenberg 2002: 111). This technological essentialism foreclosed any critique of social relations of power that created and maintained oppressive technological systems.

If the first generation saw technology as an iron cage, the foremost representative of the second generation, Jurgen Habermas, maintained that there remained a sphere of human interaction potentially free from domination and repression. Habermas posited three different forms of rationality present in modernity: instrumental, linked to the empirical sciences; understanding, linked to the historical-hermeneutic sciences; and communicative, linked to a critical–emancipatory science (Habermas 1971 [1968]: 301–317; Habermas 1989 [1962]).[7] All three have an inherent form, determined by the interests they are used to meet. Instrumental rationality is disposed towards humanity's interaction with nature and predominates in the productive sphere of society. It cannot be reconciled with the logic of the other forms of knowledge: Thomas McCarthy notes that 'Habermas's own view is that while the specific historical forms of science and technology depend on institutional arrangements that are variable, their basic logical structures are grounded in the very nature of purposive-rational action' (McCarthy 1981: 22, quoted in Feenberg 1991: 177). Science and technology have their own necessary logics, fulfilling human needs of production (Vogel 1995: 29). Habermas thereby endorses the essentialism of the Frankfurt School, but suggests that this can be quarantined to the 'system', carving out a sphere of freedom within our 'life-worlds' (Habermas 1987, 1989 [1962]).

There are clear problems with this account. Its suppression of human agency tends towards fetishism, leaving its dialectical premises in question regarding technology. There is, as a result, an inability to distinguish between technologies we may consider as harmful, such as nuclear weapons or machine guns, and those we would consider as beneficial, such as incubators or mosquito nets (Wyn Jones 1999: 84–85). A critical theory of technology that fails to recognize when technological artefacts may advance emancipation is too one-sided. Furthermore, while a primary focus of critical IR has been upon overcoming forms of exclusion fostered by sovereign political communities (cf. Linklater 1982, 1998), we should not neglect the impact that technological design and development have on subaltern social actors. The diffusion and reception of technological objects internationally is not an entirely causally determining phenomenon, but it is a significant disruptive force when introduced into different social contexts, often (but not always) linked to imperialism and domination (Anderson and Adams 2008; Adas 1989, 2006; Delbourgo and Dew 2008). Unfortunately, essentialist understandings of technology provide no purchase on these processes and as a result provide only a partial account of power in international society.

A critical theory of technology

Andrew Feenberg's work provides fruitful resources for a reconstruction of an historical materialist conception of technology that avoids the untenable determinisms of classical Marxism and the Frankfurt School. Against the instrumentalist or essentialist pictures of technology outlined in Chapter 2 and above, and in keeping with SCOT perspectives in IR, Feenberg argues for an understanding of technology as an historical process which reflects the biases of the particular social context of its creation. This 'design critique' has three primary elements:

(1) Technical design is not determined by a general criterion such as efficiency, but by a social process which differentiates between technical alternatives according to a variety of case-specific criteria;
(2) That social process is not about fulfilling 'natural' human needs, but concerns the cultural definition of needs and therefore of the problems to which technology is addressed; and

(3) Competing definitions reflect conflicting visions of modern society realized in different technical choices. (Feenberg 1999: 84)

Instead of developing autonomously according to its own logic, Feenberg stresses that 'technology is not destiny but a scene of struggle. It is a social battlefield, or perhaps a better metaphor would be a *parliament of things* on which civilizational alternatives are debated and decided' (Feenberg 1991: 14). The implications of Feenberg's first argument is that technological practices are grasped as historical, the product of particular configurations of social relationships – which lead the biases of powerful actors to be embedded within the technological code of artefacts.

This historical understanding of technological development is wider in scope than that found in SCOT approaches, with their focus upon the micro-political. Feenberg stresses that, within a given historical context, certain privileged actors influence the development of technology in a direction that meets their needs and normative values. This ability – the *power to* direct the design process – is the product of a historically enduring social structure. Within capitalist society, Feenberg argues, technologies are geared to meet the needs of rationality, efficiency, and the control of capital over labour (Feenberg 1991: 34; Feenberg 1999: 87–97; Noble 1979: 257–324). The pursuit of constant increases in productive efficiency is specific to capitalist social forms, with alternative historical contexts providing their own distinct biases towards technological innovation (Teschke 2003: 61; Brenner 1986; Wood 1981, 2002a). In contrast, as mentioned in Chapter 2, the dominant SCOT and Actor–Network approaches tend to focus on the micro-political and on specific, discrete institutional locations, struggling to account for enduring historical social structures (Elder Vass 2008; Klein and Klienman 2002; Lynch and Furham 1991; Feenberg 2002: 30–31).[8] While this work is immensely valuable, particularly for their rich empirical detail, both SCOT and ANT approaches fail to address how structurally located actors are privileged in the design process or the social processes that impel innovation. This leads to an understanding of social power in which only the exercise of power is recognized. This is important, but we must also account for the prior designation of actors as legitimate directors of material reproduction, and also outline what drives them to create technologies of one kind rather than another. Historicizing the structural and cultural context of innovation is thereby central to any account of technological development.

The second aspect of the design process is the actual physical construction of a technology. Cultural context does not lead simply to a decision to make one kind of technology, such as military technology, over another. Once a decision is taken to produce guns over butter, it still remains to be decided what type of guns, why those particular types of guns, and for what purpose – all of which still reflects an ongoing process of decision-making infused with cultural biases that become embedded in a given technology (Mackenzie 1987: 195–222). In essence, this asks that, in our accounts of the general social environment in which design takes place, we avoid functionalist explanations for the creation of specific artefacts.[9] That is, while a logic of social reproduction is in place, this logic cannot account for the precise objects that are created. For the pursuit of any overarching reproductive logic – such as market competition or peasant rent extraction – numerous technological solutions are possible. One sees this at work in Pinch and Bijker's classic account of the development of the bicycle, in which Victorian moral values became embodied in bicycle designs (Pinch and Bijker 1987: 28–50; Bijker 1995) and, anecdotally, in the range of technological solutions to any given social problem, from tanks to hatchbacks to Web browsers. What emerges as ultimately 'successful' has as much to do with political struggles and cultural values as it does with market competition.[10] For this reason functionalist explanations such as those offered by Cohen are foreclosed (Cohen 1978; 1982).[11] This points towards the centrality of 'the International' in any account of how technological design proceeds, as distinct national histories will shape the nature of objects that subsequently diffuse throughout the international system.

The third and final element of the design process is 'closure', which is comprised of two distinct practices. Closure is the process by which design ends. The first type of closure occurs when participants in the design process and society at large accept a particular configuration as meeting the needs previously outlined, and the process of technological innovation largely stops. Bijker and Pinch outline this process:

> Closure in technology involves the stabilization of an artefact and the 'disappearance' of problems. To close a technological 'controversy', one need not solve the problems in the common sense of that word. The key point is whether the relevant social groups see the problem as being solved. (Pinch and Bijker 1987: 44; Feenberg 1999: 97)

The second manner in which closure may be achieved is in the redefinition of social problems, so that the initial problem that designers sought to meet shifts, or is reconsidered, thereby ending the design process. It is through closure that technology becomes an unproblematic and particularly enduring historical structure, imparting the qualities of path dependence, noted by SCOT approaches in IR via Thomas Hughes's concept of 'momentum'. As Djelic and Quack note of path dependency in general,

> New institutional developments will only be successful if their champions can find a way to secure legitimacy. Ultimately, socialization can lead to a transparency of structuring and institutional frameworks and thus to 'invisible' reproduction. This is probably one of the most powerful kinds of stabilization mechanisms, suggesting profound entrenchment and generating great legitimacy. (Djelic and Quack 2007: 165)

Closure points towards the signal importance of symbolic politics in the construction of technological objects.

Grasping this element of the design process is central to understanding how the common misconceptions surrounding technology as either essentialist or instrumentalist come into being. Closure works to define a particular technological artefact as natural, as an accepted part of the social environment, one which no longer strikes its users as interesting or novel. Technology then becomes reified, an alienated product of human practice in which the very constructed-ness of the object is overlooked. Feenberg notes:

> Design is only controversial while it is in flux. Resolved conflicts over technology are quickly forgotten. Their outcomes, a welter of taken-for-granted technical and legal standards, are embodied in a stable code, and form the background against which economic actors manipulate the unstable portions of the environment in pursuit of efficiency. (Feenberg 1999: 97)

Technology thereby forms a largely forgotten background in which we move. Its taken for-grantedness is a significant source of its power as a part of historical structures of social relations. This path-dependent power is not unique to technological institutions, but no account of social life can be complete without an account of how the non-human world facilitates, retards, structures and allows different forms of social action. The power of objects is jointly material and ideational. The bicycle, for example, is something that we use to transport ourselves from one place to another and an expression of particular historical values that work to inform our inter-subjective meanings and understanding of the social world. A side-saddle bicycle would seem absurd to our societies now, because that is not what a bicycle *is* for us, either in the way it mechanically functions or in the values it embodies.

The path dependency of technology is not, of course, entirely deterministic. While technological institutions limit agency – captured in Feenberg's notion of bias or Hughes's concept of momentum – this is not absolute, and it is not necessary to continually build upon previously built artefacts. That is, while technological closure 'locks in' certain design choices, these choices can be undone. Feenberg's concept of 'ambivalence' effectively captures this understanding:

> [t]he lower we descend towards the foundations of rational institutions, the more ambiguous are the elements from which they are constructed, and the more these are compatible with a variety of hegemonic orders. This is the source of the ambivalence of technology. (Feenberg 1991: 83)

For Feenberg, the spring, the lever, or the electric circuit are examples of relatively ambiguous technological components – we may add to this list the digital code that comprises part of modern information communications technologies. The bias of technological objects is related to their overall complexity, with more complex objects being more heavily biased towards specific aims than less-complex objects (McCarthy 2013). For example, the average family car is a heavily biased object – it is designed to transport up to four people relatively quickly, safely, and with flexibility, and cannot be used for many other purposes: cars are uncomfortable living spaces, poor for growing vegetables, and make bad schoolrooms. However, the elements that comprise the car – the wheels, metal, engine, seats and so forth – are not as strongly biased, and can be used for any number of purposes. Attending to the ambivalence of objects ensures that technology does not appear as simply determining, and requires that we explain the mechanisms that generate momentum, rather than merely describing them.

In sum, Feenberg's argument provides the necessary conceptual tools to investigate the interconnections between technology and power in International Relations Theory. It historicizes the technological innovation, notes the centrality of cultural norms and values, and emphasizes the practice of closure as signal to securing and maintaining the path dependency of technological institutions. Historicizing innovation ensures that we do not miss the forest for the trees – that the micro-politics of technical design do not obscure the social structure that empowers some actors and disempowers others, while also imparting a rationale to the place of technological development in social reproduction. Stressing the centrality of cultural norms avoids a linear conception of technological development. Finally, stressing the practice of closure draws in the crucial role of symbolic politics in creating and legitimating new technologies. These three aspects thereby form the core of a historical materialist account of technology and social power within International Relations.

Power, information technology and 'the International'

While Feenberg's work provides a set of coordinates for consideration of the relationship between social power and information technology in International Relations, it is important to place these insights in a more sociologically grounded account, one that draws upon the insights of political economy that Feenberg has largely sidelined (Feenberg 2002: 22–23). This requires that we outline with greater precision exactly what kind of social power is operative in the construction and maintenance of information technology and how this social power operates in the international system. This section will proceed by outlining how technological development is formed by structural and productive power relations – the historically enduring power of actor *A* over actor *B* and symbolic power, respectively. As noted in Chapter 2, it is necessary to employ a broader social context of power in order to grasp the dynamics of technological design, thereby allowing us to recognize that design does not take place within a pluralist political context – as Mueller suggests of Internet Corporation for Assigned Names and Numbers (ICANN) or the Internet Governance Forum (IGF) (M. Mueller 2010) – but within a historical structure in which certain actors possess greater power to enact technological change by virtue of their structural role. Second, we will proceed to note the complications that arise once these power relations are considered in the context of 'the International'. Global politics are characterized by an uneven and combined (U&CD) process of social development in which 'advanced' states have the *power to* create technological institutions that subsequently diffuse throughout the international system. Recognizing the uneven and combined development of the International is crucial for the final section, which argues for a conception of technology as a form of institutional power – the power of *A* over *B* at a spatial and temporal distance.

Structural power: rights and resources in technological design

Structural power relations permit and motivate the development of technological artefacts by particular actors. As noted above, different historical, political, and economic structures place the right, ability, reward or sanction to enact social change in the hands of different actors (see also Hayward 2000: 35–39; Isaac 1987: 51 52, 72–94; Wartenberg 1990: 113–157). Structural power is a subset of power as domination – *power over* – in that it is historically enduring, as opposed to the episodic instances of *power over* employed by Keohane and Nye and discussed in Chapter 2. Jeffrey Isaac succinctly summaries structural power as *'those capacities to act possessed by social agents in virtue of the enduring relations in which they participate'* (Isaac 1987: 80; emphasis in original).[12] Structural power exists in two forms: internally related and externally related, or necessary and contingent.[13] Internal relations, typified by master–slave or capital–labour relations, place actor A and actor B in a relational framework in which A has *power over* B.[14] At the same time, A and B, by nature of their particular roles, have different *power to* exercise agency. A and B are necessarily related, and neither party can exist without the other – there can be no masters without slaves. Internal power relations must be reproduced for the social structure of which they are a part to be reproduced. Class relations take this form. Capital has the power – the capacity – to direct labour; its 'power to' direct the labour process constitutes a *power over* labour. This power is structurally determined while also being exercised by specific individuals (Isaac 1987: 37). Structural power exists in many forms, defining racial, gender, and class inequalities in relatively enduring forms over a period of time.

Structural power that is contingent in form is concerned not with the reproduction of the social structure but with *specific actors* within that structure. This facet of structural power is historically enduring, yet contingent in relation to the reproduction of a given social structure. Power inequality between specific states (or, similarly, specific capitals) – the power of the United States over Canada, Chile or China – is not necessary to the existence of the state system as such. The focus of our discussion throughout the following chapters will be primarily upon this second aspect of structural power. That is, we will be concerned with how the United States possesses structural power in relation to other states within international politics, rather than a more abstract concern with the structural reproduction of the system. The American government benefits from its position within a social system in which power is unequally distributed. The power of its state apparatus is constituted by its power over others, even if the capitalist state system could endure its decline. Our focus is upon the specific *power over* of specific actors, rather than the general power of certain types of social actors over other types of actors.

The central axis of structural power defining technological development lies in the social-property relations of a given society. Following Robert Brenner, social-property relations 'specify and determine the regular/systematic access of individual economic actors to the means of production and to the economic product' (Brenner 1986: 26; Wood 1981: 67–68; Rosenberg 1994: 51–54). Property relations define three different relationships: between the direct producers of goods, between the direct producers and those who exploit them, and between exploiters. Social-property relations have varied over time, with tributary relations defining most of human society historically. Capitalist social-property relations create certain dynamics amongst labour, between capital and labour, and between capitals, that define how these actors will seek to reproduce themselves (Brenner 1986: 26). One of the chief characteristics of modern capitalist society is the separation of politics and economics into formally separate spheres of social life, with the result that the 'economic' is constituted as a non-political arena of social life, in contrast to previous historical forms of social organization (Wood 1981, 2002a; Jessop 2007: 165; Poulantzas 1978). Property relations are defined through a process of struggle in which social classes fight over their composition and future direction. Benno Teschke notes:

> The time-bound balances of social forces find expression in politically constituted institutions – petrified praxes – that set the parameters for class-specific, and therefore antagonistic, rules of reproduction. Political institutions fix social property regimes, providing rules and norms, as well as force and sanctions, for the reproduction of historically specific class relations. (Teschke 2003: 7)

It is the social-property relations of capitalist society that drive capitalists' continuous pursuit of technological innovation. This logic has 'horizontal' and 'vertical' dimensions (Brenner 1976: 31; Rupert 1995: 215, footnote 2; Harvey 2006 [1982]: 98–125). Horizontally, individual capitalists in the marketplace must compete against other capitalists in pursuit of profit. This competitive pursuit of accumulation impels capital to maximize surplus value by increasing productivity, necessitating technological innovation in the production process. Failure to innovate threatens the ability of specific capitals to survive in the marketplace. One sees this process continually at work in capitalist society. Vertically, individual capitalists are motivated to innovate in order to exercise greater control over labour, to increase productivity, to reduce costs, and to increase profits. While the horizontal level of competition defines the general mechanism driving the pursuit of innovation, the vertical axis between capital and labour pushes capital to discipline labour and reduce wage costs. The classic example of the vertical process is the Fordist–Taylorist system of production, in which labour was subject to strict time management and production pressures via the assembly line. Various arguments suggest that information communication technologies have increased the power of capital over labour through reducing the demand for labour – thus weakening labour's wage-bargaining position, eroding unionization, and increasing the transnationalization of production (Kristal 2013; Mansell 2011: 24; Schiller 1999).

These relations define the field of structural power in society. By specifying who owns what, property relations delineate the right to change or maintain non-human objects, so that the occupation of a particular role – by individuals or social groups – carries with it the right to either make or accept change that is central to social power (Lukes 2005: 69). The capital–labour relation provides capitalists with property rights over the means of production, allowing them to dispose of these means as they see fit – to appropriate surplus value created in production and the right to direct the labour process. This is a central aspect of capitalist power, combining the dull economic coercion of market relations with the productive power created by labour's dispossession. Marx notes of the position of labour:

> Hence the interconnection between their various labours confronts them, in the realm of ideas, as a plan drawn up by the capitalist, and, in practice, as his authority, as the powerful will of being outside of them, who subjects their activity to his purpose. (Marx 1867: 443–450, 481–483; see also Feenberg 1991: 79; Rupert 1995: 16–33)

Self-directing productive activity, such as the ability to alter either the means of production or the goods produced, is denied to labour as a result of capitalist property relations. The creative power to control the design process rests ultimately in capitalist hands. In addition to the right to direct the design process capitalists have the access to the necessary resources to undertake new technological developments. Creating new technologies is an expensive process and requires significant material wealth. Capital is able to purchase the necessary raw materials and, crucially, the knowledge of skilled labour that allows the process of technological design to take place.

It is important to recognize that structural power, while endowing some actors with positions of dominance over others, also imposes a limit on these powers due to its very relationality. In the capital–labour relationship, capitalists cannot do anything they please to labour. Through possessing power over labour, capitalists must also recognize the limits to this power in order to maintain this privileged position (Isaac 1987: 82–89). Capital can never be completely totalizing in this respect, and the gap that remains provides the scope for resistance and change on the part of labour. It is this gap that also remains within any specific technological institution that allows for its alteration. At the same time, the limits of capitalist structural power also point towards the role of consent and the centrality of ideology in the maintenance of capitalist society (Gramsci 1971; Althusser 1969; Jameson 2011). As we will see, the norms and values attached to technological institutions are central to this process.

Productive power: defining technological design

Social-property relations are not strictly 'economic' relations. They are comprised of a number of different mechanisms by which surplus appropriation (where it exists) takes place. These mechanisms range from the strictly 'economic' right to surplus under capitalism, with its separation of the political and the economic, to the political right of appropriation characteristic of feudal social relations. Unfortunately, scholars working within the social-property relations approach – labelled 'Political Marxism'– have often failed to develop an adequate account of how various forms of social power interact to secure surplus extraction, with a heavy emphasis on coercion at the expense of ideological or organizational aspects of power (Morton 2005: 501-515). This omission is particularly surprising given the central place accorded to ideology and culture within historical materialism in the 20th century (cf. Anderson 1983). The forms of power that help construct and reproduce class relations are varied. For example, under feudal property relations, class relations were reproduced through the coercive power of military force sustained by the productive power of a particular understanding of legitimate and illegitimate forms of social organization, defined in this case by religious beliefs, an understanding of universe as hierarchically ordered, and the rights and duties of political obligation. An account of class relations absent 'the socially diffuse production of subjectivity in terms of meaning and signification' that supports these relations is incomplete (Wolf 1999).

Property relations define access to material resources underwritten by legal rights and political norms that are discursively fought over. Structural power relations are thereby legitimized and naturalized through particular cultural values and norms: for example, the liberal stress on natural rights and individual liberty strongly supports private-property relations (Becker 1977). Actors contest the meaning and validity of social practices by strategically tapping into pre-existing cultural norms and values in order to construct particular understandings of the valid forms of social and political organization (Fairclough 2003: 110–112, 214; Krebs and Jackson 2007; Williams 2007: 22–33).[15] In so doing they 'rhetorically coerce' opponents, framing issues in terms that are difficult to contest. As Krebs and Jackson note:

> While claimants may deploy arguments in the hope that they will eventually persuade, their more immediate task is, through skillful framing, to leave their opponents without access to the rhetorical materials needed to craft a socially sustainable rebuttal. Rhetorical coercion occurs when this strategy proves successful: when the claimant's opponents have been talked into a corner, compelled to endorse a stance they would otherwise reject. (Krebs and Jackson 2007: 36)

These forms of power – 'productive power' – are central to reinforcing the capitalist pursuit of technological innovation. Definitions of progress, modernity, civilization, liberty, and freedom are all key to the drive to continuous innovation that characterizes modern capitalist society. Productive power casts certain actors with the legitimacy and authority through valid inter-subjective meanings that have arisen historically.

In turn, ideas about technology are constructed which reinforce both capitalist rationality and particular values of technological design. They allow actors to naturalize a specific technology or to naturalize the process of innovation as occurring in only one specific manner (Godin 2006; Adas 1989). This is the process by which closure occurs, as outlined above. Actors draw on symbolic and rhetorical values both to promote technological design in a given direction and to end the process of technological contestation (Bijker 1995: 262–265). Agents work to fix the meaning of a technology by tying to a given artefact ideas about its moral qualities, its social utility, and its ability to promote positive and valued social outcomes. Discursive argumentation casts agents within a particular relationship to these sets of values, and thus to technology itself, depending on how actors deploy them. Pinch and Bijker's discussion of the gender norms surrounding the development of the bicycle are a fine example of this process, as different gender norms informed and validated different configurations of, for example, the Penny Farthing or the side-saddle bicycle. Representations of women's moral propriety cast them in a specific position, making their use of certain objects inappropriate and driving forward the development of objects that could sustain female moral virtue. Identities are important for the reception and promotion of technological forms – as we shall see, states that filter the Internet are often discursively constructed as anti-modern and swimming against the historical tide – and the power of discourse helps construct these subjectivities.

Any consideration of the power of ideas raises the vexed concept of ideology and the relationship between the representation of the world, the actual nature of the world, and the manner in which our representations are, in some sense, misrepresentations. The position taken here is that the power to symbolically represent the world is linked to the power to misrepresent it. This holds onto a critical understanding of ideology, whereby ideological representations are those that misrepresent or obfuscate the actual nature of reality (Eagleton 1991). These representations are not, however, necessarily conscious manipulations, although they may be. More often they are the product of a genuinely held belief about how the world is. Ideological representations will never be completely false: they are not akin to believing in unicorns or woodland faeries. Nevertheless, these genuine beliefs can be, and often are, wrong. When Republicans in the United States represent tax cuts for the top 1 per cent of society as being in the universal material interest of all members of society, this is ideological, even if the product of genuine belief: it misrepresents what is in the interest of the rest of society. When racial categories are used to suggest the superiority or inferiority of social groups, this is ideological.

Internationally, this process may be much more complex and contested due to a relative absence of shared norms, yet it still occurs. Actors draw upon different norms surrounding human rights, state sovereignty, concepts of community, the individual, freedom, transparency, and so on, in order to validate their preferred technological makeup of the Internet, as the empirical aspects of this study will demonstrate. In conceptualizing power and technology in IR, the integration of structural and productive power places the development of technology within a historical framework, opening the way to consider how these two forms of power allow certain agents to create a third form of power: the institutional power of technology. Before we can proceed to consider technology as institutional power it is necessary to locate these power mechanisms within the context of the global political economy.

States and capitals in the international politics of technology

The high level of abstraction through which we have discussed the structural power relation between labour and capital illustrates the basic dynamic that generates technological innovation in modernity, but we need to concretize it at a lower level of abstraction in order to grasp the relationship between power and technology in International Relations. To do so we need to understand how this dynamic operates within an international system characterized by multiple states and geopolitical competition.[16] Capitalist social relations are articulated in an international system composed of multiple political communities. These political communities formed as distinct territorial units prior to the establishment of capitalist social relations throughout the global economy (Comninel 1987; Teschke 2003; Lacher 2006; Rosenberg 2013: 196–198). As a result, as capitalism spread throughout the international system, from the 17th century onwards, it developed in a system of states. The historically antecedent state system thereby refracts the basic capital–labour relationship by embedding within it elements of national particularity. National particularity gives rise to the 'varieties of capitalism' one sees in the modern international system. At the same time, the unique split between politics and economics that defines capitalism generates distinct spatial relations. States' political actions stop at the water's edge, as embodied and expressed in norms of sovereign self-determination. Alongside this, however, exists a transnational economic space – the 'empire of civil society' (Rosenberg 1994) – permitting the free movement of 'non-political' capital across state borders. These spatial relations mean that territorial control is unnecessary for economic prosperity. This allows states to cooperate economically, affording joint prosperity and peace, in contrast to previous international systems characterized by territorial logics of reproduction in which the possession of territory equalled the possession of wealth (Teschke 2003; Wood 2003; Lacher 2006).[17]

The class character of the state informs its foreign policy.[18] States interact according to distinct social logics driven by their social relations, generating the distinctive forms of politics between states with shared social interests and antagonism between states with opposed interests. The state is not an instrument of classes, nor does it operate to functionally reproduce capitalist social relations. Instead, it is an institution comprised of judicial, legislative, and coercive arms, over which actors struggle for control (Jessop 1982: 221–232; Jessop 2007). This struggle both constitutes the form of the state – one can witness this in the shifting contours of the state in the transition from the Keynesian welfare state towards neo-liberal state forms in the 1970s and 1980s – and gives the state a strategic purpose, established by its dominant partners. When state actors speak they articulate the interests of a specific class or class fraction and their political projects, often belonging directly to such groups themselves (see pages 65–66 and 168–169, footnote 19). In turn, the form of the state conditions the power of specific groups within society. This viewpoint requires that we conceptualize the state in its process of reproduction rather than in the static conceptions favoured in classical Marxism or Realist and Liberal Institutional approaches in International Relations. Looking at the history of American foreign policy, for example, one can perceive a distinct change in US policy around the turn of the 20th century as the American state embraced the pursuit of the 'Open Door' internationally, in contrast to its earlier attempt to shield its domestic economy. This cannot not be 'read off' the generic character of a capitalist state – a mistake often made in Marxist theorizing (cf. Callinicos 2011) – but must be historically located in the shift in the class character of the American state: from a position of weakness to a position of international strength. We can claim that capitalist states will work to secure their economic reproduction internationally – in both its political *and* economic dimensions – but the precise character of its practices must be made at a more concrete level.

The capitalist competition for profit occurs concurrently with competition between states – again, understood as institutions – for influence over the direction of the international system. Moreover, this aspect of strategic competition locates 'the International' as internal – theoretically and empirically – to the nationally embedded development of technology (McCarthy 2013; Rosenberg 2006; Allinson and Anievas 2009, 2011). Inter-societal interaction is always present in the design and creation of technology within a national framework, acting as both a generative force for change and the framework in which change takes place. As noted above, while structural property relations set the general dynamics of social reproduction for capital and labour, the response to these requirements is inflected with their location in specific historical and cultural contexts – that is, inflected by 'the

International'. In the United States, for example, a general cultural disposition favouring lax regulation of public speech – the historical product of a particularly Lockean conception of liberalism drawn upon by the founders of the American state and firmly embedded in the First Amendment (Peters 2005: 142–167; Foley 2007: 59, 100; Hartz 1955) – is important in driving the development of communications technologies in directions that meet these values. The technological solution to the problem of offensive speech devolves to individuals for implementation through private censorship technologies, rather than through state action. This stands in marked contrast even to European states that largely hold shared liberal values, as in German support for national measures that censor neo-Nazi hate speech on the Internet. The production of a liberal-libertarian Internet is centrally informed by the 'causal fabric of "the international"' (Rosenberg 2013: 198). Empirically, this has been well demonstrated in historical studies of information technology and countless other technological objects (McCarthy 2013). Theoretically, we need to grasp the central role of U&CD and the process of diffusion as introducing exogenous elements to social development within political communities – this would not occur absent the interactive aspect of social development. The contextualization of technological development is necessarily both historical and spatial, locating technological development in the political communities in which objects are designed and developed. Alongside this, however, exists a form of technological determinism created specifically by the International.

The uneven development of the global economy, by which 'advanced' and 'backward' states coexist and interact, creates processes of comparison between states and, in turn, the emulation or rejection of 'advanced' states (Shilliam 2009: 17–18; Herrera 2006: 8, 12; Marcuse 1964: 51; McCarthy 2013). The presence of different societies with different levels of economic development and different cultural practices provides the space in which technology functions as a form of institutional power. As backward states seek to adopt advanced technology, they import technological artefacts created within dissimilar national contexts and which carry the values of that context. The drive to adopt advanced technologies is compromised by the relative material poverty of backward states. Technological development within the global political economy will not occur absent the potential for corporate profit, with the poverty of particular regions thereby setting limits to their levels of technological development. This is clearly illustrated in the literature surrounding the digital divide. For poorer regions of the globe the build-out of information communications technology has thus become a development project rather than an organic process as in developed states. These dynamics of uneven and combined development are the background conditions for technological artefacts to assume the form of institutional power internationally.

The result is a fragmented picture in which a variety of actors, with distinctive capacities created by their specific structural locations, compete to realize different sets of values in a series of overlapping issue areas. States expressing a specific balance of class forces act internationally to pursue the interests of their constituent groups. In this understanding, the actions of the US government in relation to Internet governance are not in opposition to those of American corporations or industry associations in a 'states-versus-markets' view of political economy. Approaches that suggest a division between state actors and market actors often underplay the deep integration between the two in actual policy consultation, design, and implementation (e.g., M. Mueller 2010; Mackinnon 2012). The US Department of Commerce and the National Telecommunications and Information Administration (NTIA), for example, extensively consult with the private sector in the development of policies on cybersecurity and innovation (US Department of Commerce 2011: 65–67, passim; NIST 2011). Similarly, the US Department of State actively and regularly consult the private sector on a range of policies, including international telecommunications policy and public diplomacy. For example, under the Obama administration the Advisory Committee on International Communications and Information Policy had 40 members, half of whom directly represented the private sector, with private-sector consultancies and legal firms specializing in representing the telecoms industry prominent among the remaining members (US Department of State 2012).[19] The State Department has engaged the private sector for advice and assistance in crafting its public diplomacy programmes, consulting widely with a range of corporations and industries, from Accenture and AT&T to Walt Disney and Walmart (US Department of State 2007d: 28–32). Indeed, US officials do not conceptualize a break between US government policy and the private sector in terms that even allow for private sector activity to be considered as lobbying. Ambassador Terry Kramer, head of the US delegation to the 2012 World Conference on International Telecommunications, noted that of a delegation of 100 individuals, approximately 40 were from industry and 10 were from civil society organizations (Kramer 2012). Private-sector participants explicitly had to 'sign an agreement that that says they're representing national interests' (Kramer 2012).

They were, moreover, central to US policy strategies, consulted for issue-specific expertise and explicitly utilized to conduct public outreach. Finally, a 'revolving door' operates between government and industry, with top officials responsible for US international information policies often coming from and returning to corporate life.[20] A 'states-versus-markets' approach premised upon a liberal conception of the state as a body standing above society cannot capture the policy dynamics and power relations within or between societies. This dichotomy, long-recognized as unhelpful within International Political Economy, obscures the grounding of the state within civil society as the representation of a balance of social forces. The politics of Internet governance consist in different social forces contesting the future of the technology, not in a contest between a reified and idealized 'civil society' contesting the oppression of an equally reified state. Allowing for this means that the conflict or cooperation exhibited internationally over the past and future shape of the Internet is recast as a conflict between different social forces represented by state institutions.

The institutional power of material culture

Structural power relations – considered here as social-property relations – grant certain social actors the power to design and develop technological institutions in line with their norms, values, and material interests. Via their privileged social position, these actors are also able to effectively construct and disseminate certain ideological understandings of these structural power relations. Drawing upon pre-existing cultural norms and values, powerful actors create narratives surrounding both their own dominance and the construction of physical infrastructures that attempt to legitimize this dominance. The state, as a condensation of the social forces in civil society (Jessop 1982; Poulantzas 1978), structures the ability of actors to pursue their interests through its support for certain legal, political, and social forms. In turn, the state promotes the interests of the dominant groups in civil society in their international affairs, cooperating or competing with social forces in other states in an effort to realize their aims.

Within an international system characterized by uneven and combined social development a space is created whereby the social forces acting through – and beyond – advanced states create technological objects that diffuse to less advanced states. As a result, information technology operates as a form of institutional power in the global political system. Barnett and Duvall have outlined institutional power as

[c]ontrol actors exercise over each other through diffuse relations of interaction. This power is...the formal and informal institutions that mediate between A and B, working through the rules and procedures that define those institutions, guides, steers, and constrains the actions (or non-actions) and conditions the existence of others. (Barnett and Duvall 2005: 43, 51)

Information technology possesses the character of an institution, although a diffuse one, because its norms, principles and rules – its *bias* – constrain the actions of actors belonging to the institution. As a physical structure, these principles and rules are expressed in the manner in which the structure itself is constructed: the Internet expresses its bias through its fibre-optic cables, its routers, its servers, and the code that runs the network, all of which could be configured differently. The technological is not an instrument that can be put to any use, nor is it simple destiny. Instead, it is the product of political conflict, a product with determinate effects that, nevertheless, can be altered through action upon its components (or even through neglect). Recognizing this aspect of technology as institutional power is crucial to adequately grasping the constitution of global politics, a point increasingly, if still sparingly, noted in the literature on Internet governance (DeNardis 2009, 2012).[21] The material, physical norms and rules constrain the way in which technology may be used, and thus practices that one may enact with a given technology. By including and excluding certain practices the Internet prevents and promotes goals in line with the goals of its designers.

As a technological institution such as the Internet diffuses internationally it mediates the relationship between actors in an agenda-setting manner. With forms of institutional power the relationship between *A* and *B* – between, say, the United States and Thailand – is indirect and diffuse: the United States does not possess the technological institution, Thailand retains scope for action within the institution, and the action takes places between the United States and Thailand at a distance, both temporal and spatial (Barnett and Duvall 2005: 51–52). The Thai response to the form of the Internet – with its values favouring the free flow of information due to its creation in the United States – is to censor politically and socially sensitive information, particularly regarding King Adulyadej (Ramasoota 2012). This is a contestation of the rules of the institution, yet is largely ineffective. As Ramasoota notes, with '...the robust nature of the Internet it is no longer feasible to keep the king virtually beyond criticism in the virtual world' (Ramasoota 2012: 102). This represents the power of the United States government to act upon the Thai government over time and at a distance. It is not an instrument used episodically, nor an iron cage.

Two points about this form of power are important to note. First, as mentioned in the introduction, this is a type of power that is distinct from most literature in International Relations, Strategic Studies, and related fields, on 'cyberpower'. This concept refers not to the structuring qualities of technology, but to the new capacities that the technology is alleged to generate. When scholars speak of the facilitation of the 'Arab Spring' by Twitter and Facebook, of the empowerment of the surveillance activities of the American National Security Agency, or of the (alleged) ability of terrorist groups to crash planes, episodic *power to* is the primary point of reference. Here, we are concerned with the initial creation of these capacities, with the design decisions that create an Internet with a specific form, and how this form – absent any consideration of content – determines social actions that can or cannot be undertaken.[22] We are concerned, then, with the power to create power, as it were. At the same time, however, conceptualizing the Internet as a form of institutional power is quite distinct from claims that the technology generates new forms of 'meta-power' (Singh 2002, 2013). It focuses analytical attention on the structural relationships that create institutional norms via the design of technology, and on the continued embeddedness of this power within these broader and – in this analysis – fundamental structural relations. For this reason the institutional power of the Internet is conceived as a support for, rather than a challenge to, US hegemony internationally. Second, this form of institutional power exists along both the horizontal – intersocietal – and vertical dimensions of social structure. Internationally, the institutional power of technology is, as mentioned, reliant upon the space created by forms of uneven social development. This power thereby structures processes of combination, pushing development in directions that would not otherwise be taken. At the same time, even within 'advanced' states unequal power relations mean that technological institutions structure the life choices of certain actors more than others, defined by their structural location.

As with any institution, the rules and norms of technology do not causally determine singular outcomes. Agents may adopt a technological institution but at the same time exploit aspects of its ambivalence to resist its bias or to realize alternative ways of organizing the institution entirely. However, this is a cost that the institutional bias of technology imposes on actors who reject its norms. It is necessary to dedicate both time and money to the construction or alteration of a technological institution, a price that does not have to be paid by actors responsible for its initial creation. This is a significant element of the constraining and agenda-setting power of institutions (Baldwin 1989: 147, 205–206). Actors' ability to pay this cost – in our example, the ability of the Thai government to censor the Internet – are conditioned by their own structural location and their power capacities, constituting a specific cost–benefit matrix for all actors using the technology rather than a singular effect that can be theoretically established a priori. As we shall see in Chapter 4 below, actors are placed in a bind in which they either accept the bias of the Internet, reject it and thus forego its benefits in terms of economic development, or attempt to alter the technology at significant cost. Depending upon the actor, different options will have different faults or benefits, presenting agents with a unique field of alternatives. This unique field of alternatives prevents clear causal accounts of a Humean-type, as found in debates over whether or not the Internet causes democracy (Shirky 2011; Morozov 2011; Farrell 2012). Embedding responses to technological institutions within wider structural power relations helps us grasp these dynamics.

There is a further element of the institutional power of the Internet. The use of a technology enacts its norms. Actors are forced to perform the bias of the technology, to perform the norms that the technology embodies. Terry Eagleton, drawing upon the work of Slavoj Zizek, notes this point:

> Ideology, in other words, not [sic] just a matter of what I think about a situation; it is somehow inscribed in the situation itself. It is no good reminding myself that I am opposed to racism as I sit down on a park bench marked 'Whites Only'; by the act of sitting on it, I have supported and perpetuated racist ideology. The ideology, so to speak, is in the bench, not in my head. (Eagleton 1991: 40; see also Hall 1985: 99–104; Thompson 1978: 8–9, 17–19)

Two effects result. First, even if we disagree with the values of certain technological objects – the racism of the bench, for example – we may nevertheless enact them in practice. Second, limits are placed upon the concepts and arguments we can make about the character of an object and the types of politics it can be used to foster. The United States government can correctly point towards the Internet as promoting the free flow of information. Obscuring the process of design, these claims can naturalize information technology but remain entirely accurate about the capabilities that the Internet generates – one cannot accurately say that the technology does not meet these goals. Structurally powerful actors create the technological institutions which are subsequently discursively contested, granting to their arguments an ontological legitimacy denied to others.

An interesting question arises at this point regarding the attribution of responsibility and power to actor A – the United States in our example – in this institutionally mediated relationship with other actors. If the United States creates a new technology and Thailand chooses to adopt it without direct compulsion by the United States, is this still a power relation? That is, can the United States be held to be in a power relation with Thailand unintentionally and thus be responsible for unintended effects? Two points are important here. First, as we shall see below, actual historical relations between social actors are often characterized by a conscious drive to diffuse technological innovations throughout the international system. Liberal developmentalist logic, the requirements of capital accumulation and the drive for 'spatio-temporal fixes', and the general ideological linkage of modernity and progress with technological innovation all lead to a general international environment in which technological diffusion is actively promoted (see Rostow 1990; Harvey 2006 [1982]; Adas 1989). Intended effects are present throughout the international politics of technology, as we shall see in chapters 4, 5, and 6.

Second, even in the absence of intended effects, the power of the United States to alter Thailand's social choices, for better or for worse, still comprises a power relationship. The presence of unintended effects speaks to the structural power of an agent – their social gravity – in a telling manner. An agent with the ability to create a technological institution sets the rules by which other agents act and, in locating responsibility for this context, we would be right to attribute it to this actor, regardless of the intent, in both practical and evaluative terms (Morriss 2002; Lukes 2005; Connolly 1983). Again, conceptualizing power as capacity permits the recognition of an actor's capacity to shape the policies of others, even in the absence of an observable exercise of power.

Conclusion

This chapter has presented a historical materialist conceptualization of the relationship between power and technology in international politics. It has accomplished this task through an initial discussion of the dominant understandings of technology within historical materialist thought, noting that they reproduce the instrumentalist and essentialist determinisms of IR Theory outlined in the first chapter. I have argued that both 'orthodox' Marxism and the Critical Theory of the Frankfurt School have relied on a singular understanding of technology that has skewed their analyses. They have portrayed technology as a determining force, cutting agency out of their perspective and weakening historical materialist work both theoretically and practically.

In order to shift the debate within historical materialism it is necessary to turn to the work of Andrew Feenberg and his central concept of technology as 'biased but ambivalent'. Feenberg provides the conceptual resources needed to rethink the role of technology in international politics. First, he places technological design within its social and historical context. This enables Feenberg to note how structural relationships systematically exclude some actors from the design process, a significant improvement over the pluralist Social Construction of Technology approaches noted in Chapter 2. It allows Feenberg to present some overarching rationale to technological innovation which is often absent in the detailed micro-analyses of the Science and Technology literature. Second, Feenberg's concept of bias allows us to retain the deterministic and path-dependent influence that technology does play in social life but, crucially, when combined with the idea of ambivalence he retains a space for change and for the exercise of agency. 'Biased but ambivalent' thereby retains the important notion of technology as a form of social power and enables us to chart the effects that technological institutions produce in their use in society while avoiding the problems of simple determinism.

While Feenberg's work lays the foundation for my conceptualization of technology as a form of power in international politics, it has required a more detailed consideration of social power mechanisms in order gain any analytical purchase. Conceptualizing technology as a form of institutional power within international politics meets this aim. This move has required a number of related arguments.

First, in order to understand technological development it needs to be placed within the context of enduring structural-power relationships. These relationships, discussed through the abstraction of capital–labour social property relations, provide both the generative impetus to technological innovation and a general impulse to design certain kinds of technology through the horizontal and vertical pressures these relations exercise. They empower certain roles with the right and ability to guide the technological design process, while excluding others, favouring the norms of dominant actors in the process.

Second, it is important to note that these structural power relations are supported and furthered by the productive power of discourse. Discursive power, mobilized by agents drawing on particular cultural values in specific formations, allow actors to portray hierarchical social relations as materially beneficial, as modern, progressive, or democratic. These discourses are also central to the definition of both what goals a technology will be designed to meet and to closing down the process of innovation. Conflicts over the meaning of technology are as central to how technology is created as structural power relations.

Third, I have noted that these processes, discussed abstractly, take place within an international political economy characterized by economic and geopolitical competition. The pressures driving innovation are not limited to the goal of profitable accumulation, but are also refracted through states political and cultural aims. Numerous actors are involved in technological design internationally. The interplay of power relations between these different actors is central to any analysis of technological institutions. It helpfully avoids viewing technology as the product of either a political or an economic imperative, directing our attention to the conflict at the heart of these interactions.

Finally, the chapter introduced a conceptualization of technology as a form of institutional power in international politics. This concept allows us to see technology not as a tool, nor as a systemic property, but as a politically contested institution that mediates the relationships between actors in a way that benefits some and disadvantages others. Viewing technology as institutional power retains the understanding of technology as structuring social life, but also allows for the exercise of agency within this structure.

This procedure of conceptual clarification has suggested a picture of how power and technology can be analysed within IR, the task to which we now turn. The following chapters will outline, through an extended empirical examination, the manner in which the Internet functions as a form of institutional power in international politics. Chapter 4 will outline the historical and structural contexts in which the Internet was developed and the character this granted to the institution. We will note how the Internet's hardware and software architectures function to favour the free flow of information, a benefit to some states and capitals and a drawback for others. Chapter 5 will draw out the centrality of productive power in the process of technological closure, as the United

States seeks to forward one particular understanding of the Internet as valid by drawing on internationally legitimate symbolic resources. Chapter 6 will extend this insight further by playing on the tensions within the US approach and the contradictory and complementary aspects of their discursive closure.

4
US Foreign Relations and the Institutional Power of the Internet

Introduction

With the theoretical framework in place it is possible to outline how the different facets of social power have enabled the United States government to construct and maintain the Internet in line with its foreign policy aims. This chapter will demonstrate how these aims – the pursuit of an international system comprised of liberal capitalist democracies – have informed the construction and reproduction of the Internet. This will be undertaken by first outlining the nature of the Open Door policy and its central role in American grand strategy, up to and including the Obama administration. The story told here is one of the overall continuity of American foreign practices. While certain changes are apparent both within and between administrations, with the Bush administration being a standout in this regard, these changes take place within coordinates established by the set of cultural values and material interests that comprise the Open Door. Second, we will note how American grand strategy, driven to open markets to foreign capital and to open polities to become liberal democracies, has informed international communications strategy and policies in their political and economic aspects. Third, we will proceed from the discussion of American policy to note how the bias of the Internet meets these goals, acting as a form of institutional power for the United States internationally. The formal political and economic equality of the Internet, expressed in the end-to-end principle, masks the manner in which the technology favours powerful actors in the global political economy. While anyone may create and transmit content, the financial and technical resources of large corporations ensures their dominance of both content and application creation. Considered in these terms we can see how the Internet reinforces the power of the United States through its institutional rules, which disproportionately benefit the United States in economic and political terms. The analysis of this chapter thereby sets out the object of American foreign policy discourse and practice discussed in Chapters 5 and 6 – the achievement of technological closure surrounding the Internet in order to secure this form of institutional power.

The Open Door tradition

The purpose and aims of American foreign policy engender highly contentious debate. Whether American aims are driven by identity or interests, whether they are prompted by security concerns or the pursuit of avarice, whether US rhetoric matches the reality of practice, all these issues form central axes of conflict among scholars studying US foreign relations. We cannot hope to engage comprehensively with this topic in a sustained and comprehensive manner – the material is simply too vast to cover here, and this discussion will not, therefore, partake of sustained engagements with alternative interpretations of American foreign policy and its drivers.[1] Instead, what is offered is a condensed – but considered – argument that American foreign policy is informed by the aims of the Open Door approach to foreign policy. This policy is generated by the structural pressures of capitalism (horizontal and vertical, as noted in Chapter 3) and by the specifically American response to these pressures – a response informed by a liberal democratic American political culture.[2] US policy in general pursues the twin aims of opening markets to international capital and opening polities to conform to liberal democratic principles.

The argument that American foreign policy is driven by the pursuit of the Open Door finds its classical expression in William Appleman Williams *The Tragedy of American Diplomacy* (1972 [1959]).[3] In this work, Williams outlined the driving force behind American foreign policy as an extension of Frederick Jackson Turner's 'Frontier Thesis', first expressed in 1893, which contended that the United States pursued continuous expansion across the North American continent – and, in Williams's further development, across the globe and into Empire (Williams 1980) – in order to meet the needs of domestic political stability. American society, Turner and Williams argue, is based upon the successful expansion of the capitalist economy in the United States. Domestic division and discontent are ameliorated and contained due to a form of class compromise in which the continual expansion of the economy and the continued growth of material wealth function as compensation for unequal political and economic relations within the American polity. In essence, Jackson and Williams suggested an early form of Fordist class compromise existed in American society, by which the militancy of labour is contained by a continual growth in wealth – expansionism thereby allows the United States to avoid domestic economic crises which create instability. In contrast to his contemporary Louis Hartz, who located the supine character of labour in the absence of feudalism and the domination of liberalism in the United States, Williams attempted to locate this process in both the ideological dominance of liberalism and the material practices of US foreign policy.[4]

For Williams, the tragic character of this diplomatic practice was due to its irreconcilable tensions. American foreign policy was not driven by material greed, but by a political culture in which the pursuit of American material wealth, vital to domestic stability in the United States, fused with the missionary impulse in American thought – classically identified with Woodrow Wilson – in which the United States sought to universalize its way of life for the benefit of other peoples. Williams outlined the dilemma:

> By the time of World War I, therefore, the basic dilemma of American foreign policy was clearly defined. Its generous humanitarianism prompted it to improve the lot of less fortunate peoples, but that side of its diplomacy was undercut by two other aspects of its policy. On the one hand, it defined helping people in terms of making them more like Americans. This subverted its ideal of self-determination. On the other hand, it asserted and acted upon the necessity of overseas economic expansion for its own material prosperity. But by defining such expansion in terms of markets for American exports, and control of raw materials for American industry, the ability of other peoples to develop and act upon their own patterns of development was further undercut. (Williams 1972 [1959]: 88)[5]

The tragedy is the result, jointly, of American ideals and American practices: the need to pursue material wealth, and the belief in the universality and validity of these practices juxtaposed against the willingness to allow other societies to choose their own way of life. Williams identifies John Hay's 'Open Door notes,' which outlined American policy towards China in 1898 as the embodiment of this approach. In a period of inter-imperial rivalry over China, the Open Door policy forwarded a strategy of non-territorial imperial expansion: to open markets to the penetration of American capital while not excluding the capital of other states (Williams 1972 [1959]: 51).[6] It avoided promoting exclusionary territorial expansionism as practiced by European states, thereby seeking to avoid the problems posed by such inter-imperialist competition. American policymakers, and their supporters within US industry, could be confident that the overwhelming size and strength of American business would lead to its domination of open and fair markets – no politically constituted policy of discrimination was necessary, as the mechanisms of the market would meet the needs of US capital.

Williams's basic framework has been subject to substantial criticism. Williams's terminology has been noted as slippery – 'empire,' 'expansionist,' and 'imperialism' were held to be ill-defined and analytically inadequate, lumping together disparate concepts and phenomena (J. Thompson 1973).[7] The Open Door analysis has been viewed as monocausal and economically determinist, despite the role of ideas in Williams's work, and despite the complete absence of economic concepts of overproduction, the falling rate of profit, or the technical composition of capital, which characterize economically driven historical-materialist accounts (cf. Brenner 2002). Perhaps most centrally, Williams has been criticized for overemphasizing the centrality of economic motives over national security concerns in the thinking of US policymakers. Gaddis, for example, stated in his overview of the revisionist debate that US policymakers were as concerned, if not more concerned, with military threats to the United States: '[E]conomic instruments were made to serve political ends, not the other way around as the Leninist model of imperialism would seem to imply' (Gaddis 1983: 175, 180).

While some of these criticisms are well-founded – Williams's terminology was indeed slippery, and his argument could have been more rigorous, particularly in its periodization – other aspects of these critiques promote a truncated understanding of national security. There is an effective acceptance by Williams critics that politics and economics are two separate realms. The resulting understanding of national security lacks depth. The United States is not concerned only with maintaining its territorial integrity absent any concern over the form of life inside the state; not just any form of political order is an acceptable price to pay for the US populace and its policymakers in order to achieve security. Fear of the development of a garrison state in the pursuit of national security has historically been crucial to US policy decisions (Leffler 2011; Craig and Logevall 2009). A foreign policy that maintains and extends capitalism internationally is seen to secure capitalism at home. As Michael Foley has noted:

> Capitalism in the United States represents far more than a set of economic arrangements. It denotes an entire way of life. American capitalism draws so closely upon the indigenous values, ideals, and traditions of the republic, that the dynamics of capitalism and the United States are almost invariably depicted as interchangeable categories. (Foley 2007: 213)

The maintenance of capitalism is not simply an added extra, but a central element of national security policies seeking to secure an American way of life in which capitalism – and a specific kind of capitalism at that – is central. Williams's approach was holistic, grasping these features in a way that his critics did not. Moreover, many of Williams's critics, and to some extent Williams himself, understate the logic of capital in structuring US policies. The structural pressures imposed by capitalism on specific capitals – the horizontal pressures of market competition mentioned in Chapter 3 – press towards the expansion of markets and the expansion of commodification in social life (Harvey 2006 [1982]; Arrighi 2005: 23–80; Brenner 1998). Different historical periods have seen the pursuit of different solutions to this pressure. In the early post-Second World War period, a combination of support for European reconstruction, including tariffs, coincided with the growth of domestic Keynesianism and higher wage levels to deepen domestic American commodification. For the past 30 years, increasing financialization combined with the transnationalization of production and the pursuit of global free trade to meet the socially necessary rate of profit. US policymakers can solve the problem of accumulation in a number of ways, but a solution to this problem must be devised if American capitalism is to be sustained. Objective structural pressures must be accorded a place in any account of US foreign policy.

Despite the criticism of Williams and his 'Wisconsin School' colleagues, and the weaknesses in some aspects of Williams's work itself, the understanding of American foreign policy as driven by the pursuit of the Open Door has found broad acceptance. That the United States is driven to open markets and to create liberal polities is a position shared by scholars of diverse backgrounds and perspectives (Augelli and Murphy 1988; Colas 2008; Dueck 2006; Jahn 2007; Layne 2006; Ikenberry 2006; Ruggie 1997; Smith 2000; Walker 2009). For example, G. John Ikenberry and Christopher Layne both conceptualize the United States as a liberal hegemon which has sought to extend its power internationally in order to liberalize the global political economy, despite deep differences over whether or not this has been achieved or whether or not this represents a positive or negative outcome. Indeed, Layne, a Realist critic of crusading liberalism, is worth quoting at length on the merits of an Open Door explanation of US policy:

> I believe that the 'Open Door' explains America's drive for extraregional hegemony. The Open Door incorporates both economic expansion and ideological expansion and links them to U.S. national security. Open Door economic expansion created new interests that had to be defended by projecting U.S. military power abroad, shaped policymakers' perceptions of how those interests were threatened, and led to a new conception of America's security requirements by transforming the goal of U.S. grand strategy from national defence to national security. 'National security,' Melvin P. Leffler observes, 'meant more than defending territory. Rather, it meant defending the nation's core values, its organizing ideology, and its free political and economic institutions.' The Open Door is as much about ideology as it is about economic expansion and the distribution of power in the international system. Indeed, these factors are linked inextricably, because U.S. strategists believed that the nation's core values could be safe only in an international system underwritten by hegemonic U.S. power and open to both U.S. economic penetration and to the penetration of American ideology. (Layne 2006: 8–9)

Despite disagreeing with Layne as to what US policymakers *should* be doing, Ikenberry agrees that the basic precepts of the Open Door thesis drive American foreign relations. He notes five central elements that comprise US liberal grand strategy: the belief in the correlation between democracy and peace; the interconnection between free trade, economic openness and democracy; the need for institutions to corral conflict; and the need for shared norms and values within security communities (Ikenberry 2000: 14–24). It is these coordinates that set the template within which American foreign policy officials move and, beyond that, which structures dominant views within the United States of how its external relations with other states should be conducted. It is crucial, as we consider how the institutional power of the Internet – expressed through its bias – supports US foreign policy goals, to grasp this point.[8]

Bush and Obama: changes within a liberal constellation

While the Open Door thesis may find favour in describing the traditional impulses of American foreign policy, it may still be argued that during the period under study – and for the Bush administration in particular – these drivers did not function. Indeed, the widespread claim, made by opponents and proponents alike, of a 'Bush Revolution' in foreign policy suggested that the post-9/11 environment ushered in a new period in American foreign policy (Daalder and Lindsay 2003). The claim has been made that the Bush administration represented a 'neo-conservative moment' (Fukuyama 2004; Williams and Schmidt 2008) or a 'Caesarist moment' (Paul 2006), a regime seemingly different in quality from all preceding administrations. Post-9/11 American foreign policy pursued objectives different in kind, not in degree, from the traditional conduct of diplomacy, a claim viewed alternately as a necessary or unnecessary evil (Singh and Lynch 2008; Lieber 2005; Mearsheimer 2005). The Obama administration has been viewed by some as a continuation of Bush era policy, rhetorically distinct but essentially wedded to the new realities of 21st-century global politics (Ali 2010). The overarching suggestion is that the threat of terrorism from non-state actors and their potential ability to acquire weapons of mass destruction have introduced a rupture in American foreign conduct, legitimizing new, illiberal, domestic and international policies in a drive to secure the homeland.

There are a number of issue areas and strategies across which these issues can be judged. Whether policies are pursued in a unilateral or multilateral manner, whether they push towards isolationism or internationalism, or whether they are idealist or realist in orientation suggest a sample of the vast range by which policy approaches may differ. This discussion here cannot, due to constraints of space, deal with these complexities in the detail they deserve. Simply put, while arguments asserting a 'Bush Revolution' are well argued and often contain substantial insights into the character of the Bush-era foreign policy, they extend their arguments too far when claiming this was outside of the liberal policy constellation within which American administrations move. The poverty of the Bush administration's rhetoric and image management was certainly remarkable – rarely has an administration been so ham-fisted or inept. Yet, for each aspect of Bush foreign policy described as beyond American traditions historical precedents are numerous. American policy in Latin America – always falling, it seems, outside of the comparative historical record – has often been 'preemptive', unilaterialist, interventionist and crusading (Robinson 1996; Stokes 2008). Claims that the Bush administration was 'Wilsonianism with teeth' (Mearsheimer 2005) precisely tend to forget the rather toothy policy of Wilson himself in the Western Hemisphere.[9] The Bush White House's unwillingness to be bound by international treaties, such as the International Criminal Court or the Kyoto Protocol may indicate a poor handling of its international legitimacy but, again, the United States has been here before: with the League of Nations in the 1920s, the United Nations Economic, Scientific and Cultural Organization (UNESCO) (Finnemore 1993), the Ottawa Treaty on Landmines, and any number of other international treaties and agreements, either ignored or ratified only with substantial amendments.[10] The Bush White House did not pursue a foreign policy that was fundamentally neoconservative or fundamentally different from US foreign policy conduct in the past (Dueck 2006: 141–171; Jahn 2007: 88; Lieber 2009; Leffler 2004: 22–28; Singh and Lynch 2008; Stokes 2005: 39–53; Wood 2003). It was not a neoconservative administration (Parmar 2009: 177; Hurst 2005), nor did it adopt a Realism of the Nixon-Kissinger mould (perhaps the administration farthest outside US foreign policy tradition since 1898). The militancy, crusading character, universalism, rhetoric, and political economy of the Bush administration was not entirely novel by historical standards, even if, in its specific articulation, it represented a unique approach.

And, as much as the Obama administration has altered aspects of Bush-era behaviour, particularly rhetorically, it does not represent an approach to the world outside of established US foreign policy tradition. Obama, as with his predecessors, continues to promote the expansion of liberal democratic capitalism globally. Despite calls for retrenchment (MacDonald and Parent 2011), the US military is set to maintain forward deployments for the foreseeable future. While lacking the spectacular failure of intervention in Iraq, the Obama White House has continued American traditions of intervening into the affairs of states in the global South – in Libya, Somalia, Yemen, and Pakistan, alongside a continued presence in Afghanistan. Democracy promotion remains high on the list of the administration's priorities, even if no 'Freedom Agenda' is announced (Bouchet 2013; but see Lindsay 2011). The Obama administration has engaged in multilateralism to a greater degree than did the Bush administration, but this should not be exaggerated. While multilateralism was in evidence over the intervention in Libya and a renewed commitment to the UN (Murray 2013: 152, 156, 159–160) it has been less prevalent over, for example, drone strikes in Pakistan or cyberconflict (Murray 2013: 160; Skidmore 2012). Spreading a specific blend of neoliberal capitalism also continues unabated with the signing of new bilateral free trade agreements that open markets in Colombia, South Korea, and Panama. The primary points of differentiation stressed by commentators are oriented towards Obama's development of a pragmatic realism, in contrast to Bush-era idealist foreign policy, stressing his 'nonideological' approach (Indyk et al. 2012: 31; Gerges 2013; Lindsay 2011). Aside from the conservative bias that stresses US policy as non-ideological, characterizing Obama's policy as Realist stretches the meaning of the term beyond its utility. Restraint is not realpolitik, and the centrality of liberal humanitarian values to the 'Obama Doctrine' (Murray 2013) suggests the administration is not working with a limited conception of the national interest. What this argument tends to leave out is that these oscillations take place within a fundamentally liberal framework. Realist thought, often understood as non-liberal, must instead be recognized as a species of liberalism (Williams 2005). Once grasped, we being to see Obama's policies as shifts within the larger continuity. This should not be surprising. For, despite the optimism that greeted Obama's capture of the presidency, altering the fundamental precepts of a state's grand strategy cannot be achieved quickly.

Free markets, free societies, and the free flow of information

Just as the overarching goals of US foreign policy have remained largely consistent historically, a similar continuity is present in America's international information-communications policies. The United States has consistently viewed the 'free flow of information' globally as an avenue to open up other states, to liberalize their polities. Edward W. Barrett, assistant secretary of state for public affairs in the Truman administration, asserted that for the United States 'truth is our weapon'. Central to the process of realizing American goals in an era of interdependence, he argued, was the free flow of information:

> It involves the need for the full, free, and continuous flow of ideas across boundaries. Only through the interchange of ideas can the free nations progress together toward a common understanding, and a mutual plan of operation to achieve a common cause. (Barrett 1983: 10)

During the Kennedy administration these values were emphasized in relation to satellite technologies, as Lyndon Johnson, Walt Rostow and the State Department outlined the economic, political and security benefits of free communications for the United States (Slotten 2013: 327, 330, 343; Latham 2011). George Shultz, Secretary of State under Ronald Reagan, repeatedly emphasized the importance of information flows in undermining the stability of the Soviet Union (LaFeber 2000: 12–19). Shultz wrote: 'The combination of microchip computers, advanced telecommunications – and a continuing process of innovation – is not only transforming communication and other aspects of everyday life, but is also challenging the very notions of national sovereignty and the role of government in society' (Shultz 1984–1985: 715). Shultz viewed these technologies as a testimony to the values of entrepreneurship, linking these values to technological innovation and creativity and, in turn, the economic growth that this confluence of forces occasions (ibid.). Moreover, Shultz did not limit the benefits of these technologies, or the manner in which they should be developed, to economic prosperity alone. He extended the importance of these technologies and of the free flow of information to their political effects in liberalizing global politics. Schulz asserted, in a passage that bears prolonged quotation:

> This points to another advantage the West enjoys. The free flow of information is inherently compatible with our political system and values. The communist states, in contrast, fear this information revolution perhaps even more than they fear Western military strength. We all remember the power of the Ayatollah's message disseminated on tape cassettes in Iran; what could have a more profound impact in the Soviet bloc than similar cassettes, outside radio broadcasting, direct broadcast satellites, or photocopying machines? Totalitarian societies face a dilemma: either they try to stifle these technologies and thereby fall further behind in the new industrial revolution, or else they permit these technologies and see their totalitarian control inevitably eroded. In fact, they do not have a choice, because they will never be able entirely to block the tide of technological advance.
> The revolution in global communications thus forces all nations to reconsider traditional ways of thinking about national sovereignty. We are reminded anew of the world's interdependence, and we are reminded as well that only a world of spreading freedom is compatible with human and technological progress. (Schulz 1984–1985: 716)

As with Shultz's remarks on innovation, this passage could be taken verbatim from policy discourse during either the Bush or Obama administrations (see Chapters 5 and 6). It illustrates the continuity of aims in US international communications policy. Through organs such as the Voice of America and the United States Information Agency the US government consistently pressured the censorship regime in the Soviet Union (Taylor 1997: 28–57; Arndt 2005; Dizard 2004; Cull 2008). As the Cold War ended, the American stance on the importance of the global spread of information did not, extending from radio, satellites, and television to encompass Internet communications. The Clinton administration, and in particular Vice President Al Gore, promised that the growth of the Internet and open access to information promised a 'new, peaceful world revolution' (Dyer-Whitherford 2000: 34; Latham 2011: 193). The free flow of information internationally was and is promoted to achieve American foreign policy goals in liberalizing the international system and expanding capitalism globally.

The importance of the free flow of information – and, thus, an Internet with norms and rules that support these aims – remains central to American foreign policy and its diplomatic conduct. The Bush administration sought to re-emphasize the centrality of public diplomacy, occasionally labelled 'strategic communication,' as part of the war on terror and an attempt to win 'hearts and minds' (Mor 2006; Kennedy and Lucas 2005; Edelstein and Krebs 2005). The motivation for this process is the same as it was during the Cold War: a belief that the United States benefits from spreading the 'truth' via information networks (White House 2006a: 45; White House 2006b: 17). Indeed, the administration often explicitly identified the continuity of aims in its information diplomacy between the Cold War and the 'war on terror'. David A. Gross, former US Coordinator for International Communications and Information Policy, noted the centrality of Shultz's vision for a new information environment (Gross 2006a). One of the first reactions of the Bush administration to the crisis provoked by 9/11 was a concerted attempt to emphasize the importance of 'Telling America's Story.' A new undersecretary for public diplomacy and public affairs, Charlotte Beers, was appointed in October 2001 in the hopes that her experience in advertising would enable the State Department to transmit the American message more effectively (Kennedy and Lucas 2005: 317). The White House created the Office of Global Communications in 2003 (defunct by 2005) in order to facilitate this process of 'truthfully depicting American and Administration policies' (White House 2003). The Bush State Department, after 2001, repeatedly acknowledged the need to update and improve its public diplomacy programs, the central element being the use of new communications technologies – as did administration figures Condoleezza Rice, Donald Rumsfeld, and Robert Zoellick (Department of State Advisory Commission on Public Diplomacy 2005: 7, 11, 23; Beers 2001:

29–32; Hughes 2007: 19–22; Department of Defense 2008; Gross 2005; Rumsfeld 2005). The push towards re-emphasizing public diplomacy was articulated within the framework of the Open Door. As the Advisory Commission on Public Diplomacy noted:

> Among other things, long-term public diplomacy seek to increase mutual understanding across cultures to maximize prospects for peace and development; foster support for values such as freedom and democracy and human rights; enhance trade opportunities; and promote positive international relations. (Department of State Advisory Commission on Public Diplomacy 2005: 11)

Seeking to harness the power of Disney, NBC, and MTV to craft US government messages, officials believed that the entertainment industry and its products, spread by open communications networks, could function as a form of soft power and enhance America's image – and security – internationally, calling industry groups 'America's best ambassadors' (Hughes 2007; Glassman 2008; Sullivan 2008).

This is not to suggest that the administration was successful, or that it pursued effective policies that would enable it to meet its aims.[11] Public diplomacy efforts were repeatedly undermined by the administration itself, by the aggression and condescension of Rumsfeld, Wolfowitz or Bolton, and by deeply unpopular policies abroad, engendering significant criticism from the US foreign policy establishment and resentment overseas (Kennedy and Lucas 2005: 320–321). Nevertheless, for the Bush administration the free flow of information was conceptualized as important to the achievement of opening markets and spreading liberal democracy. At the same time, and quietly running beneath these goals of strategic communication and public diplomacy, there lay another element of the need for an open Internet: the need to monitor and gather intelligence in the 'War on Terror' (Deibert 2008). This need would, in time, generate one of the biggest threats to the legitimacy of American Internet governance policies and, thus, its productive power: Edward Snowden's revelations about National Security Agency wiretapping during Obama's second term (see Conclusion).

The Obama administration continued this emphasis on the role of public diplomacy, stressed as a 'national security imperative' (McHale 2009). Secretary of State Hillary Clinton's 2010 Quadrennial Diplomacy and Defense Review (ODDR) underlined the need to 'Make public diplomacy a core diplomatic mission' (Department of State 2010: viii, 60; Comor and Bean 2012). The role of a free flow of information is key to facilitating this ICT-enabled discourse. Keeping pace with the development of social media, this has involved using Twitter, Facebook, YouTube, and other applications to reach out to core target audiences in ten different languages. In contrast to the first Bush administration, Obama's foreign policy team has tried to ensure that public diplomacy focused upon dialogue as much as selling 'Brand America'. To this end the administration has instituted 'Digital Outreach Teams' in the Middle East (Khatib, Dutton and Thelwall 2012). These policies may not be effective – their utility remains contentious (Comor and Bean 2012; Morozov 2011) – but belief in their effectiveness remains an important driver of US Internet foreign policy under the Obama administration, helping to generate the pursuit of the 'free flow of information' for the Internet.

Pursuing net dividends: saturation and market expansion

Economically the centrality of the Open Door for international communications programs has taken on increased significance since the 1970s. The Keynesian consensus – domestic and international – that broke in the early 1970s, introduced a period in which profit rates either became stagnant or fell, introducing a crisis of profitability in the United States and elsewhere. A squeeze on the rate of profit in the manufacturing sector caused by global overproduction led to a decline in growth rates across Western economies, but it was particularly acute in America (Brenner 2002: 16–60; 1998).[12] In the face of this global downturn, neoliberal accumulation strategies were promoted which aimed to both undermine the power of organized labour and increase capital mobility. This was achieved by simultaneously attempting to break the power of organized labour, as exemplified in the anti-union actions of Thatcher and Reagan in the 1980s, promoting the transnationalization of production, and by promoting the financialization of the global economy (Harvey 2005; Gamble 2009). Digital technologies have been central to these processes, allowing businesses to realize reduced labour costs, reducing the power of organized labour, and accelerate the turnover of financial capital (Castells 1996: 5–6, 18–20, 52; Schiller 1999; Tal 2013: 369–382; Harvey 2005: 3–4, 68–69). Domestically, the United States pursued the liberalization of the telecommunications market in an effort to generate competition, while internationally it pressured other states to follow suit (Cowhey and Aronson 2009: 150–159; Hills 2007). With profit rates stagnant in other areas of the economy, significant amounts of capital moved into the telecommunications sector in the 1990s, following deregulation and privatization in the 1980s.

The historical context in which the Bush administration took office was characterized by ferment within the broader political economy of telecommunications and 'e-commerce' (Noam 2006). US policy officials were acutely conscious of the importance of the ICT industry to the general prosperity of the American economy. John Marburger, Director of the Office of Science and Technology Policy in the Bush White House, noted in 2003 that an estimated 40 per cent of productivity growth between 1995 and 2002 had been down to communications technology (Marburger 2003; Gross 2006a; Sullivan 2008). However, the hype of the dotcom boom during the late 1990s had inflated stock-market values for both telecoms and Internet applications and content services to the extent that, at the height of the boom in the spring of 2000

> telecommunications companies produced less than 3 per cent of the country's GDP, yet their market capitalization, the value of their outstanding shares, had reached a staggering $2.7 trillion, or close to 15 per cent of the total for all US non-financial corporations. (Brenner 2002: 292; OECD 2007)

As Noam noted, 'Everybody built capacity to overwhelm competitors and gain size' (Noam 2006: 277; Noam 2009: 275–276). The asset bubble generated by market competition collapsed in the middle of 2001, leaving Internet and telecoms companies facing substantial losses and overcapacity in domestic broadband provision. The interlinked dotcom and telecoms crash saw the loss of 180,000 jobs and $1 trillion of stock-market capitalization (Noam 2006: 272). Subsequently, market consolidation occurred, with growth in the concentration of ownership across Internet sectors – backbone, Internet Service Providers, search engines, content providers, and so on (Noam 2009: 273–293; Simmons 2010; World Bank 2006). The development of 'Web 2.0' saw excess capacity dissipate, and spurred a renewed, but less-frenzied, round of investment – although the problem of infrastructure buildout in rural areas perpetuated the American digital divide (GAO 2007). Overseas markets thereby took on increased importance to realize high rates of profit in the face of domestic market stabilization and opposition to alternative accumulation strategies, such as differential pricing on US networks.

The 2007–2008 crisis reinforced the centrality of open doors, as US policymakers, led by the Obama White House, increasingly stressed the centrality of export-led growth to power economy recovery, exemplified by the National Export Initiative launched in 2010. The White House stressed the need to double exports by 2015 as crucial to economy recovery. The Obama administration has noted that, with its $12 billion export surplus, 'copyright-intensive' products within the information-technology sector are central to rebalancing the entrenched US trade deficit (US Trade Promotion Committee 2012: 9). IPR violations and protectionist filtering practices threatens these industries, prompting a strong American response to such practices (see Chapter 6). While open doors are central for telecoms and copyright-intensive industries, the importance of the continued expansion and deepening of ICT markets extends beyond these sectors to include the service sector, retail, computer equipment manufacture (personal and business), financial services, and any number of other areas of the economy which rely upon global information networks. The Obama administration asserted as a policy priority that 'technical projects that the United States supports will by design enhance security and commerce, safeguard the free flow of information, and promote the global interoperability of networks' (White House 2011a: 15, 17–18). This policy is structurally driven by the needs of US capital, alongside political and security concerns. US capital drives for the continued functioning of the Internet on a non-discriminatory basis, and the US government supports these aims.

These are the overarching goals of the United States government's information policies, generated by structural imperatives and inflected by a specific American foreign-policy culture. I will now outline how the Internet's rules and norms, expressed in its hardware and software architecture, functions to support and further these aims. This points towards the conceptualization of the Internet as a form of institutional power for the United States in global politics, with the rules and norms of the network acting, indirectly and at a spatio-temporal distance, to pressure others to conform to American political goals.

Opening doors at a distance: the power of the Internet

It is necessary to outline how the Internet's physical and software infrastructure – the cables, routers, servers, software, and applications that comprise the Internet – operate to favour the goals of American foreign policy in opening markets and liberalizing polities. These material features comprise the rules of the Internet as an institution, expressing norms and principles via their technological makeup. These norms and principles are not a given, but are themselves the product of the creation of the Internet within a specifically American context (Townes 2012; Mowrey and Simcoe 2002; Abbate 2000). As rules, these physical features enable some actions and constrain others for actors who take part in the institution – in this case, for actors who use the technology. This discussion will also draw out the relationship of this technological–institutional power to intersecting aspects of global structural power and highlight that the power of the Internet works to reinforce the position of dominant social actors globally.

The Internet is comprised of a number of layers, both hardware and software, which comprise it as an institution. At the most fundamental level is the physical architecture of the network – its cables, routers, servers and computers. This aspect of the institution is often underplayed in social-science analyses of the Internet (DeNardis 2012), which has a tendency to focus upon content rather than content-delivery, although this has changed significantly in recent years, as noted in Chapter 2. In a basic but important sense, the physical nature of the technology is dependent on the infrastructure present in a geographical location, making the buildout of hardware and infrastructure needed to power the network easier or more difficult. Two aspects of this geographical requirement are important. First, a given location will be more or less expensive to create the necessary infrastructure given its topographical qualities. Second, a given location will also be more or less profitable for investors: investors will expect a higher return on investment, in general, within developing economies (to a point, as we shall see). They will also find laying fresh infrastructure in the developing world to be at times more profitable than augmenting existing infrastructure in the developed world. These features – the uneven and combined development of the global economy – create pockets of informational inequality: the 'digital divide', which has been the focus of much concern on the part of academics and policymakers (WSIS 2003; May 2006: 123–128; Wade 2002; Leyne 2009). Thus, as we consider the specific form of Internet power, it is important to remember that material infrastructures representing the heritage of world economic development continue to shape current socio-technical dynamics. Furthermore, as Internet governance has emerged as an arena of geopolitical struggle, the physical routes information must take to complete its journey have become increasingly contested, with the Brazilian government's decision to force Internet companies to route information around the United States – requiring new physical cable networks to do so – a prime example of this phenomenon.

The Internet was designed to facilitate the secure free flow of information between networks using different hardware. It was initially conceived, not as a military device – it was not created in order to have a secure communications network in the event of nuclear war, despite the pervasiveness of this story (Murray 2007: 60–64; Mowrey and Simcoe 2002: 1371; Townes 2012) – but as part of a military-funded research network created to link together disparate research institutes and their computer networks. This occurred during the US budget crunch of the late 1960s, as Lyndon Johnson's 'guns and butter' policy generated the need for cuts to US spending on scientific research (Boffey 1971: 874–876). The cost of providing new identical computers for all of the Department of Defence's Advanced Research Project Agency (DARPA) sites was prohibitive, and thus the sharing of hardware, via networks, between diverse sites became an important task (Murray 2007: 60–64).

In order to do this the network was designed to be dumb. That is, there is little in the network itself that performs any substantial function, such as checking the content of information packets or discriminating between different types of information sent over the network. Designated the 'end-to-end' principle, this seeks to have information processed at the edges of the network, not in the middle as in traditional network designs. This principle remains the central feature of the network today, although it is increasingly under threat due to filtering and proposals to alter 'network neutrality'. The routers for the network were designed to route information from the inquiring computer to the host computer and were not initially designed to discriminate between packets passing through them, although, again, this has been compromised internationally with the rise of filtering. Servers developed to host information, and are often the end-point of general users network requests: we tend to contact servers that host information rather than other users on the network directly. Central to the network are Domain Name Servers (DNS) which perform the function of matching an IP address to its alphabetical designation – that is, 123.456.789 'resolves' as the address for www.example.co.uk. Domain Name Registries match domain names with addresses. The number of possible addresses represents a significant challenge to controlling information on the network, particularly as IPv6 comes to be adopted (see DeNardis 2009).

Above the dumb physical infrastructure lies the core of what we have come to know as the Internet, the Transmission Control Protocol/ Internet Protocol (TCP/IP). These two protocols form the core of the protocol layer of the network and are perhaps its most distinctive feature; as Lawrence Lessig noted, 'these components of the network are fixed. If you required them to be different you'd break the Internet' (Lessig 2006: 145). TCP/IP functions to package content, apply its address, and move it from the sender to the receiver along the most efficient route. TCP/IP was designed to route around network blockages in order to reach its destination without being resent or simply lost. The survivability principle is key to the network overall – if part of the network's functioning is impeded it still allows for messages to get through (Abbate 2000; Clarke 1988: 106–114). Above the protocol layer is the applications layer, the software architecture of the Internet which is designed to be compatible with TCP/IP and facilitate the process of information retrieval and storage. Applications are devoid of content as such. Instead, they allow content to be displayed or found in particular ways, such as Google's PageRank algorithm or Facebook's social networking application. Neither of these create content. Rather, they provide a platform for user-generated content, analogous to providing the paper, ink, and printing machines to newspapers. Finally, above the applications layer is the content layer, the actual information provided via the functioning of the other layers. It is important to note that the structuring quality of these layers flows upwards, with each layer's capabilities determined by the one below.

For early proponents of the revolutionary character of the Internet, it was the combination of the end-to-end principle with the Internet protocol suite that led them to argue that the Internet cannot be censored or controlled. These pronouncements, while overegged and subject to unwarranted enthusiasm, do point to an important element of the Internet's institutional power. That is, the Internet was designed to allow for the free flow of information, and for the majority of its history it has indeed allowed for open communications, with limited prospects that anyone could technically restrict information flows in the face of actors determined to communicate across the network. As a result, the network almost appears to have no rules, a particularly seductive vision for some Internet libertarians and their vision of a sovereignty-free cyberspace. As Jack Goldsmith and Timothy Wu note of the Internet's creators and their creation, 'In effect they built strains of American libertarianism, even an 1960s Idealism, into the Universal language of the Internet' (Goldsmith and Wu 2006: 23; Barnbrook and Cameron 1996). Mueller and Bendrath note that the norms of the network embodies political freedom and economic openness (2011: 1147) – that is, the norms of the Open Door. However, as Goldsmith and Wu emphasize, and as many detailed empirical studies have made abundantly clear, the picture of an Internet free from the direct control of states is no longer accurate, if it ever was (Deibert et al. 2008, 2010, 2012). Technological measures such as filtering compromise the openness of the network, as does the mooted move towards ending net neutrality. The Internet remains biased towards openness, but with sufficient ambivalence still remaining at the lower levels of the network – due to the absence of legitimate technological closure that could secure its momentum – that the free flow of information may be stymied.

The creation of an Internet biased towards a free flow of information was the product of a culturally specific American context. Throughout the history of the Internet's development, the norms and values of the American state and American society set the framework within which the technology developed (Cowhey, Aronson and Richards 2009: 105–125; M. Mueller 2010; Singh 2008: 233–235; Mowrey and Simcoe 2002; Murray 2007; Townes 2012). While one could certainly not argue that the Internet's evolution was determined since its inception – it is impossible to imagine its initial creators envisaged its form today – it is certainly the case that, as the technology developed, it presented actors with a series of choices as to its continued progress. Dilemmas presented by these forks in the road – presented, that is, by a technology's inherent ambivalence – were resolved in favour of the policy aims of the American state, aims that were, at first, domestic, broadening to a concern with the international as TCP/IP diffused internationally (Townes 2012; Drezner 07: 108–109). Here, the salience of non-decisions is apparent, as at each fork in the road the progress of the network was examined by the Department of Defense's Communications Agency (DCA) without action being taken to alter its course (IETF 1981, 1985; IEN 1980). Moreover, the US fought for a particular shape of the network, embodied in the TCP/IP code, against alternatives when they presented themselves, such as the X.25 standard promoted by the ITU or proprietary standards advanced by IBM or Xerox (Drezner 2007: 107–110). The shape of the network was the product of American scientific research institutions within the enabling conditions set by the American state, including both decisions and non-decisions (Townes 2012). In this process the United States government remained the key actor creating the Internet as an institution, embedding within its architecture the rules and norms of its foreign policy culture of the Open Door.

Disconnection costs: rejecting Internet values

The ability to censor information, to discriminate between different applications linked to the network, has required that actors who are part of the institution must undertake to work against this principle by instituting physical changes to the network that will allow for discrimination between different packets, or instituting software controls which attempt to filter content. The rule as it has stood throughout the history of the Internet is that information could flow across the network regardless of content – there was no mechanism built into the network to check the content of messages. Actors who have wanted to use the Internet but not abide by this rule have had to make changes to the functioning of the network that actors who support the values of the institution – the values of the free flow of information – have not had to undertake. If a state is comfortable with information flowing freely within and across its borders, the end-to-end principle is largely not an issue in political terms, and no action is required to resist the institutional rules of the network. This is, by and large, the situation with the United States, which primarily filters based upon concerns over child pornography on a local level.

If a state is uncomfortable with the free flow of information, it must take some action to counteract the bias of the network. The number of states in this category is significant, and ranges from French and German censorship of Nazi websites to Thai censorship of material criticizing King Rama IX and to the famous 'Great Firewall' of China. The cost imposed on such states is an expression of the institutional power of the Internet. This is power at a spatio-temporal distance between, for example, the United States government on the one hand and the Iranian government on the other. The United States – or, more accurately, a specific fraction of American capital acting through the state as an institution – benefits from its position as creator of the Internet by its ability to set the rules, rules which other states must either accept or reject. Understanding the network on these terms clarifies how specific forms of social power – also described as altering opportunity costs – as the 'second face' of power, or as 'institutional power', operate vis-à-vis the Internet (Baldwin 1989; Baratz and Baruch 1962; Barnett and Duvall 2005). The ability to filter the network represents pushback against these norms, and a pushback against American policy. The categories of content subject to filtering extend across a wide range of both subjects and Internet applications, including, among others: free expression and media freedom; political transformation and opposition parties; human rights; women's rights; gay/lesbian content; pornography; anonymizers and circumvention tools; Voice-over Internet Protocol; search engines; translation; peer-to-peer (Faris and Villeneuve 2008: 5). The arms of American public diplomacy, such as the Voice of America, Radio Farda, Radio Sawa, or other channels for strategic communications, are often captured in these filtering nets, imperilling the ability of the United States to 'Tell America's Story'. However, while the network exhibits this ambivalence, it also requires significant time and effort to realize it, alongside social pressures – both domestic and international – against censorship policies in both their political and economic dimensions (see Chapters 5 and 6). It is in this sense that the rules of the network exercise power in favour of US foreign policy interests. In trying to alter the technology's bias, these actors must pay a cost in time and labour to prevent the free flow of information.

Three aspects are important here. First, as Corrales and Westhoff note, states require some level of economic development in order to carry out filtering in the first place. For example, Cuba, with its limited economic resources, for a long time lacked the capacity to filter the Internet and therefore decided not to implement the technology widely (Corrales and Westhoff 2006: 926). Estimates of the cost of filtering are often difficult to make given the lack of transparency of host governments about this practice (itself indicative of the productive power of anti-censorship norms surrounding the Internet). In China, the country which has attracted the most attention regarding censorship, estimates suggest that the government employs anywhere from 30,000 to 100,000 people to implement their filtering practices (Corrales and Westhoff 2006: 928; Dann and Haddow 2008: 220; Reporters without Borders 2009; *Economist* 2013). The financial cost is inexact, with estimates being complicated by the presence of 'dual use' technology and by the externalization of filtering costs onto market actors, making the implementation of filtering technologies and practices the cost of doing business within the Chinese market, as the Google case of 2010 illustrated. Estimates of the cost of Chinese state censorship vary substantially, with some estimates suggesting $770 million had been spent up to 2002, while others argue that it has cost $1.6 billion in total since 1998 (Bao 2013; *Economist* 2013).

Second, the cost of filtering extends beyond the financial expenditure on technical measures. The practice of Internet filtering requires both time and resources, but it also constitutes subjects in relation to the institution and, through the institution, to other actors. Just as the United States constitutes itself as a specific kind of global actor in its creation and promotion of the 'free flow of information' – detailed in greater depth in Chapters 5 and 6 – actors who censor the Internet undergo the same process. In some sense, states that block the Internet, and the social forces these states represent, cast themselves in opposition to the information they are blocking, and constitute themselves as actors resisting certain norms and values. Thus the Saudi government acknowledges its censorship of pornography as an effort to maintain the Islamic character of the country (Saudi Arabia 2013). Public speech is not, for such states, a place for the free debate of a range of opinions. Instead, it is to be harnessed towards particular, communally valued ends, an undertaking that requires that free speech be curtailed. The network thereby forces an engagement with these issues and an active stance towards the liberal conception of the public sphere which the Internet's rules promote.

This dilemma – again, created through the encounter with the technology and its socially constructed norms – also defines the relationship between the state and the citizenry of censoring states in a complex fashion. It suggests that the citizens of a censoring state do not have the need, or the ability, to decide their opinions about information for themselves. The attitude of censoring governments suggests that the technology of the Internet presents citizens with choices they either do not want, in an organic link between people and state, or cannot make, in a more paternalistic model. This has generated substantial discontent amongst civil-society groups in such states (Howard 2010; Mackinnon 2012). The norms of the technology have, as Howard notes in relation to the Middle East, elevated the Internet as a 'site of political contestation between the state and civil society, and between secularism and Islamism' (Howard 2010: 132).[13] This aspect of the technology has obviously generated the most heat in recent years, particularly surrounding claims of a 'Twitter' revolution during the events known as the 'Arab Spring'. Yet one does not have to buy this to recognize that the values of the technology introduce contestations over the shape of the public sphere in a hitherto novel manner. What is important to recognize for our purposes is this as an outcome of American institutional power operating at a distance, and that, as we shall see in Chapters 5 and 6, US foreign policy officials work to legitimize and, crucially, reproduce these technologically expressed norms through their policy statements, narratives, and practices.

Third, the norms of the technology alter the opportunity costs of actors seeking to filter the network, in addition to the economic cost of filtering programs and the social strain of censoring. There are two aspects to this, the first based in problems of technological adaptation, the second in the location of the network within the global political economy. First, as Zittrain and Palfrey note:

> Every system suffers from at least two shortcomings: a technical filtering system either underblocks or overblocks content, and technically savvy users can circumvent controls with a modicum of effort. (Zittrain and Palfrey 2008: 34)

While they note that ordinary citizens may not be either resourceful enough or dedicated enough to employ circumvention measures, the burden clearly falls upon the censoring state:

> For example, a previous version of the SmartFilter service provides the choice of blocking or allowing all URLs in the 'anonymizer/translator category'. Even though a state may wish to block anonymizers in order to prevent circumvention, that same state may wish to preserve access to translators as a useful tool. (ibid.: 39, 45–46)

Censoring states face a choice between using certain aspects of the technology that meet some of their aims but not others – the United States does not face this choice. There are also potential costs in speed, with the implementation of a network with tight bottlenecks and filtering technologies (Murdoch and Anderson 2008: 68–69). These technical difficulties are often compounded by the dominance of American companies in producing censorship software. Zittrain and Palfrey note: 'The blocking in states using these commercial filters therefore tilt heavily towards evaluating – and in turn prompting blocks of – English language sites' (Zittrain and Palfrey 2008: 39). As a result, information that the censoring state wants blocked – information in the local language – is less easily stopped, although the precise nature of this opportunity–cost dilemma is structured by a given state's technological capabilities.

Beyond the technical opportunity costs are the larger opportunity costs created through the centrality of the Internet to the global economy. Countries adopting the technology of the Internet but seeking to limit its full functioning are placed in the predicament of not only incorrectly filtering content, but also of foregoing certain economic opportunities. This dilemma is increasingly recognized by both academics and policymakers alike (Drezner 2007: 95; Wu 2006–2007; Liu 2011; Mueller 2013; ONI 2012; Locke 2011; see Chapter 6). For example, Iran has outlined increasing access to information-communications technologies as a key aspect of its economic development, while at the same time attempting to restrict access due to political concerns (ONI 2009). Authoritarian states, states that US officials would prefer were liberalized and marketized, face a choice between accepting an opening to the market but blocking the free flow of information imperfectly and at some cost (a cost often off-loaded onto market actors, potentially discouraging Foreign Direct Investment) or foregoing an opening to the market by not adopting the technology – but avoiding the perceived risk of democratization. Corrales and Westhoff summarize the reaction of authoritarian states to the agenda set by the technology:

> In short, there is variation in the ways in which authoritarian states control the Internet. The poorest, low-trade, least market-oriented authoritarian regimes deploy the most draconian policies (complete blockage). Less poor authoritarian regimes have an economic interest in the Internet, so they supply it cautiously (i.e., restricting access and content). High-income, high-trade authoritarian regimes that are growing fast and pursuing market-oriented policies (such as China), on the other hand, have the largest appetite for internet technology, so they supply it (i.e., have lax access restrictions) while spending heavily on restricting content. (Corrales and Westhoff 2006: 928; see also Howard 2010: 10)

This effectively outlines the dilemma faced by states uncomfortable with the cultural values embedded within the Internet. The choice of whether or not to adopt the Internet, and the manner in which this occurs, takes place due to an agenda set by the technology – the 'moment of determinism' (McCarthy 2013) – and which reflects the interests of American grand strategy in liberalizing the global political economy.

The Internet as a market and the uneven global economy

Theoretically grasping the nature and extent of the Internet's institutional power is further deepened and extended if we go beyond the purely formal aspects of its technological rules to consider their substantive content. If, as Lessig has argued, 'code is law', then, as Marx argued, the substantive content of the formally equally Internet 'law' is its reproduction of substantive inequality (Lessig 2006; Marx 1976 [1867]: 280; Wood 1981). That is, it is necessary to consider not only the institutional rules of the network, but also the structural power relations that operate to favour powerful actors at the expense of the less powerful. The rules and norms of the Internet, constructed around the end-to-end principle, secures a form of formal equality for actors engaging with the technology. All actors who use the technology are in principle able to create information and applications for the network. However, in the competition for limited attention spans and limited market shares, only large, economically powerful companies have the financial resources necessary to develop popular Internet applications and bring them to market. Despite the popular image of Internet companies created by 'two guys in a garage', successful companies require a massive influx of capital in order to create, develop, and promote their applications. Google was the product of two graduate students – from Stanford, one of the finest universities in the world –using an initial $25 million in start-up capital. Facebook, the poster child for 'Web 2.0' and its vision of user-created content, had similarly humble upbringings: it originated, as we know, from Harvard, again with substantial financial backing. These processes are integral, not incidental, to the creation of applications and content.

Underdeveloped states that adopt the Internet to realize economic benefits face an unequal playing field. It remains the case that the network is dominated by economically powerful actors. This power ranges from the capacity of 'Tier-1' networks – of the 12 such networks, 8 are American – to shape peering arrangements (Singh 2008: 35–181; Wade 2002: 454–455) to the dominance of Internet traffic by large corporations. While the former is distinct from the technically embedded norms of the network, the latter is very much created and maintained by the purely formal equality of the end-to-end principle. American companies remain dominant in the provision of web browsers, applications, and content. Outside of China, which has created a strong domestic profile for its web companies via discrimination against foreign competitors, American companies are strikingly dominant. A few examples are illustrative. In India, the top 25 Internet sites by traffic are dominated by American corporations, with Google, Facebook, YouTube, LinkedIn, Twitter, and Ebay featuring (Alexa 2013). Brazilian and South African traffic is similarly constituted, with over 50 per cent of their top 25 sites owned by American companies (ibid.). Google, Facebook, Apple and Amazon – the Internet's 'giants' – dominate the global digital economy, with Apple's market capitalization alone accounting for 1.1 per cent of the global equity market (*The Economist* 2012). Global media ownership figures from 2011 note 16 of the top 30 global media companies by revenue are American, with Google again top (Zenithoptimedia 2013). MSN, Google, Facebook, Yahoo! and Amazon dominate Internet traffic to the extent that they seem to be altering the configuration of the network, potentially eroding the dominance of Tier-1 networks (Shavitt and Weinsberg 2012) while enhancing their oligopoly of content provision (Palacin et al. 2013).

Web content is dominated globally by large media conglomerates with their headquarters in the United States and Europe – Time Warner, Viacom, Bertelsmann, Disney, and News Corporation, among others (Arsenault and Castells 2008; Curran 2013; *Columbia Journalism*

Review 2010, 2013). Within any particular country in the developing world the dominant websites in terms of traffic are American creations, with the partial exceptions of China and Russia. The applications that global users encounter when they use the Internet are applications created by American corporations. While the formal rules of the network encourage informational equality, the disparity in resources globally leads to the substantive domination of the Internet by already dominant social actors. Far from creating a level playing field, as liberal authors often suggest, the rules and norms of the network reproduce substantive inequalities. There is, therefore, a digital divide not only in terms of access to information but in terms of production of content and the economic benefits that such production creates. There may be no satisfactory way around this technological dilemma – one would not wish to suggest that positive discrimination on the network is feasible. In any case, movement towards such substantive equality would, at this point, require significant alteration in the capitalist social relations that underpin the norms of the Internet. Such a prospect will not be realized in the near to medium term.

Conclusion: closure and the Open Door

The argument so far has suggested the dominance of the United States government and American capital in setting the rules and norms of the Internet. The network functions as from of institutional power in global governance which supports and facilitates both market liberalization and political liberalization globally through its institutional rules. The structural power that created the network – generated by the uneven development of the capitalist global economy – flows through the network. Engagement with the norms of the network produce specific relational identities according to their acceptance or rejection, a manifestation of the productive power of material objects. These facets of social power support the aims of the United States' Open Door approach to foreign policy.

However, resistance to these aims is clearly possible and desirable for some social actors. States are able to resist the American drive for the free flow of information via the ambivalence still present in the technology. Filtering practices, while incurring a cost in resources, are able to limit the free flow of information and do allow states such as Burma, China, Iran, Saudi Arabia, Thailand, and Tajikistan, among others, to restrict information flows within their countries. As we shall see in the following chapters, the United States government has attempted to counter this practice by designating it as an illegitimate, unjust denial of human rights and freedoms as enshrined in the UN Declaration of Human Rights and as promoted by facets of global civil society. This uses the productive power resources provided by these norms in an attempt to close off alternative conceptions of how the Internet can and should be structured. At the same time, though, the United States faces a dilemma in its treatment of its own corporations, as US capital can, and has, undermined the goal of openness by creating and maintaining filtering networks for other countries. The most high-profile examples are the conduct of Yahoo! and Google prior to 2010, but this practice is more widespread. In weighing how to respond, American policy officials thereby face a dilemma, trying to strike an uncertain balance between the political and the economic goals of the Open Door foreign policy. The tension between these goals will shape the future of US policy in this area, but the precise nature of this negotiation is uncertain. The role of the state, mediating the diverse political and economic needs of American capitalism, will be central, but the form of this mediation remains underdetermined.

5
Pursuing Technological Closure: Symbolic Politics, Legitimacy, and Internet Filtering[1]

Introduction

The institutional power of the Internet for US foreign policy cannot function in the absence of a supporting ideological construction which legitimizes a specific form of the technology. The norms and values of technological institutions must be continually reproduced (Sims and Henke 2012) – the momentum of a technological institution relies on precisely these forms of reproduction. Symbolic politics are central to this process (Althusser 2008 [1971]). This chapter and the following will outline how US government discourse attempts to secure an Internet with values that reflect its interest in the promotion of liberal capitalist democracy globally. We will see that US foreign policy officials use a variety of discursive strategies and construct a number of interrelated narratives to assert that the Internet must be a medium for the 'free flow of information'. Drawing upon dominant norms in international society the US government asserts that the free flow of information guarantees the right to freedom of speech and promotes open democratic government. In the process, the US government casts alternative arrangements – those which would interrupt the free flow of information due to social, cultural, or political concerns – as illegitimate.

We will examine these narratives in relation to Internet filtering. Filtering represents an attempt to subvert the open flow of information. In an effort to delegitimize this practice, which is seen to operate against its interests, the US government employs two primary strategies. First, US discourse links the free flow of information to the provision of universal human rights, drawing upon the symbolic capital provided by international organizations, human rights treaties, and Western non-governmental organizations. Second, US policy discourse links the denial of the free flow of information to the denial of democracy. US officials appeal to the unprecedented position of 'democracy' as a legitimate value in international society to support its policy position in favour of an open Internet. In contrast to the discourse around intellectual property rights and its reliance upon claims to scientific authority over how technological innovation works, US arguments surrounding Internet filtering centre upon claims to moral and normative validity. The relationship between the two central concepts of the US story – that between liberal freedoms and democracy – elides the continually contested nature of their articulation, portraying them as necessarily universal and thereby outside history. A clear value is accorded to the Internet as a technological object that promotes liberty, democracy, and international peace, as long as its form remains unchanged.

These constructions are mobilized to support and legitimate American foreign policy practices. The final section of this chapter notes the manner in which this discourse – assigning negative values to filtering policies and thereby constituting filtering states as illegitimate both in relation to international society and in relation to their own population – validates US policies of funding and developing filtering circumvention technologies to restore the bias of the Internet in places where it has been undermined. The ability of states to filter the Internet remains, but at a higher cost. Here the structural power of the US government, its productive power, and the institutional power of the Internet's form, combine to exert pressure against norms and practices of state sovereignty and self-determination as classically understood.

One final issue must be mentioned before proceeding to the substantive analysis. In discussing freedom of speech and expression, no normative claims are made as to the validity of censorship or the validity of the free flow of information – while the analysis critically examines US policy, this should not be taken as an endorsement of the policies of states that censor information. These issues are very important and deserve to be debated at length, something not possible at present and which must thereby be postponed.[2]

Human rights and Internet openness

Perhaps the most significant element of US discourse is the constant linkage between the free flow of information and an open Internet with the goal of preserving and promoting universal liberal human rights to freedom of speech and expression. American policymakers, in both the Bush and Obama administrations, continuously emphasize the link between the free flow of information with freedom of expression and human rights. In crafting this narrative, US officials tap into the international legitimacy of the human-rights regime (Beitz 2001; Donnelly 2003; Hafner-Burton, Tsutsui and Meyer 2008; Hamelink 1994: 284–294; Hurrell 2005: 36).[3] For example, in preparation for the World Summit on the Information Society (WSIS), US policymakers set out the value of the free flow of information in relation to human rights.

> The US believes that the WSIS should affirm the right of all individuals to freedom of opinion and expression, including freedom to hold opinions without interference and to seek, receive and impart information through any media regardless of frontiers, as set forth in Article 19 of the Universal Declaration of Human Rights (UDHR). We believe that the WSIS draft declaration of Principles and draft Plan of Action should refer to these rights as stated in the Universal Declaration. Rather than seeking to create additional rights at the WSIS, States should implement the obligation that they have assumed under human rights treaties. In this vein, we believe that individuals should have the freedom to communicate, access information, and pursue development. (US Department of State 2003a; see also Marburger 2003; Shiner 2006; Bush 2008b; Clinton 2010a, 2011a; Posner 2011a; Baer 2011b)

The principle expressed here – the importance of freedom of speech and expression as a universal human right – is constantly expressed throughout US discourse. Its initial crystallization occurred at the end of the first phase of the WSIS. The US government stated that 'States have affirmed their commitment to freedom of the press, as well as to the independence, pluralism and diversity of the media. The US believes that the principle free flow of information [sic], as enshrined in the UDHR, lies at the heart of the Information Society' (US Department of State 2003b). The 'moral touchstone' of international society (Beitz 2001: 269), the Universal Declaration of Human Rights (UDHR), is deployed to make the case for an open Internet. The UDHR, and in particular Article 19,[4] is used to reinforce the legitimacy of a specific technological configuration for the Internet. US officials assert that they are not attempting to create new international norms or constitute new human rights practices. Daniel Baer, Deputy Assistant Secretary in the Bureau of Democracy, Human Rights and Labour in the Obama administration claimed that

Article 19 of the UDHR is, in retrospect, kind of amazingly prescient about the protection of freedom of expression through any medium regardless of frontier. And through any medium and regardless of frontier, we think we don't need any new principles. We have existing principles, and we think human rights apply online just as they do offline. (Baer 2011b; see also White House 2011a: 9; Posner 2012a)

In this manner, US officials can claim that they are merely asking states to conform to already-existing international principles when they push for the free flow of information. That the technology represents a step change in what this norm means via its ability to rapidly spread massive amounts of information is sidelined, despite claims to the revolutionary nature of the Internet found elsewhere in the US policy narrative. That the norms of international society are the products of specific historical contexts and thereby open to renegotiation is underplayed by the claim to the continuing validity of Article 19 as drawn up in 1948.

This sits in tension with other aspects of the US discourse. While an open Internet is linked to the provision of human rights, US policymakers simultaneously work to undermine the legitimacy of the right to self-determination for other states. Censoring states are identified as violating their commitment to free speech, a commitment which has been redefined in the process of arguing for a specifically liberal interpretation:

> The Internet is arguably the greatest facilitator for freedom of expression and innovation in the world today. The US recognizes the importance of freedom of expression and ideas and the free flow of information on the Internet to economic development and its influence in facilitating greater social and political debate. We also recognize that numerous governments around the world unduly restrict freedom of expression on the Internet despite their international commitments to freedom of expression, such as those made at the WSIS and as found in the UDHR and the International Covenant on Civil and Political Rights. (Gross 2006a; see also Shiner 2006)

The status of the UDHR and the Covenant as legitimate norms within the international system permits the US to undermine competing conceptions of sovereignty. Ambassador David Gross, US Coordinator for International Communications and Information Policy and the lead American official on communications policy during the Bush administration, clearly outlined this perspective:

To summarize, there is in the UDHR that was adopted at the United Nations back in the '40s, both in Article 19, what we believe is a very clear and very important statement on freedom of expression. There is another article in the same document, Article 29, which refers to things such as community values and laws and things of that nature.

And we believe that those concepts are compatible with each other, of course. We all live in a world of laws. But we don't think people should misunderstand the import of Article 29 as it related to Article 19. We do not view Article 29 as in some way in balance with Article 19. (Gross 2003a)[5]

The identification of a particular configuration of the Internet architecture as meeting universal human rights grants the technology a powerful identity and role within the international system. In US policy discourse this takes precedence over competing norms of self-determination. Traditional norms of national sovereignty – expressed in Article 29 and envisioned to allow political communities to decide for themselves how they will live – do not justify censorship or filtering. The limits to communal rights of self-determination are reached when they violate an individual's right to freedom of speech and freedom of expression and, crucially, this explicitly includes a technological makeup of the Internet that locks 'people inside a world of government-controlled content cutting them off from [the] rest of the world' (Posner 2012a). US policymakers place their arguments about the valid architecture of the Internet within the large stream of post-Cold War attempts to construct a norm of 'conditional sovereignty' based upon states' abilities to realize liberalism (Franck 1992; Ignatieff 2002; Teson 2003). Addressing the World Telecommunications Standardization Assembly in 2008, Gross made this link explicit:

As was made clear in our deliberations, by 'Member States' we mean not only the governments but also the citizens of those states. Therefore, all agreed that we are to refrain from impeding the access of any citizen of our countries to public Internet websites. (Gross 2008)

Sovereignty hereby becomes defined as liberal sovereignty: states which are not liberal and do not enact liberal policies are not properly sovereign. American policy officials resist suggestions that states may censor information as an expression of self-determination or their right to control information flows within their borders, rejecting any suggestions that rights are culturally specific (Baer 2012). For example, at the Organization for Security and Cooperation in Europe (OSCE) meetings in Vilnius in 2011, US officials pushed for a declaration to acknowledge the right of Internet freedom and states' duties to protect this right. American policymakers refused, when pressed, to agree to the non-interference in the domestic affairs of states in order to meet these aims. One, US Assistant Secretary of State Daniel Baer, asserted:

> I think that the question about non-interference, when I said that that can be code for other things, one of the things that some countries have used that as code for is allowing massive censorship of the online space or allowing shutdowns on the online space. And for that reason, language like that, when introduced in the context of conversations about the online space, it can be deeply concerning. And so that would be one reason why using language like that in this context would be something that we might have significant concerns about. (Baer 2011b; see also Clinton 2011b)

In this manner, Russian concerns about allowing the free flow of information, linked to concerns over domestic political stability (Myers 2011), are pushed aside and the right to promote individual liberty internationally asserted. In January 2010, in her most famous speech on Internet governance, Secretary of State Clinton proclaimed the explicit goal that the United States would take active steps to 'advance freedom' on the Internet, outlining a range of US policies to meet these aims (Clinton 2010a). No right to enforce the norms of Article 19 through interference in the domestic affairs of a censoring state exists in international law, yet this argument still operates to legitimize these practices, as outlined below. The push towards conditional sovereignty, led by the United States and supported by Western governments in general – half of the OSCE's member states supported a declaration (Myers 2011) – exercises significant symbolic pressure upon authoritarian governments.

In the context of debates over the form that Internet architecture should take, we thereby see a series of relational identities attributed to people, states, and objects constructed to reinforce US long-term strategic aims. States which are non-liberal and which deny freedom of speech and expression are not properly sovereign. Instead, sovereignty is conceived in a liberal fashion to rest in the hands of the people. Individuals within states are redefined as proto-liberals denied the right to access information, which they would presumably otherwise seek out (DeBrix 2008: 8–11). The Internet is about empowering these individuals, a frequent refrain for Obama administration officials (Posner 2011f). This expresses the deepest roots of American political culture and thought, based in Lockean liberalism, and 'as prevalent today as they were in the eighteenth century' (Foley 2007: 40; Hartz 1955). In this understanding, which largely constitutes the common sense of the American foreign policy community, individuals have a natural right to liberty, including the right to free speech, expression, and association. Being natural, these rights are not historically or culturally specific. Instead, they are the possession of all human beings in all places at all times. Governments that deny these rights are, for Locke and for US foreign policy officials, illegitimate and lacking the central prerequisites of sovereignty. The American attempt to universalize these values – central to American foreign-policy practice (Hunt 1987: 42; McCrisken 2003: 11; Westad 2006) and including, as we shall see, the provision of anti-censorship technologies – rests upon this claim.[6] The right to pursue the global expansion of liberty, one of the foundational norms of American foreign relations, is expressed throughout these arguments (Hunt 2009: 41–43, 192; Smith 2012).

In turn, of course, the social basis of censoring states is redefined. Offending states are portrayed as having no roots within civil society; instead they sit on top of it and act as a fetter on the realization of the natural rights of the population. The cultural roots which may lie behind certain policies are sidelined, as is the notion that different communities may legitimately believe in and pursue different forms of life – forms of life that may proscribe certain forms of information in pursuit of communally held norms and values. As individuals cannot abrogate their liberty, governments that fail to secure this liberty cannot claim to act upon the sovereign will of the people. The technological structure of an open Internet is granted primacy over the sovereignty of states, characteristic of the drive to ensure the penetration of international institutions into the domestic constitution of societies internationally (Slaughter 2004). Priority falls upon ensuring that the makeup of the technological institution meets the needs of liberal individuals over and against the actions of governments. In relation to the technological development of the Internet, the construction of illiberal regimes as illegitimate allows for the US government undertaking practical action to promote the free flow of information, thereby undermining the control of sovereign governments over the information flows into and out of their countries. The policy is legitimate because it represents 'the peoples' interests, rather than the interests of an authoritarian government.

This narrative goes further to invoke two more symbolically powerful elements in support of the free flow of information. First, US officials make strong knowledge claims about how the Internet and international society must function, a claim to epistemic authority. Attempts to filter the Internet 'indicate a basic lack of understanding that free speech – whether it's supportive speech or subversive speech – is harder than ever to supress in the Digital Age' (Posner 2011f); states 'who seek to impose their control over the Internet will only be further removed from its awesome potential' (Strickling 2012a). US officials repeatedly claim that authoritarian states do not understand how the information society must enable the free flow of information in order to function. In other cases the functioning of the Internet and its norms are presented as receiving broad acceptance, particularly when arguments are directed towards states in the developing world that may be useful allies in Internet governance disputes with authoritarian governments. Obama administration officials express this via the principle of 'trust', one of their two 'dominant principles in relation to Internet governance' (Strickling 2011b, 2012a, 2012b; Clinton 2010a). A failure of trust has the potential to destroy the functioning of the network: 'If foreign governments do not trust the Internet governance systems, they will threaten to balkanize the Domain Name System which will jeopardize the worldwide reach of the Internet' (Strickling 2010b, 2010a). Absent trust, users will not post information, content providers will not produce content, and corporations will not exploit the potential of the network to its fullest (Strickling 2010b). Trusting a technology is central to accepting its purposes and agreeing to its politics. It suggests a settled area of normative agreement, placing the operation of a technological institution in functional terms. It is necessary to know a technology works in order to use it: no one would ever get into a car if they were uncertain about its safety – but acceptance that a technology 'works' rests upon acceptance of its purpose (Pinch and Bijker 1987: 30). The idea of trust suggests agreement about the shape of the Internet.

Second, US officials appeal to History in support of their knowledge claims. Gross, for example, invoked a teleological conception of history in favour of the American vision of the Internet when he asserted that censoring countries are attempting to resist historical progress: 'These countries are attempting – vainly, I believe – to deflect the course of history' (Gross 2003b). Similarly, George Bush asserted that 'Historians will...point to the role of technology in frustrating censorship and central control – and marvel at the power of instant communications to spread the truth, the news, and courage across borders' (Bush 2003).

Obama's Assistant Secretary of State, Michael Posner, asserted that 'History is on our side here' (Posner and Crowley 2011). Attempts to censor the Internet are linked to the Cold War and the effort of the Soviet Union to impose forms of censorship, a continuation of the US policy outlined in Chapter 4. A phrase such as 'information curtain' alludes to this, as 'citizens of some other countries remain trapped and isolated behind firewalls' (Posner 2012c). Blogs and social networks have been described as 'modern-day samizdat' (Posner and Ross 2010). Mobilizing the end of the Cold War ties US Internet Freedom policy to two strong symbolic markers – that which generally is in accord with the social movements involved in the struggle against Stalinist communism and claims to historical inevitability and their resonance with an 'end-of-history' thesis. For officials in the Obama administration, these claims are expressed through 'sustainability', a concept that links both a claim to expert knowledge and to historical prescience. Thus, censorship, 'ultimately, it won't be a sustainable way of managing the Internet' (State Department 2011; Posner 2011a; Clinton 2011a; Baer 2011a). It is a "fool's errand," one that did not work for either the Qaddafi or Mubarak regimes (State Department 2011).

These claims to knowledge and authority enact a powerful form of symbolic politics crucial to the process of technological closure (Bijker 1995: 263–265). They suggest that only states that recognize this necessary historical process and conform to it are modern and progressive. The end point of international politics is redefined in liberal capitalist terms. Interestingly, US actions are not asserted to be part of creating this future as such. Instead, they are more often cast as moving with the tide of history. Making these developments the outcome of history, rather than the outcome of agents actively seeking these results, effects a naturalization of these deeply social processes (Fairclough 1995: 104–115; Fairclough 2003: 141–153). The ongoing political contestation over the cultural norms and values that adhere to the Internet, currently in full swing, are not configured as a contest between potential alternative forms of political organization, as within the narrative no true historical alternative actually exists any more than a genuine alternative to liberal sovereignty exists. As an interlinked system of signification, American officials quite effectively shut down other avenues of argumentation. The existing bias of the technology – again, a bias created through the Internet's historical development in the United States – further supports these reifications. That is, the Internet *is* biased towards the free flow of information, but this is the outcome of agency, not historical inevitability or of an exogenous technological rationality. The unequal capacity of agents to create new technological institutions – structural power – creates a material world that enables certain productive-power narratives which then support and reproduce these institutions in turn. Within the policy discourse, however, the conjuncture between US arguments and technological potential appears to be causally unrelated, despite their inseparability in practice.

American officials outline this narrative in a broad number of fora, both domestically and overseas. They explicitly identify specific states whose policies transgress these norms and values, a set of states ranging from traditional US allies such as Turkey, potential allies such as Vietnam, clear antagonists Syria and Iran, to the most high-profile case, China, among many others (Melia 2010; Baer 2011a; Posner and Dibble 2011; Posner and Feltman 2011; Posner 2011c; Clinton 2011a, 2011b). Importantly, the US government has institutionalized the push for the free flow of information within its human rights foreign-policy apparatus – Internet freedom has been included as a category of investigation and reportage within the State Department's Human Rights Reports since 2006; the Global Internet Task Force (GIFT), established in 2006, draws together and coordinates State Department policy;[7] the Office of the Coordinator for Cyber Issues was created in February 2011 to pull together policy on Internet freedom and cybersecurity; and funding for circumvention tools has become more embedded with US policy practice (see below). This institutionalization is reflective of a broader narrative that equates the worst and most violent forms of state oppression with violations of Internet freedom: 'Egyptians need the freedom from fear that the State security police will knock on their door in the night or hack their Facebook page' (Posner 2011b). Indeed, for the Obama administration it is evident that free expression is a precondition for the promotion of these other rights (Clinton 2009; Posner 2011a). Drawing upon the work of the transnational NGOs that have helped to promote these norms internationally – some of which were created by the US government, while others are substantially funded by it – these reports set out to detail the violation of Internet freedom across the world and include details about the technological infrastructure of the Internet, beyond direct blocking, as evidence of the denial of human rights (Department of State 2007b, Department of State 2012 Country Reports). For US policymakers the technological form of the Internet is fundamental to realizing a just world.

An Open Door foreign policy contains, of course, both political and economic aspects. In keeping with the pursuit of a quintessentially liberal vision for the Internet, American officials restrict the applicability of the 'free flow of information' to a strictly formal right to access information. That is, while everyone in principle should have the right to access information regardless of nationality, race or class, it is not necessary to ensure that the ability to access information is guaranteed for all. This is a strictly political definition of equality (Wood 1981; Marx 1867). Actions undertaken to enforce intellectual property rights on the web maintain its expression of liberal equality. The extension of substantive equality of access threatens the profitability of information capital internationally by undermining intellectual property rights and, for US officials, undermines the very process of technological innovation itself (see Chapter 6). This policy stance is a manifestation of the paradoxes of liberal capitalist democracy (Mouffe 2005). US officials understand this policy as pursuing and enabling forms of 'economic freedom' (Locke 2011). This is, of course, a highly contentious argument – the notion that actors with unequal resources and capacities experience the same freedom, as opposed to privilege, in market exchanges – yet it is consistent in US policy overall.

'21st century democracy promotion'

In the pursuit of technological closure about the valid configuration, meaning, and use of the Internet, democracy and its symbolic deployment are central to US rhetorical strategy. The Internet is said to enhance democratic politics and be enhanced by them in turn. This causal narrative suggests that democracy is enhanced by the free flow of information, as an open Internet creates the digital equivalent of a town square or Athenian agora. This public space allows for democratic participation and transparent government that responds to the needs of the citizenry. The resultant 'marketplace of ideas' tests the validity of political principles. In the American vision, as in American culture and political thought more generally, democracy is quintessentially liberal democracy, promoting and perpetuating the very individual rights that constitute it in the first place – as Michael Posner notes of the US position: 'We believe that Internet Freedom is essential to 21st century democracy promotion' (Posner 2011e). Thus, while we may separate out the symbolism of liberal human rights from democratic values for heuristic purposes, in practice they are inseparably intertwined. Moreover, in American foreign policy they combine with a belief that democratic societies that recognize liberal values are more peaceful, stable, and secure (Smith 2007). This specific articulation of democratic peace theory is, in many ways, foundational to US Internet policy and lends content to the American conception of 'cybersecurity', as we shall see in a moment.

The initial causal claim of US policymakers is complex and – unlike many other aspects of the discourse – often inconsistent. US officials often argue that the Internet has caused an expansion of democracy globally. Condoleezza Rice asserted that the Internet is 'possibly one of the greatest tools for democratization and individual freedom that we've ever seen' (Dobriansky 2008; Posner and Crowley 2011; Locke 2011). Indeed, while US officials are aware of criticism of claims that the Internet causes democracy (cf. Morozov 2012) they nevertheless claim an association between the free flow of information and democracy. Thus, David Gross has noted that

> [...] because that naïve view became outdated so quickly, people assumed that the Internet and other new forms of communications were not really having a major impact on the political process – at least to advance liberty and democracy. Fortunately, that limited view has turned out to also be wrong. (Gross 2006b)

The American narrative traces out an historical process whereby the expansion of new information-communications technology, and primarily the Internet, is central to increasing the number of democratic governments:

> I do not believe that it's an accident that we have more democracies now in the world than ever before at the same time that information is able to flow more freely. More people have access to information than ever before, which empowers people, and the access helps support and encourage democracies around the world. (Gross 2006b; McHale 2010a)

The nature of this claim is quite clear – the relationship between a free flow of information and increased democratic governance is a *necessary* causal relationship. The amount of information available within a given polity is claimed to be internally related to the nature of that polity. The Internet, and particularly social media, 'empower' – the word features repeatedly throughout the discourse, as noted below – individuals to pursue democracy. While US officials often claim that Twitter or Facebook did not cause the Arab Spring – Secretary Clinton, speaking of the marches and protests in Egypt in January 2011, explicitly denied this in asserting 'The Internet did not do any of those things; people did'[8]

(Clinton 2011a; Posner 2011f) – their overarching narrative belies this understanding.

This is evident in the repeated metaphorical casting of the Internet as a public square or 'town hall' (Posner and Chamberlain Donahoe 2011; Posner 2011i). The image of the town hall is one of democratic participation. Within the ideal-typical town hall, or in the public square, political debate is not subject to coercion, and is open to the participation of all. Individuals meet to engage in rational argumentation, with the aim of reaching some form of consensual agreement over their differences. The town hall, in this idealized picture, does not necessitate that individuals hold any specific beliefs and, in keeping with the understanding of technological instrumentalism noted above, is also neutral. This procedural democracy suggests the ability of the Internet to allow both for individuals rights to free expression and the uncoerced pursuit of varied forms of political life. In the most philosophically informed treatment of public diplomacy, James K. Glassman, Under Secretary for Public Diplomacy in the Bush administration, looked to ancient Athens to reinforce the characterization of the Internet as democratic:

> The Internet world of Al Qaeda is one of direction: believe this, do that. The Internet world of today is one of interactivity and conversation: I think this, your ideas are unconvincing, I need more information to make up my mind, let's meet at 3pm Thursday for a peaceful protest. In fact, the Internet itself is becoming the locus of Civil Society 2.0. This new virtual world is democratic. It is an agora. It is not a place for a death cult that counts on keeping its ideology sealed off from criticism. The new world is a marketplace of ideas, and it is no coincidence that Al Qaeda blows up marketplaces. (Glassman 2008)

The Athenian democratic ideal is mobilized to suggest the potential of the Internet to realize a timeless human aim, contrasted, in this case, against the coercion and violence of non-democratic and non-liberal terrorist organizations. This powerful claim suggests that an Internet biased towards the free flow of information upholds principles of plurality and free association. It does not, as such, represent a threat to regimes that may not favour specific American political or cultural values – censoring states should not, in a recurrent characterization, have anything to fear from an open Internet.

An open Internet, US officials assert, increases the transparency of a society by making more information available to both citizens and government.[9] This allows citizens to make informed choices and engage in more informed public deliberation – Gross notes 'democracy is strengthened by access to knowledge' (Gross 2005). Transparent government allows citizens to hold their government to account, as citizens are aware of how government is, or is not, meeting its obligations (Posner 2011b; Clinton 2010a). Linking this argument to claims about American history lends these claims some legitimacy. The Internet 'has tremendous capacity to empower citizens by expanding access to information and encouraging participation in government' (Beaird 2003; United States of America 2005; McHale 2009b). Posner, in remarks stressing these values as those of the international community, emphasized that young Internet entrepreneurs had 'developed tools with unprecedented potential to empower people around the world to participate in a truly democratic process' (Posner 2011f; McHale 2011c). If US officials explicitly deny that the Internet causes revolutions, they nevertheless suggest – overwhelmingly – that it alters the social context within which revolutions and democratization may occur. As we have noted in Chapters 2 and 3, it is this alteration of social context that must be accounted for in any account of how technological institutions exercise power.

More than empowering people to participate in forms of governance, however, the US narrative relies upon a crucial spatial metaphor, that of a 'marketplace of ideas' that the Internet, as a town square, creates (Clinton 2011a; Locke 2010; McHale 2011c). The metaphor of a 'marketplace of ideas' is suggestive of a process whereby ideas, like commodities or firms, compete for market share. And, just as markets are seen to weed out successful from unsuccessful products via this functional mechanism, so too are ideas weeded out according to their success in the democratic marketplace. This simple yet powerful notion challenges filtering states to subject their values to the crucible of democracy. The American faith in the universality of its values promotes a similar faith in the outcome of this competition. As a challenge to censoring states the value of this construction is evident. Beyond this, functional narratives exclude human agency in their explanations of social outcomes (cf. Elster 1982 and McLaughlin 2004). Problematic for understanding the historical development of ideas, it is – more importantly for our purposes – a strong claim to the validity of the technological form of the Internet. If the Internet creates a marketplace for ideas, it also thereby creates a neutral mechanism for adjudicating between which ideas survive and which fail. Claims to the form of the Internet as neutral, allied to the technological instrumentalist understanding mentioned above, are broadly evident in the American narrative (State Department 2011; Biden 2011; Posner and Crowley 2011). This is not a political process, but merely an efficient – indeed, technical – manner in which human beings can pursue their desired forms of social organization and governance.

By tying the technology of the Internet together with the expansion of democracy internationally, the United States is drawing upon perhaps the most powerful form of symbolic capital and legitimacy in international politics in the post-Cold War world (McFaul 2004–2005; Hobson 2008; Clark 2009). Democracy and its promotion have become cornerstones of international political practice and rhetoric. The World Bank, the United Nations, the European Union, the OECD, and a litany of non-governmental organizations all incorporate the spread of democratic values as a central goal of their policies (Abrahamsen 2000: 31–36; Guilhot 2005; Tilly 2007: 186–190). Clark nicely sums up the place of democracy within international society, noting, 'It is not just that democracy is becoming more prevalent, but that it now enjoys a status as an authoritative principle of international life (Clark 2007: 154). The link between liberty, democracy, and the Internet is subject to serious disagreement and ongoing contestation (Noam 2005: 57–58; Dahlberg 2007; Prior 2007; Faris and Etling 2008; Rohlinger and Brown 2009; Morozov 2011; Farrell 2012; MacKinnon 2012). Any clear assertion of an actual existing link between the free flow of information and the creation of liberal democracies is premature. Nevertheless, as a rhetorical strategy designed to achieve strategic goals, these assertions are very powerful, as their respective elements – causal designations claiming knowledge of how the world works alongside the attachment of valued democratic ethics to the technology – come together in a complex and cohesive story. In the contest over the meaning and future development of the Internet, the attachment of democracy to the functioning of the technology carries significant symbolic weight, much more so than alternative values such as sovereign self-determination as traditionally understood.

As with the discourse around individual rights, this narrative extends beyond generically linking the Internet and democracy to specifically targeting states undertaking filtering practices. In this narrative, Internet filtering and censorship – a technological change to the rules of the Internet as an institution – represent a denial of democracy. For example, in regard to China:

> We should all recognize that despite the growing number of Internet users, internet censorship limits democratization because it prevents Chinese citizens from having access to a variety of sources of

information and the freedom to discuss these matters. (Rumsfeld 2005; see also Gross 2006b and Bush 2008a, 2008b)

The free flow of information is not cast simply as a means to the ends of goals such as economic development – although it is also portrayed in that light throughout US policy statements – but is configured as a fundamental human right, an end in itself. The formulation is universalist, extending the Western, and more specifically, American, view of human rights as the necessary basis for evaluating both sovereignty and the technical configuration of the Internet. The right to free speech as a settled norm of international society dating back to the Cold War (Hamelink 1994: 284–289) makes American arguments difficult to resist. Essentially, censoring states have few places to go in making their case in favour of self-determination within the realm of information-communications technology.

The United States government increasingly articulates a coherent vision for cybersecurity based upon the extension of liberal democracy and the free flow of information globally. In a particularly interesting example, Secretary Clinton argued:

> Information freedom supports the peace and security that provides a foundation for global progress. Historically, asymmetrical access to information is one of the leading causes of interstate conflict. When we face serious disputes or dangerous incidents, it's critical that people on both sides of the problem have access to the same set of facts and opinions. (Clinton 2010a)

Expressing a specifically liberal faith in historical progress linked to technological development, this passage also clearly articulates how the free flow of information can generate global peace and stability. This formulation relies upon specific, and contested, understandings of interstate war as the product of information failures (Fearon 1995; Gartzke 2007). It is important to understand the 'town square' metaphor in this light. It is not merely that individuals can exercise their natural right to freedom of expression, but that the exercise of this freedom creates greater peace and security and promotes 'global understanding' (Posner 2011i). Censorship is both a denial of human rights and a threat to international order. Cybersecurity, for US officials, is not only the protection of property rights, although it is primarily that; it is also the stability that the free flow of information promotes by promoting liberal democracy. Given the importance granted to these priorities as national security concerns, it is perhaps unsurprising that the United States seeks to circumvent censorship policies where possible.

'With great code comes great responsibility'

Michael Posner's pithy reformulation of Franklin Roosevelt delivered to Silicon Valley in 2011 (Posner 2011i) perfectly encapsulates the relationship between the American understanding of what the Internet can achieve and the responsibility to ensure that this potential is met. US officials do not merely seek to rhetorically coerce other actors, but to use this coercion to legitimize their policy practices in turn. The symbolic power of the US discourse operates beyond the level of rhetoric to legitimize material practices carried out by the US government that attempt to promote the free flow of information internationally. The US frames these polices as an attempt to realize the values of human rights and democracy internationally via the free flow of information. These practices work to re-establish the technological bias of the Internet by undermining practices of technological resistance, expressed via filtering, which other states have enacted.

The American government has been active in funding the development and spread of anonymizers and circumvention tools for the Internet since at least 2001. These applications are designed to allow for individuals – within states that enact filtering – to access banned or monitored material anonymously, thereby evading electronic eavesdropping, or to skirt around filtering technologies by accessing blocked material via another route.

The US government has funded these projects, both directly via the Department of State – whose Bureaus of Democracy, Human Rights and Labour (DRL) and Economic, Energy and Business Affairs (EEB) have primary responsibility for Internet freedom policies – and the United States Agency for International Development (USAID), as well as through the Broadcasting Board of Governors (BBG), the body that oversees the Voice of America and its news outlets, such as Radio Farda and Radio Sawa. The BBG is nominally independent from government, but in practical terms is a division of the Office of International Information Programs housed within the Bureau of Public Diplomacy and Public Affairs in the Department of State. The BBG has had its Internet Anti-Censorship division since 2002 (BBG 2013). A number of projects have been funded through the BBG to private sector software developers. In 2001, the BBG provided $100,000 to Safeweb, Inc. (a private company formerly funded by the Central Intelligence Agency), in order to develop circumvention technologies to route around the Chinese Internet firewall (Lum 2006). This particular application proved unsuccessful, but the programs have expanded since then. Two companies, Dynaweb and Ultrareach, received between them $500 700, $827 326 and $727 003 from the BBG in 2003, 2004, and 2005, respectively, while a very small amount was given to Anonymizer, Inc., for work specifically on Iran (Lum 2006). In April 2003, the BBG commissioned Peacefire.org to create a circumvention tool (Murray 2007: 48). From 2006 to 2009, the BBG donated $500,000 to Tor, perhaps the most popular Internet anonymizer, while Tor attracted smaller amounts of money from 2001 to 2006 from the Defense Advanced Research Projects Agency and the Office of Naval Research (ONR) via the Naval Research Laboratory (Tor 2009). The BBG spent an estimated $2 million per year during the 2000s on proxy networks to enable Internet users in China and elsewhere to access its websites (Lum et al. 2012).

Funding for circumvention tools has expanded considerably under the Obama administration, alongside a greater acknowledgement of these programs in US policy statements. In 2011 and 2012 the BBG received $10 million and $9.1 million respectively, for its Internet anti-censorship projects (Lum et al. 2012). US State Department officials claim that $50 to $70 million has been spent on funding technological solutions to Internet censorship (Baer 2011a; Posner 2011f) – including money for training in the use of these applications – while in 2012 the Congressional research service estimated that the State Department and USAID had spent 'more than $100 million on Internet freedom programming since 2008' (Moloney Figliola 2013). This money has been used to

> support a dozen different circumvention technologies: a 'panic button' app for mobile phones; a 'slingshot' program to identify censored content that users are searching for in a particular country and fling it back over firewalls where ordinary citizens can get it; and training programs to help activists operating in these repressive areas to keep operating, thwart surveillance and protect their privacy. In short, we're funding a whole slew of tools and techniques that *empower* users to gain access to information, organize them, tell their *own* stories and stay safe online. (Posner 2011f)

Officials estimate that this money has helped train 7,500 activists in techniques to skirt firewalls (Baer 2011a). These funding streams have coincided with the creation of organizations designed to institutionalize such streams, ensuring sustained sources of funding and support for anti-censorship activities. The Freedom Online Coalition, created in December 2011 and comprising 21 governments,[10] is designed to coordinate the activities of private and public-sector actors to promote Internet Freedom. In late 2012, the Freedom Online Coalition subsequently supported the creation of the Digital Defenders Initiative (DDI). Its activities include: establishing Internet connections when these have been cut off; providing personal protection for bloggers and journalists; development of mobile applications that can be used in 'mesh networks'; and supporting digital activists with secure hosting and Distributed Denial of Service (DDoS) mitigation (DDI 2013).[11] These numbers are, of course, small as a proportion of the State Department budget and as a proportion of the budget specifically allocated to public diplomacy projects. The small amount of funding and labour required to create and support these technologies is representative of the institutional power of the Internet and the manner in which its makeup favours the free flow of information – and thus US foreign policy goals – over those of censoring states.

The rationale for these actions, as Murray notes, was the drive to free up information, with the BBG focused upon its specific information programmes. Thus, in regard to China, Murray notes:

> In justifying their actions, Ken Berman, program manager for internet anticensorship at the Bureau said, 'the news is highly censored. The Chinese government hams all of our radio broadcasts and blocks access by their people to our Website. We want to allow people there to have the tools to be able to look at it'. (Murray 2007: 48)

On top of supporting the development of these technologies, the BBG and the Voice of America actively work with citizens within China and other states to provide information via the Internet by more straightforward practices. Upon finding that certain words are subject to filtering on a given day, the Voice of America alters its subject headings, alters characters, and changes the Web addresses from which it sends information in an effort to bypass censorship techniques (State Department official B). This allows the 'multi-millions' of messages that the public diplomacy apparatus of the US government sends each day to gain a greater chance of reaching their destination (State Department official B; Lum et al. 2012). The sheer volume of information, and the ability to adapt the message and its sending location, allows the US to circumvent censorship controls with some measure of success – roughly 80 to 90 per cent of messages sent via these channels reach their destinations (State Department official B).

The symbolic power of the US foreign policy discourse licenses these practices. They rely upon the universality of human rights and the validity of democracy as internationally recognized norms. These efforts are direct interventions into sovereign states' societies: they are beyond mere interactions in their deliberate attempts to deny sovereign states the ability to enact their laws on their own soil. This process of intervention is best illustrated if we imagine the opposite situation occurring: if the Chinese, or Iranian, or Saudi governments sought to enact filtering on the Internet in the United States to block access to information on the Falun Gong or the Green Movement or pornography, there is little doubt we would conceptualize this as a form of intervention into domestic US affairs. As forms of intervention go this is relatively mild. Nevertheless, it is important to recognize that these actions are not legally sanctioned by international society and do represent a transgression of the – perhaps waning – norms of state sovereignty. In the contest over the technological form of the Internet, funding circumvention technologies re-establishes the bias of the network in line with US foreign policy aims, and physically seeks to close off alternative approaches to the network.

US government discourse provides ample justification for these actions. The free flow of information and the right to freedom of speech and free expression are defined as universal human rights, beyond the rights of communities.[12] Non-liberal states are constructed as illegitimate due to their denial of these rights, and thereby fail to meet the condition of sovereignty that liberal states have constructed. A gap is created between non-liberal states and their citizens, so that American policy makers are able to portray their practices as helping to secure individual liberties against authoritarian governments. In turn, these practices will, it is asserted, help realize the equally universal value of democracy. Utilizing dominant post-Cold War norms, the symbolic power of US discourse allows the United States to legitimately undertake practices that may otherwise be open to question. Yet, while US officials stress the legitimacy of these actions and, as we have noted above, the unsustainability of censorship practices, they elide the connection between the two. Representing unsustainability as the outcome of an individual striving for human rights and a naturalized bias of the network, the discourse does not outline how US actions practically intervene in this process.

Conclusion

The symbolic politics surrounding the Internet are crucial to the future direction of its technological development. The argument of US foreign policy officials that an Internet characterized by the free flow of information meets international norms of human rights and democracy is an attempt to secure the form of the technology in a manner which meets the specific US vision of how international politics should be organized. American officials are attempting to enact a form of technological closure, drawing creatively upon the symbolic resources of international society – resources it has been central in constructing and institutionalizing – in the process. Their narrative outlines the American conception of the Internet's form as one that supports the natural rights possessed by every individual, is historically irresistible, promotes democracy and transparent government, and fulfils the norms and values of the international community. This, implicitly, of course, defines opponents in the opposite relational terms (Hansen 2006: 16–20). States that seek greater control over the Internet in order to censor its content are rights violators, backward, and anti-democratic, with opaque decision-making. If successful, the institutional power of the Internet, its bias, will support American foreign policy aims in the long term.

This is, though, only one aspect of the American Open Door Internet policy. While US officials push for the free flow of information, this is defined in purely political terms. That is, American policy seeks to ensure that no one is politically disqualified from accessing information, just as in a liberal democracy no one is politically disqualified from voting. The requirements of capital accumulation, however, place a limit on how freely information can be accessed in substantive terms, as not everyone has equal access to the resources needed to purchase information protected by paywalls and patents. These economic imperatives form the other core component of the United States' approach to the Internet and its architecture; its discursive legitimation is the subject of the following chapter.

6
The Narration of Innovation in US Internet Policy

Introduction

As the United States government has attempted to mobilize international norms in the promotion of its political vision for the Internet, it has drawn upon values surrounding economic development, material progress, and innovation. The flat, formal equality that characterizes the Internet leads to misrecognitions of the substantive inequality that the rules and norms of the network maintain.[1] The network, by not actively discriminating against information, ensures a form of liberal negative freedom over its wires. This enhances and maintains the structural power of capital, and specifically American capital, in the Internet economy (Curran, Fenton, and Freedman 2013: 4–7; Mansell 2011; cf. Mueller 2010: 133).[2] The formal equality of the network hides the substantive inequality which shapes the design and development of Internet hardware and software architectures, favouring actors in dominant economic positions over those with fewer resources. Again, we see here the need to place the development of the Internet within a wider context in which structural power positions are considered. Globally, this formal equality favours Western, and particularly American, corporations, due in large part to their historical advantage as first movers in the sector.

This chapter will illustrate the role that the productive power employed by US policymakers has played in buttressing and reproducing this structural relationship, via US policy discourse on innovation and free markets.[3] The focus of this discussion is directed primarily at the innovative activities that take place in the applications and content layer of the network, rather than at the level of control protocols that are the primary responsibility of the Internet Corporation for Assigned Names and Numbers (ICANN). In response to potential challenges from Internet piracy and protectionist policies in the developing world, US government discourse suggests that only measures that support the ends of the Open Door approach to foreign policy – specifically, open markets – are appropriate for regulating the current and future development of the Internet. In turn, these arguments find institutional support through the institutions of the global economy, specifically via the World Trade Organization (WTO). The chapter will demonstrate that the exercise of productive and structural power supports and maintains the institutional power of the Internet in line with American foreign policy aims and reproduces the material culture of the Internet along liberal capitalist lines. In contrast to dominant portrayals of the Internet as a threat to the American state and American capitals this analysis refocuses on the impact of the technology on 'backward' states.

This chapter examines these forms of power in relation to Intellectual Property Rights (IPRs) and the Internet. US discourse endorses a picture of market-based, incentivized innovation as the only workable method of technological development – in contrast to state-led or non-proprietary developmental alternatives. Free-market-based technological development is, of course, faced with the twin challenges of software piracy, which undermines the necessary rate of profit for corporations, and national protectionism in the developing world, which seeks to support indigenous Internet industries via active government discrimination and the promotion of national champions (Shadlan, Schrank and Kurtz 2005: 46, 49–50; Drahos 2002: 767–768, 773–774, 779–794). Both practices threaten the Open Door by undermining the ability of US capital to profitably expand globally. The drive to institute strong property rights is necessary to ensure that actors may commodify programs and applications and gain a profit from them. This is not without contradictions and tensions, and the manner in which these tensions play out will be central to the ongoing development of the technology.

The overarching theme of strong property-rights protection within US policy discourse is constructed through a complex process outlining the benefits of this approach and the costs of alternatives in relation to innovation and economic development. A story is told in which property rights create both the necessary incentives to innovate and the potential for economic development in contrast to the politically driven motivations of state-interventionist policies that retard innovation, or the economic and security threat posed by piracy (the 'most pervasive cyberthreat today', according to the Department of Defense) (DoD 2011: 4). Within this overarching narrative a number of discursive and rhetorical features are present, such as a process of relational identity construction for market-based actors, states, and software 'pirates' which draws out the validity of the former in relation to the latter; the (re)construction of the historical record of both the development of the Internet and the American history of intellectual property rights enforcement, and claims to knowledge and authority in relation to how technological innovation occurs. Present throughout is a recourse to symbolic resources which resonate deeply within American political and foreign-policy culture, such as the universalization of American values, while also drawing upon international norms and treaties to burnish US government claims for market-led development.

This chapter will present this argument as follows. First, it will outline different approaches to the innovation of information technology, contrasting and comparing these models. Second, the chapter will outline how private property rights are comprehensively tied to innovation by US officials. After noting this, the foundation of US discourse, we will move, third, to note how officials characterize the role of government in the process of innovation in an effort to suggest that the state-led development is ineffective in generating innovation. Fourth, the chapter will note how 'piracy' is mobilized as a threat to American national security, both in terms of economic prosperity and via its linkages to terrorism. This leads US officials to argue that, historically, America strongly protected IPRs, universalizing (and reimagining) this history while arguing that the strong protection of IPRs is the only path to economic success for developing states. Finally, the chapter will outline how US structural and institutional power in international society is supported by, and supports, this narrative. This will demonstrate how the productive power of American discourse is deeply enmeshed with structural and institutional power more broadly.

Property rights and models of software innovation

The issue of how innovation in the architecture of the Internet does and should take place has been the subject of significant and ongoing controversy within the areas of Internet law and governance. Central to this controversy is the issue of property rights, and especially the place of intellectual property rights in software code and their benefit, or harm; to the process of technological innovation. Two primary means of innovation have been debated, 'free and open source' (FOSS) or 'commons' software development versus proprietary software development (Benkler 2003; Lessig 2004, 2006; Spinello 2003; Weiser 2003; Zittrain 2006; Anderson 2009; Mueller 2010: 129–157). The free software development model is most closely associated with Richard Stallman and the Free Software Foundation. Using the GNU-General Public License (GNU-GPL),[4] adherents to the free software model seek to ensure that the source code and the object code of software programs, which include Internet applications, remain accessible to the general public and, in particular, other programmers who may wish to alter and adapt the code to suit their purposes. Free software advocates stress the collaborative nature of software development and the necessity for 'open' software applications in order to facilitate innovation (Zittrain 2006). The free software model implies that innovation is most likely to occur when everyone can access and alter software and hardware. To this end, adherents to the free software model seek to use copyright law to ensure that any code produced by free software developers remains free to alter, in order to maintain freedom to innovate in the digital realm, a freedom threatened when code becomes subject to ownership rights and the limitations this entails. Anyone familiar with the Apple business model will recognize these limitations, whereby 'closed' technologies prevent innovation by anyone but the original developer.

The proprietary software model adheres to a different picture of technological development, one informed by an understanding of innovation that places the need for economic incentives at the centre of technological development (May 2000: 16–44; Richards 2004; Becker 1977). In this understanding, authors – as individuals or as a corporate body – must have some incentive to undertake the research and development necessary to produce new digital products. Profit-making is central to the motivations driving investors in this framework. Proprietary software is developed more conventionally than FOSS software. Programmers work as salaried employees of a corporation which responds to market pressures – the horizontal pressures discussed in Chapter 3 – and ownership rights belong to the corporation. The right to alter the code of software produced in this manner belongs exclusively to the creators of the programme or application. Jonathan Zittrain notes that 'Proprietary software in mass distribution almost uniformly reserves all rights to the author except a license to "run" the software on the purchaser's computer' (Zittrain 2004: 269). The value of proprietary software lies in the ability to charge a fee for this license, to charge royalties or, increasingly, through patent-protected business models (such as Amazon's one click application) that create exclusivity (US Copyright Office; Drahos and Braithwaite 2002: 173). Proprietary innovation depends on keeping access to its code limited in order to create and preserve revenue streams. The ability to access and, potentially, freely copy a given programme or application prevents the developer from recouping their research and development costs, reducing the incentive to innovate to zero (Zittrain 2004: 267–269; Weiser 2003: 579).

While the extension of intellectual property rights globally represents an extension of the formal equality of the market (in which everyone has the right to participate), it also represents an extension of substantive inequality, in which the *ability* to participate – the *power to* participate – is highly stratified (Deibert 2008: 142; May 2007). That is, while the playing field of the international digital economy is formally levelled as IPRs spread, in practice certain actors still enter the game with substantially greater resources than others. Typically, this stratification is discussed through a focus on barriers to market entry and thereby accounts for unequal resources between capitals, but not between capital and labour. As noted in Chapter 4, American capital will remain the guiding hand of the Internet economy for the foreseeable future (Cowhey and Aronson 2009: 14–15). In response, a third model of innovation is occasionally pursued by states in the developing world trying to counteract their structural disadvantages, a form of import substitution. For example, China and India have utilized a strategy of state-led economic development in the information technology sector, subsidizing and promoting national champions and sector-specific development domestically (Shadlen et al. 2005; Saraswati 2008; Lu and Weber 2008: 81–82; Segal 2010). These policies are often combined with lax enforcement of intellectual property rights, allowing for the dissemination of protected works throughout a given economy and allowing for some degree of 'catch-up' within the sector – thereby denting the profit margins of Western multinationals in the process. These practices undermine the formal equality of the network. US policymakers – and industry associations – argue that these practices are an 'unfair advantage' for some capitals, stressing formal rather than substantive equality (Locke 2011; White House 2011a; IIPA 2011). State-led development may represent the greatest threat to the dominance of American capital in the information economy, and the source of the greatest strain in the United States relationship with other states regarding the governance of the Internet.

Intellectual property rights structure the process by which technological innovation takes place in relation to the Internet's software architecture. Arguing for one method of innovation over another – FOSS over proprietary, or state-led over open market – favours certain groups of actors as the primary agents of software development. Free and opensource software development favours non-profit software development groups. Proprietary software development favours large software corporations that have gained a significant first-mover advantage and market share or have the financial resources to buy up rivals. State-led development favours national capitals over foreign competitors. As we shall see, the discourse of the US government largely favours one method of development – proprietary software development– over the others. The productive power of its discourse works to legitimize and naturalize this model over its alternatives in an attempt to close off alternative understandings of how the political economy of the Internet could develop. It is to this discourse that we now turn.

Linking property, the private sector, and innovation

The discourse of American policy officials surrounding property rights in the information economy is characterized by a strong and consistent argument in favour of intellectual property rights protection. Aimed primarily at states which have yet to reform their domestic structures in line with those of developed countries, and pushing for a process of policy harmonization and convergence which also occurs across other issue areas (Phillips 2007; US Trade Promotion Coordinating Committee: 2, 7–9, 11, 18, 50–54; US Intellectual Property Enforcement Coordinator 2013), this rhetoric is comprised of a variety of discursive techniques and rhetorical strategies. At its most basic level, this involves the consistent and comprehensive linking of certain predicates to the key agents, actions, and objects upon which the discourse of Internet governance centres.

In the summer of 2002, in preparation for the first leg of the World Summit on the Information Society (WSIS)[5] in 2003, Ambassador David Gross, Coordinator for International Communications and Information policy, noted the need for 'private-sector led innovation' as the private sector 'has the flexibility and resources to offer innovative solutions' (Gross 2002, 2003).[6] The linking of innovation to the private sector and to the incentives that are required for innovation, is at the centre of US policy, and resonates, repeated as a key theme, throughout policy discourse. Richard Beaird, Deputy Coordinator for International Telecommunications and Information Policy at the time, stated that 'We should never lose sight of the fact that the private sector is the primary investor in, and innovator of, infrastructure, products, content, and services' (Beaird 2002; see also United States of America 2003a, 2005;

Gross 2007c; Sullivan 2008; White House 2011a: 9, 21–24; White House 2011b: 17; Bryson 2012). In this narrative the private sector is not one innovator among many, including universities and government, but the prime mechanism by which technological development occurs. Beaird noted, again in the run-up to the 2003 Geneva Phase of the WSIS, that the private sector is one of the 'fundamental building blocks of the information society' (Beaird 2002). Precisely how fundamental was emphasized by the US government in its 'Guiding Principles' document released in 2004, prior to the Tunis phase of the WSIS in 2005, in which the US outlined seven core principles to guide policy discussions. Of these seven principles, four emphasized the need for the private sector to be as free to innovate as necessary. For example, the document argues:

> To maximize the economic and social benefits of the Internet, a clear, market-based, legal framework and supportive policy environment that promotes and ensures effective and efficient competition. The United States believes that full competition is the cornerstone of a healthy, robust Internet market. Innovation, expanded services, broader participation, and lower prices will arise most easily in a market-driven arena, not in an environment that operates under substantial regulation. (United States of America 2004)

It goes on to note:

> The private sector is the primary investor in and innovator of Internet infrastructure, products, content and services. They are the primary stakeholders who build, operate, and maintain the IP based networks that collectively form the Internet and are largely responsible for its commercial success. Consequently, it is imperative that private sector leadership in these areas be maintained and encouraged. (United States of America 2004)

US policy officials thus repeatedly and comprehensively link the private sector and markets to qualities of innovation. Mentions of the private sector are, throughout US discourse, linked to flexibility, dynamism, and efficiency and subsequently accorded primary status as the actors who must be entrusted with innovation. Support for the private sector is support for technological innovation, while other possible means of innovation are either sidestepped or mentioned only in passing, as occurs with FOSS approaches. For example, in the Obama administration's 30-page *Strategy for Cyberspace*, open-source software development – noted as 'vibrant' and 'community-driven' – is mentioned once; the 'private sector' is mentioned 19 times as a key to innovation (White House 2011b: 8). The process of defining the characteristics of the private sector is central to the overall thrust of US Internet policy. Its power lies both in obscuring the potential of other forms of technological innovation and in producing practices consistent with US policy interests and values.

With the private sector as the primary source of technological innovation, US policymakers argue that the role of government is to create the necessary regulatory environment within which the private sector can flourish. Government has a role to play in creating the conditions for innovation, a role acknowledged with significantly greater frequency and emphasis during the Obama administration (White House 2011b: 10–11). This consists first and foremost in the provision of strong intellectual property rights. Universal private ownership rights are linked to innovation throughout US discourse – 'intellectual property agreements provide a valuable mechanism through which to protect intellectual investment and encourage the creation and dissemination of works' (United States of America 2003). Again, at the most basic level of linked predicates the causal relationship between innovation and property rights suggested is clear: 'intellectual property rights fuel knowledge creation and innovation' (Gross 2003; US Department of Justice 2006: 13); further, 'innovation evaporates when innovators lack protection for their ideas' – intellectual property must be protected 'as surely as the products of our physical capital' (Gross 2005a). Gross heavily stressed the role of IPRs during the first World Summit on the Information Society (WSIS), stating, 'We think that being committed to intellectual property rights, so as to promote and give economic incentives for the promotion of content, is extraordinarily important' (Gross 2003; United States of America 2005).[7] The power of these formulations derives from existing norms and values within international society – norms the United States was often central in crafting, and expressed in agreements of international organizations such as the OECD, APEC, the World Bank, and of course the WTO's TRIPs agreement (Strickling 2011d, 2012c; cf. OECD 2008; World Bank 2010; WTO 1996: 320; Padovani 2005; Sell 2003: 20–21, 60–74; Muzaka 2011: 763–766).

This understanding of the private sector as uniquely innovative relies on an implicit understanding of human rationality. Markets are able to promote innovation, in the US government's understanding, because they provide incentives, via profit taking, to create new technologies. Without this incentive provided by the market – for which private property rights are the prerequisite – neither companies nor individuals would be willing to undertake the necessary labour to create new Internet innovations. As one US government official has stated:

> If you think about it the number of ideas, good ideas, that are never commercially viable is enormous and so unless you can capture the economic benefit of your idea, it will never be more than an idea... Because there is – it's a funny thing – there is this notion, generic notion that with the information technology revolution and the development of the internet that everything should now be free. And the problem with that is if everything's free nothing will ever happen because there is no incentive for anything to happen, so no new infrastructure will roll out. If infrastructure companies can't make a return on their investment, they'll never do it... no one will produce new TV shows if they can't actually get a return on their investment... It costs money to do those things and so ultimately everything can't be free. (White House official 2008)

Two claims are being put forward through the linkage between the private sector and technological innovation. The first concerns the character of labour itself, derived from a particularly Lockean understanding of innovation, property, and human motivation. This suggests that labour is not something that human beings voluntarily engage in, and it is not an activity which is enjoyed or constitutes an expression of self-actualization (Becker 1977: 35–36).[8] As a result we arrive at the second assumption, that without the necessary material reward individuals will not be encouraged to undertake labour which leads to productive and innovative activity. Material incentives as provided by strong intellectual property rights are thereby central to technological innovation. Christopher May effectively summarizes this argument:

> Drawing from Locke the notion of reward for effort in improvement... it is often asserted that without IPRs there would be little stimulus for innovation... Thus, not only does intellectual property reward intellectual effort, it actually stimulates activities that have a social value, and therefore serves to support the social good of progress. Underlying this argument is a clear perception of what drives human endeavour: individual benefit. Only by encouraging and rewarding the individual creator or inventor (with property, and therefore market-related benefits), can any society ensure that it will continue to develop important and socially valuable innovations,

which will serve to make society as a whole more efficient. (May 2007: 26–27)

Interestingly, however, while the premise of human rationality may have roots in Locke, the argument put forth is primarily utilitarian in character. That is, US policymakers promote strong intellectual property rights because this is the only manner in which material wealth can be created. US officials tend not to suggest that private property rights lie at the core of an ethical society, in contrast to certain liberal and libertarian political theorists (e.g., Nozick 1974). Instead, the justification is the *necessary* character of innovation itself; technology and material wealth can only be created through the private sector. Even when US officials point to the link between intellectual property rights and individual liberty, the understanding promoted is not that private property fosters liberty, merely that it is not inconsistent with it (Department of Commerce 2012: 7–12; Locke 2011).

When this argument is applied to the private sector it is certainly accurate, as the private sector will not create new Internet applications if there is no profit motive present. What occurs in US officials' discourse, however, is the naturalizing of one form of technological development, that of free-market capitalism. This form of innovation is asserted to be the essence of innovation and is stripped of its historically embedded character. The argument requires that the central role of the private sector is accepted first, after which the necessity for profit incentives to drive innovation follows naturally and, indeed, necessarily. This is a problem-solving approach to technological development. It is not a false representation so much as a partial one.[9] Indeed, the prime example of a technology not initially developed along these lines is the Internet itself. Linking the private sector, innovation and private property requires that cooperative motivations and their contribution to technological development receive less emphasis than their role merits.

Between politics and piracy: locating the identity of the private sector

US policy discourse extends beyond the simple linkage of the private sector to innovation in pressing for the provision of strong intellectual property rights to govern the development of the Internet architecture. While outlining the necessity for a private-sector-led approach, the discourse creates a relational field, casting the private sector in opposition to both government and to some aspects of civil society labelled as pirates. Beyond simple predicates, the discourse places the United States policy positions within a field of constructed identities that outline why other actors must not be given responsibility for guiding technological development of the Internet.[10] We will now discuss each of these in turn.

US officials distinguish between how markets choose among different technological options and how governments choose among different technological options. The former is seen as a technologically neutral process, non-political. Technological options, in the form of different standards, applications and software, are produced by various private-sector actors in competition with each other, and the market chooses among the alternatives. Markets thereby create the space for citizens to exercise freedom of choice.[11] The proper role for government is not to interfere in markets or consumer choice but to allow this process to work naturally. The Department of Commerce outlines this philosophy:

> And so we also wouldn't advocate a particular solution, we wouldn't advocate proprietary solutions over open source where people should be able to choose...The role of government should be sort of a playing field so that customers can choose. If you would like to have Microsoft that's fine, but if you would like to be able to use open source Linux systems that is also fine...I think our role is to make sure that folks can pick whatever is the best solution. (Department of Commerce official 2008; see also Zoellick 2004)

In contrast, the decisions of governments are described as 'political' (US Department of State and Department of Commerce officials 2008). Governments choose technologies to suit political aims and goals, while the operations of markets work to choose the best technologies available. US officials thereby outline the 'importance of voluntary, market-driven standards in competitive telecommunications markets as being the most efficient method for ensuring that the new technologies provide the economic and social benefits to consumers in every market' (Gross 2004). Government intervention in the process of Internet architecture development creates 'uncompetitive national champions'; they enforce 'closed markets' and 'non-market driven standards' (Gross 2004; Locke 2011; Department of Commerce 2011: 15). Government is portrayed as stagnant, a lumbering bureaucratic hindrance within the fast-moving stream of Internet development – 'glacial' is the adjective that the Obama administration favours – in contrast to the dynamic and flexible private sector (Strickling 2012c;

Biden 2011). This is explained as the 'natural urge of governments to maintain and expand bureaucracies' (Strickling 2012a). Lawrence Strickling, Assistant Secretary for Communications and Information and the administrator of the NTIA under the Obama administration, effectively captures these tropes in the following statement on the multi-stakeholder model of governance: 'We can choose to expand bureaucracies. Or we can choose to expand jobs, economic development and wealth and fundamental rights and freedoms for all' (Strickling 2012a). Part of this construction relies upon characterizing the Internet and technological development in a particular manner: as rapid, fast-changing, evolutionary, dynamic, and so forth, qualities also used to describe the private sector. This characterization of information-communications technology and its development are evident throughout US policy statements, as US officials note a 'rapidly changing, globally interconnected digital society' (Zoellick 2004; see also Strickling 2011c, 2012c); 'it is such a dynamic space, constantly changing, that governments, by their nature, will not be able to keep up with the changing technology' (Gross 2003); 'nothing in history matches the expansion of the Internet' (Beaird 2008). In this environment, stagnant and rigid government is not up to the task of Internet governance or technological development.

In a series of comments to the foreign press prior to the second leg of the World Summit on the Information Society, Assistant Secretary of Commerce Michael Gallagher outlined the view of the United States, in contradistinction to proposals from states that pressed for greater oversight over the Internet, in clear and frank terms:

> Governments are not capable of change at a rapid enough level to meet the demands of growth that we have seen in the Internet ... combinations of them [government and bureaucracies] are only going to make things slower and make the Internet more vulnerable than it is to the threats that are out there today ... And by projecting this notion of a world cup of bureaucracy sitting on top of the Internet is only going to disincent that investment that we very much want to see, not just in Europe, but around the world. (Gallagher 2005)[12]

The American government thereby creates a distinctive representation of government within the Internet ecosystem. An innovative dynamic private sector, embodying human rationality in its practice of incentivized invention, is able to swim in the fast-moving stream of the

Internet's technological advancement. Attempts by governments to direct this process can only act as fetters upon the path of market-driven innovation.

These representations are often wielded against opponents of US policy. State-led development strategies, such as those pursued at times by India and China, are particular targets of this American rhetoric (Locke 2011; Kirk 2011). In these formulations the strategic character of US discourse – the attempt to leverage productive power – is striking. For example, Gallagher, in a heavily sarcastic comment at the same press conference mentioned above, characterized European Union proposals for greater government involvement in public-policy issues related to the Domain Name System, the root zone file, and other measures, as akin to George W. Bush's 'Axis of Evil':

> And I would say that if the EU wants to cast its lot with digital trailblazers like Iran, Syria and Cuba, then that's their choice. But I would suggest that when they're doing that, it's a step toward preserving their 1.3 percent GDP growth rate and their unemployment rate that approaches 9 percent. In fact, to be competitive in the world of tomorrow and looking forward, it's going to take a much more nimble approach to policymaking than an additional layer of bureaucracy over the top of things that are already working very well. (Gallagher 2005; see also Rice 2005; Strickling 2011a)

Assistant Secretary Gallagher of course knows that the EU is not like Iran or Syria in any respect, yet ties these actors together in a narrative construct in order to make a powerful symbolic argument, mobilizing productive power to meet specific policy aims.[13] The legitimacy of the EU policy proposal – a call for greater government involvement in the regulation of the Internet, ultimately unsuccessful at WSIS – is called into question through its purported similarity to the aims of 'rogue states' and its creation of economic lethargy. A causal claim is employed to suggest that EU proposals for greater government oversight for the Internet is directly related to its slow rate of economic growth and its unemployment rate. The effect is to outline the EU in particular – and government in general – as specific types of actors unsuited to direct involvement with the development of the Internet's architecture. At the same time this representation creates a misrecognition of the role of the state in the development of the Internet, a process of historical forgetting that is central to discounting the place of government in creating and guiding the development of the Internet. Thus, even between liberal states with widely shared cultural norms and values, productive power is mobilized to push for technological closure.[14]

In place of an interventionist government impeding technological progress, the United States discourse articulates a role for the state as an overseer of the process of technological development. There are differences of emphasis between the Bush and Obama administrations on this issue, with the Obama administration stressing the need for state involvement more broadly than Bush administration officials (Department of Commerce 2012: v–vii, passim). The Obama administration clearly outlines the need for the public sector to support innovation through increased research funding, greater support for science, technology and engineering education, and support for infrastructure construction and maintenance. For the Obama administration the private sector cannot innovate without a solid foundation laid by the state, a foundation that markets cannot themselves provide. This reflects, perhaps, that officials in the Obama administration 'get it' more clearly than those of the Bush years – they understand how capitalist innovation must occur and the necessary role of the state. Despite these differences, however, the essence of the US discourse has remained the same: the role of government is to create the environment for innovation to occur.

The threat of Internet piracy

State-led technological development is not the only obstacle to the reproduction of US high-technology capital and the pursuit of an Open Door international system. Indeed, state-led development has a significantly lower public profile than the other primary hindrance to the US grand strategy of private-sector-led technological development – Internet piracy. If state-led technological development threatens to create uncompetitive national champions unconducive to economic growth, this threat to US capital is indirect. That is, open markets are a requirement for continued profit taking by US capitals, but a failure to realize profit in this manner may simply push US capital to pursue other strategies of reproduction. Internet piracy, on the other hand, directly threatens US high-technology capital by stealing and disseminating technological products – both hardware and software – that already embody significant sunk capital. Piracy does not represent an alternative strategy of innovation, being parasitic upon the very provision of private property rights it violates. Solutions to piracy may take a technological form, altering the character of the network, through filtering of sites that host pirated material, a solution debated and ultimately rejected by the United States

Congress in early 2011. However, piracy may be ignored by developing states in an attempt to accelerate processes of technological diffusion. In order to ensure that the future development of the Internet is led by the private sector and enables a free flow of information that includes commodities, American officials mobilize productive power in creative ways. The result is a discourse that relies upon an ahistorical depiction of US economic development – creating a misrepresentation of how innovation occurs in order to further technological closure.

The principal elements of this discourse, articulated with great consistency between the Bush and Obama administrations, have relied upon securitizing moves to create a specific discourse of 'cybersecurity' around IPRs, a discourse and set of policies supported and promoted by industry lobbying organizations such as the International Intellectual Property Alliance (2003).[15] Labelling Internet piracy as an existential threat to the American economy and society, the United States Trade Representative outlines the 'Global Scourge of Counterfeiting and Piracy' as a serious threat to stability and prosperity internationally (USTR 2003). The threat is not merely economic. Jon Dudas, the Under Secretary of Commerce for Intellectual Property and the Director of the United States Patent and Trademark Office (USPTO), stated:

> As former U.S. Attorney General John Ashcroft reported: 'In addition to threatening our economic and personal well being, intellectual property crime is a lucrative venture for organized criminal enterprises. And as law enforcement has moved to cut off the traditional means of fundraising by terrorists, the immense profit margins from intellectual property crimes risk becoming a potential source for terrorist financing'. (Dudas 2005; see also Pinkos 2005; Intellectual Property Task Force 2010: 4)

In a post-9/11 environment the representation of piracy relies upon a powerful symbolic linkage between the violation of intellectual property rights and the fear of and threat from international terrorism. Thus officials from the Department of Commerce argue that 'intellectual property crimes risk becoming a potential source for terrorist fundraising' and represent 'threats to US economic interests and our national security' (Pinkos 2005). The Obama administration organized a symposium specifically on this topic in June 2010, led by the Intellectual Property Centre of the US government and with attendees including the Immigration and Customs Enforcement (ICE), the Department of Justice, INTERPOL and the City of London Police. Despite the occasionally tenuous nature of these claims – the RAND report approvingly cited by ICE actually states 'researchers found no evidence terrorists are widely involved with film piracy' (RAND 2009), and two of the three cases noted are quite outdated – the symbolic power of this construction is evident. This is not a novel strategy – the UK's Federation Against Copyright Theft has used similar constructions for years – but it is effective in drawing upon globally legitimate norms surrounding international terrorism to promote a specific political economy of technological innovation (Chowdhury and Krebs 2010; Lowenheim and Steele 2010). Aside from extending this label to include actors who may seek to circumvent digital-rights protection to material on which they have 'fair-use' rights (May 2007; Lessig 2004), tying IPR violations to terrorism stresses the illegitimacy of practices that may, in certain circumstances, represent state development strategies. As Daniel Drezner has noted, 'Economically, these governments [developing states] prefer lax standards as a way of accelerating the transfer of technology and lowering the cost of acquiring new innovation and ideas' (Drezner 2008: 102). Enrolling the social sanction against terrorism in the cause of protecting IPRs effectively leverages the productive power of international norms centred upon the use of violence in the cause of US Internet foreign policy. It attempts to prescribe how innovation should occur and who may legitimately innovate by narrowing the rhetorical options with which opponents of the US approach can respond.

IPR violations are portrayed as a threat to American national security in general. The strength of the threat to the American economy is heavily emphasized in order to make the connection solid and tangible: in one instance, Commerce officials note three times over the course of Congressional testimony that pirates are 'robbing billions of dollars' from the United States (Pinkos 2005). Again, this is not a simple economic issue. The Department of Defense emphasized in its Strategy for Cyberspace: 'As military strength ultimately depends on economic vitality, sustained intellectual property losses erode both US military effectiveness and national competitiveness in the global economy' (Department of Defense 2011: 4; see also White House 2011b: 4). The central role of digital IPRs to 'national economic security' is expressed in the increased focus by USTR's Special 301 reports on Internet marketplaces (White House IPEC June 2010: 9; USTR 2012). As we shall see, US policy officials use a number of policy measures to support their drive for technological closure that are legitimized, in some measure, by these representations.

Alongside these securitizing moves, US officials universalize this specifically American national-security priority into a global-security priority. As Terry Eagleton notes, 'An important device by which an ideology achieves legitimacy is by universalizing and legitimizing itself. Values and interests which are in fact specific to a certain place and time are projected as the values and interests of all humanity' (Eagleton 1991: 56). This is undertaken first by recasting the history of American economic development and, second, by linking economic development to IPR protection in the developing world. Officials' representations use the prosperity of the United States and its pioneering role in Internet development to suggest that the American approach to innovation is valid for all social actors. Here we see, as outlined in Chapter 3, how the structural power of a certain class – American high-technology capitalists, via the state – can promote a specific cultural conception of how innovation has and should occur. US officials reconstruct intellectual property rights as eternally valid rules for development. American history is recast to suggest that the United States has always valued the strong protection of intellectual property, with these norms central to its very foundation. Stephen Pinkos, Deputy Undersecretary of Commerce for Intellectual Property during the Bush administration, linked strong intellectual property rights to the founding of the American republic. Pinkos stated:

> The United States has long been concerned about IP protection dating back to the founding of our country. For example, Gilbert Stuart's Athenaeum portrait of George Washington was replicated without authorization by a Philadelphia merchant, who was later sued for copyright infringement. (Pinkos 2005)

Similarly, the Obama White House *Strategy for American Innovation* has stated:

> The U.S. Constitution empowered Congress to create effective intellectual property rights – helping add 'the fuel of interest to the fire of genius,' in President Lincoln's words. Americans later seized on the Industrial Revolution – an explosion of innovation – propelling a young country with democratic ideals to unprecedented economic heights and providing a powerful example for other nations to follow. (White House 2011a)

Domestically, the rhetorical power of these statements is clear. The value Americans accord to President Lincoln and, more intensely, to the Founding Fathers and the Constitution, proscribes attempts to transgress these foundational principles. Given that an estimated 21 per cent of software used in the United States is pirated, the mobilization of these symbols is understandable (Yu 2005: 126). Despite this, an alternative framing based around the First Amendment proved successful in halting the extension of property rights via the Stop Online Piracy legislation in 2012 (Sell 2013). In an international context these specific symbols may lose their effectivity. Instead, they suggest a measure of authority and expertise based upon historical experience and the immense material well-being the US economy has generated. American officials argue that this is, indeed, the case, suggesting that the 'soft power' of the United States is enhanced by the example of its creative industries – backed by intellectual property rights protection (Locke 2010a).

These formulations rest upon, and create, misrecognition of the actual historical experience of US economic history. Each instance in which a Founding Father enunciated vague support for intellectual property rights may be met by its opposite. Peter Garnsey has noted, in his study of the development of property rights from Roman Law to the Age of Revolution, that 'Jefferson left out property (with the connivance of colleagues) because he held that to designate it as an unalienable human right was philosophically unjustified and politically unwise' (Garnsey 2007: 225). Lincoln's view of property was similarly conflicted (Garnsey 2007: 225).[16] While the patent system developed and became institutionalized around 1840, the protection of copyright was significantly less embedded. For the majority of the 1800s piracy and copyright infringements were widespread, and significant portions of American society benefitted from the piracy of foreign works (Buinicki 2008). Examining the debate over the validity of enforcing international IPRs in the 19th century, Buinicki notes: 'Throughout the debate, opponents of international copyright suggested that they were on the side of American citizens, enlisting their support to stop any measure that they claimed would hinder the education of the American public and endanger democracy' (Buinicki 2008: 160). Moreover, it certainly remains unclear that the protection of patents was responsible for technological innovation given the central role of technology transfer between Britain and the United States and the strong role of personal knowledge in technological diffusion in prompting material innovation (Rosenberg 1970; Pollard 1981). Neither does it address whether the specific institution of intellectual property rights generates economic growth – again, this is a highly contentious area of debate, with the role of slavery, imperial expansion, abundant land, market compulsion, and geopolitical security forwarded as alternative explanations (E. Williams 1944; Post 1995,

2011). The reconstruction of American economic history is part of the naturalization of strong intellectual property rights protection that is relatively recent historically, perhaps dating no earlier than 1982 (Sell 2003: 12).

Combined with a reconstruction of American intellectual property rights protection is the second aspect of this discourse, centred upon liberal development policy. US policymakers stress the need for the developing world to apply the 'rule of law' and develop practices of 'good governance' (United States of America 2003; Zoellick 2008; Beaird 2008). President Obama has asserted that 'Assuring the free flow of information, the security and privacy of data, and the integrity of interconnected networks themselves are all essential to American and global economic prosperity, security, and the promotion of universal rights' (White House 2011b: 3). Or, in Vice President Joe Biden's typically direct phrasing: 'We're working for the 5 billion people who will join cyberspace in the years ahead so that they'll be able to experience the open, free and secure Internet. For their sake and for ours, we've got to get this done' (Biden 2011). Following the US lead, states will lay the foundation 'that will allow them to fully realize the benefits of an economic upsurge connected with global trade' (Zoellick 2008). The state cannot be removed from the process of economic and technological development. It must create the regulatory environment in which the private sector can flourish, which requires privatization, liberalization, and opening markets to international trade and foreign direct investment. David Gross asserted:

> The commitment to liberalization and competition in the ICT sector opens the door to productivity gains and sustainable wealth creation through increased private investment... [countries need to] build an environment to [sic] private sector investment and that are adaptable to technological innovation to experience the great benefits of the networked economy. (Gross 2002; see also White House 2011; Locke 2011; Strickling 2012; BSA 2012b)

The stress on liberalization, privatization, and open markets articulates a vision of the correct policy framework that states should enact. Based upon the primary characteristics assigned to the private sector, property rights, government, human rationality, and the nature of innovation itself, it represents the economic aspect of the US Open Door policy, a complement to the pursuit of the free flow of information outlined in the previous chapter. This overarching policy framework is articulated with the input and support of American high-technology companies, including Adobe, Apple, Cisco, Microsoft, Google, IBM, Oracle, Verizon, and Yahoo, among others (Department of Commerce 2011a, 2011b; IIPA 2003; Department of State ACICIP group) – and often with statistics taken directly from industry groups (e.g., Pinkos 2005).[17] It is clear that American officials recognize the centrality of the Open Door to the continued reproduction of American high-technology capital. US policy officials repeatedly stress the benefits that strong IPRs and open markets bring to American business and the country as a whole (Zoellick 2008; White House official 2008; White House 2011a). The United States relies on strong intellectual property rights to protect the R&D investments made by its corporations.[18] Removing the state from economic interventions internationally – undermining protectionist measures undertaken by developing states – is a central condition for US capital to reproduce itself globally. US government policy discourse is generated, in part, by this structural imperative, but we must be careful not to understand this as distinct from national security concerns. The ability of US capital to reproduce is central to the security of the American way of life, as fears over the development of a garrison state have historically articulated (Craig and Logevall 2009). As failed states became synonymous with the threat posed by non-state terrorists in the post-Cold War period the fusion of liberal developmental and security logics fused ever more tightly, extending the traditional American fear of instability and revolution (Paris 2006; Duffield 2001; Hunt 2007 [1989]). Grasping the social character of national security allows us to recognize the interrelationship between IPR protection, development policies, and national security.

An Open Door foreign policy is not, for US officials, mutually exclusive with the interests of other states. These rhetorical arguments cannot be read off structural pressures or reduced to disingenuous statements. US policy officials offer these prescriptions in recognition of their importance to US capital, but also in a genuine attempt to aid developing countries in improving their communications and Internet software and hardware, their economic development and, subsequently, their political stability. The threat of Internet piracy is a threat to this integrated vision of global security. In contrast to approaches that seek to compartmentalize this issue area (e.g., Mueller 2010), it is important to recognize that Internet governance is one element within a larger grand strategy that seeks to universalize American political culture. This missionary impulse, persistent in the history of American foreign relations (Williams 1962; Hunt 2007 [1989]; Smith 1994; Ekbladh 2010), informs US rhetoric and its representation of the threat of intellectual property theft. A holistic grasp of American grand strategy allows us to recognize that US officials conceive private-sector-led development of the Internet as a necessary measure to ensure continued technological innovation, economic growth, and international peace and security.

Not by narrative alone: technological closure and structural power

In seeking to secure property rights against violation by pirates or other actors, and thereby secure the 'neutral' character of the Internet's political economy, the United States mobilizes its contingent structural power in conjunction with the symbolic power of its narrative. As noted in Chapter 4, the size of the American market grants it significant leverage in its trade disputes with foreign governments. Withholding access to the American consumer is such a significant threat that some scholars have referred to the Special 301 – the United States Trade Representatives' mechanism for withholding access to American markets – as the 'H-bomb' of trade policy (Yu 2000: 138).[19] For example, the Special 301 allowed the United States to impose tariffs of $75 million on Ukrainian products in 2003 following a failure of that state to crack down on optical media piracy and to implement effective IP laws (USTR 2003). The structural position of the United States, its power over others in the global political economy, grants the US government greater capacity to reproduce international order in line with its preferences.

This power, coercively employed via the Special 301, is further supported by the institutions of the international system, with the World Trade Organization and its Agreement on Trade Related Aspects of Intellectual Property Rights (TRIPs) playing a central role alongside organizations like the Internet Governance Forum (IGF).[20] TRIPs functions as a form of institutional power in that its norms and rules force actors joining the WTO – a goal for most states – to adopt property-rights protection in line with the interests of Western, and particularly American, foreign policymakers (Sell 2003: 75–93; Matthews 2002: 7–45; Drezner 2008: 101–103). TRIPs requires that states treat nationals of other countries – in essence foreign multinationals – on equal terms with their own corporations. Failure to do so can see the offending state challenged under the WTO's stringent dispute-resolution mechanism. The loss of a WTO dispute carries an obligation to alter the offending practices within a set period of time or face further material repercussions, an outcome that is seldom necessary but which has been used, most recently against China, when IPRs have been systematically violated, as outlined below. American structural power and its institutional power located in the norms and rules of international organizations further its ability to create the material culture of the global political economy. These actions rely upon the rhetorical coercion of US discourse for legitimacy, and support that legitimacy in turn.

This is most starkly, and usefully, illustrated via the complex relationship between the United States and China over the provision of intellectual property rights in software and protectionist measures in general, including Internet filtering as a form of protection for domestic industry. The history of American intellectual-property-rights disputes with China stretches back over 30 years to the inception of market reforms in China in the late 1970s, beginning with the Agreement on Trade Relations between the United States of America and the Peoples' Republic of China (Yu 2000: 136). From that period to the present the United States government has engaged in an ongoing struggle over the form IPRs should take. This is, in some respects, a proxy for the divergent models of development both states promote and their distinct material interests in stronger or weaker IPR protection. A cyclical pattern of US pressure, Chinese resistance, and tacit compromise resulted each time the issue flared (Yu 2000; Kshetri 2009: 156–159; Drezner 2008: 103). Beginning in the 1990s, however, IPRs took on increased importance within US foreign policy (Shadlen et al. 2005: 46). The prominence of intellectual property as an issue for US foreign economic relations has continued to grow in importance through the Bush and Obama administrations, with an increasing emphasis on digital media, such as software products (USTR 2005). China, which acceded to the WTO in 2001 (ratified in 2002) had, of course, also accepted TRIPs as part of this accession. It was thereby required under WTO rules to enforce IPRs on software as a condition of its membership of the organization. Joining the WTO also meant that fellow members could take China to the WTO Dispute-Resolution Mechanism if treaty obligations were not being met.

The Bush administration believed this to be the case. China's lax protection of software IPRs – connected to its censorship regime – was alleged to function as a form of trade protectionism. It undermined the profitability of US corporations in China while at the same time boosting Chinese domestic industry through the informally supported transfer of technology. While not a direct trade barrier, the failure to enforce strong IPRs for material not yet approved for distribution in China functioned to indirectly discourage trade. This undermined the functionality of the end-to-end principle of the Internet without offering any alternative. Pirates, who had previously physically copied software in the form of CD-ROMs, now downloaded copies online and distributed them online (Ma and Gao 2012). In response, the United States began, as it had previously, to increase pressure on China by amplifying its rhetoric and signalling its displeasure through Special 301 reports. The seriousness with which the United States viewed the problem of inadequate IPR protection was emphasized in 2005, when the USTR extended its normal 301 review process to include an 'out of cycle' review of Chinese intellectual property rights protection. The review noted that even though China had made some progress on IPR reform: 'The United States remains gravely concerned, however, that China has not resolved critical deficiencies in IPR protection and enforcement, and, as a result, infringements remain at epidemic levels' (USTR 2005). The out-of-cycle review called on the Chinese government to honour its TRIPs obligations. Accession to the WTO had exposed the Chinese government to the institutional power of its rules and norms. TRIPs, formulated in the interests of Western developed states, has granted the US government power at a spatio-temporal distance as it has sought to pursue technological closure.

The threatened initiation of an IPR dispute in the WTO prompted a change in Chinese domestic property rights law as China lowered the threshold of criminal responsibility for IPR violations a couple of days before the US initiated the dispute (Zhu and Liu 2008: 197). In this instance, however, the tit-for-tat process did not take place. Instead, the United States followed through on its threatened action, initiating a dispute with China over its protection of intellectual property rights in the summer of 2007 (WTO 2009; Li 2010). The main points of contention between the two parties centred upon the threshold for criminal prosecutions of software piracy and the failure to provide copyright protection for works that are censored in China – including works that are in the process of being reviewed by censors (Li 2010: 640). The United States maintained that Chinese authorities must lower the threshold for criminal prosecutions of software piracy, as their failure to do so was allowing for large-scale piracy and cost American businesses millions (USTR 2008). The failure to protect intellectual property rights, the USTR argued, was preventing market access by American companies and represented a barrier to free trade (USTR 2007). US policymakers thereby resorted to the WTO dispute resolution to restore profitable market access for American corporations. In January 2009 the WTO found in favour of the United States, agreeing that the Chinese government had failed to meet its multilateral obligations, although not on the crucial point of the thresholds for criminal prosecution.

The WTO ruling chipped away at one aspect of China's state-led development strategy. As Adam Segal has noted, in line with Drezner's remarks above:

> Keeping out foreign companies and growing domestic ones also helps China avoid a technology trap, where Chinese producers dominate at the labor-intensive, low-value end of production while paying expensive royalties to Japanese, European, and US patent owners. (Segal 2012)

If poor protection of IPRs is becoming less feasible for China – Segal also notes the significant technical weakness reliance on pirated software introduces (ibid.) – 'networked authoritarianism' seems to offer no real solution (MacKinnon 2012).[21] Chinese Internet censorship and filtering practices have been increasingly viewed as an attempt to protect domestic industry by restricting the market access of foreign capital (Wu 2006–2007; Calinoff 2010; Liu 2011; Ting 2011; Mueller 2013: 181–182). Filtering actively blocks applications and content rather than passively allowing their theft. Catherine Liu has noted that the blocking of YouTube, Facebook, and Twitter resulted in gains in market share for their China-based equivalents Youku and Tudou, Ren Ren Wang and Kai Xin Wang, and Sina (Liu 2011: 1205–1206). By requiring the censorship of foreign websites, Chinese authorities protect and promote their domestic Internet software industry. This is, however, contrary to China's WTO commitments to ensure national treatment for foreign corporations. As a result, filtering as a form of protectionism or 'affirmative action' for Chinese companies is subject to legal action via the WTO, due to the necessity of national treatment (Ting 2011: 293–294). The United States and the European Union threatened such action in 2008 over Chinese censorship of financial services information originating from Bloomberg, Dow Jones and Reuters, leading to the removal of the Chinese measures (Ting 2011: 296; USTR 2008). Chinese authorities thus face a dilemma. They may choose to force all companies to conform to domestic censorship laws and apply the same restrictions in all information available in-country, meeting the aim of political censorship while still extending national treatment. Or they may filter information from foreign corporations, both censoring and securing the protection of domestic industry at the cost of WTO disputes and, possibly, their international reputation. In this manner, US institutional power expressed through the rules of the WTO practically supports American policymakers' claims about the necessary interrelationship between private sector innovation, open markets and economic development.

Conclusion

This chapter has outlined the role of US narratives surrounding innovation, private property rights, and the market as central to the American attempt to secure the market-opening power of the Internet for US capital. US officials articulate a complex discourse comprised of a number of layers and rhetorical strategies. First, we have noted how US officials outline the private sector as the primary driver of technological innovation. This claim is rooted in a liberal-Lockean understanding of human rationality in which actors will only attempt to innovate if they stand to materially benefit from the process. This requires the provision of strong intellectual property rights; without strong IPRs innovation and its partner, economic growth, will stagnate. Second, developing this foundation, the chapter outlined how US officials cast government in a quite specific role as the enabler of technological innovation. Government itself cannot innovate, lacking the dynamism of the private sector, but it can provide the environment in which innovation takes place. The discussion then noted, third, how threats to this model of innovation, represented by Internet piracy and state-led development projects, are cast as illegitimate. Piracy is linked to the threat of international terrorism, while state-led development is represented as contrary to the necessary course of economic development. Jointly, terrorism and underdevelopment represent a threat to global stability, which strong IPR protection may help to overcome. Finally, I have noted that the productive power of US discourse, with its echoes in the norms of the economic institutions of international society, is supported and furthered by those very institutions. Thus WTO rules and norms support and further American aims of opening markets to US capital internationally. The power of discourse is supported and furthered through structural and institutional power within the international system.

The technological rules of the Internet which open markets to the penetration of foreign capital – its institutional power expressed on behalf of the American state and American capital – are thereby strengthened and reproduced. The material culture of the Internet, its material expression of particular values, remains resolutely liberal and capitalist in form despite the ongoing and potentially transformative challenges that the network now faces. It is in the interstices between liberalism and capitalism wherein the future form of the Internet is currently being contested via these mechanisms of power. The productive power of US discourse, drawing on global norms and values, finds its material expression in the institutions of the global economy. The net result is pressure upon foreign governments to conform to the American vision of an Open Door Internet, to maintain the technological bias of the network towards American norms, values, and interests.

7
Conclusion

Technological design, development, and diffusion is a complex historical processes. Technological objects are not created according to any ahistorical rationale of efficiency and do not possess any necessary form beyond that given to them by human beings. The course of technological advance is multi-linear and under-determined. Technological design is imbricated with social power relations, and it is these power relations, in their varied facets, that lead to certain design decisions being taken over others. Social property relations – the institutionalized right to command, control, and dispose property – are the primary axes that determine how technological institutions develop. At all moments in the process of technological development, capitalists possess the capacity to shape the design process to meet the needs of capital accumulation. While capitalists possess this right, it is important to note that it is ultimately sanctioned by the power of the state. The role of the state, as an institutional apparatus embedded in civil society, is thereby critical; an alteration in the social basis of the state will produce a concomitant alteration in the technology a given social order creates. If structural power forms the analytical starting point for analyses of technological creation, productive power – the ability to legitimize both structural-power relations and the technological institutions they generate – remains central. This is particularly so for the course of technological reproduction. Reproduction requires the acceptance of a given set of social relations and their technological manifestations. Only through the interaction of these two facets of social power can technological institutions form a type of power, institutional power, which may shape the actions of other social actors at a spatio-temporal distance.

The field of Science and Technology Studies has outlined (some) of these aspects of social development in significant detail, and

International Relations Theory would do well to continue its incipient engagement with this scholarship – of which this book is a part – in order to further its study of the politics of the non-human world and the International. The converse is also true, though, and this needs to be emphasized. To this end, while this book has engaged with the STS literature on the politics of technology, it has also asserted that we cannot understand how technological objects are designed and developed if we neglect the role of inter-societal multiplicity: that is, if we neglect the International. Undertaking this analysis entails relating struggles over technological design to the nature of the state and its role within a competitive international system (Krasner 1990; Cowhey 1990). It is important, though, that such studies do not limit themselves to incorporating a generic assumption of anarchy and geopolitical competition. The picture of international society that a particular community of technological designers holds, and how that community should relate to other communities, is central to an investigation of the development of technological institutions and artefacts. This extends beyond security-relevant objects to the more mundane artefacts of everyday society. For example, it is not only Americans' visions of themselves, but their understanding of themselves in a global society that gives shape to their construction of technological artefacts from their inception. Or, to draw upon another (admittedly anecdotal) example, the Nazi embrace of aesthetic modernism and technological development occurred within a racialized cosmology of global society that influenced their reaction to Western liberal material culture, spurring on the creation of alternative technological orders (Evans 2005: 322–338).

The book has laid out an historical-materialist approach to the conceptualization of power and technology within International Relations Theory. This analysis stresses both ideational and material aspects of technological development in global politics. Thinking of technology as an institution allows us to grasp that non-human objects exercise institutional power between political communities. Refracted through the presence of multiple political communities, 'backward' communities encounter these technologies, diffused throughout the system by geopolitical pressures and the pressure of capitalist reproduction, as shaping their social development. As a result, it has argued that it is necessary to reconsider how technology as a form of power is conceptualized. In order to undertake this reconsideration, however, rethinking how technology is understood within the field of IR was required. Only if technology is recognized as the product of social construction – as not following a teleological path – can it be understood as a form of power;

without this reconceptualization the necessary link between power and agency cannot be made.

The book has explored these arguments as follows. Surveying the field in Chapter 2, three approaches to information technology were found to be dominant within the discipline: technological instrumentalists, optimistic technological essentialists, and pessimistic technological essentialists. The first group of scholars outlined technology as politically neutral – technological objects do not cause social or political change. This argument emphasizes the centrality of human agency. Discussion focused upon the work of Robert Keohane and Joseph Nye. Their primary argument is that the growth of information technology has made 'soft power'– the power of attraction possessed by certain actors and their ideas – increasingly important in global politics. This argument, impressive in its clarity, unfortunately does not offer any account of how information technology has been developed. This process was not, and is not, predetermined by any technological rationale. An explanation of Internet governance seems impossible or, at least, entirely irrelevant, within this framework. The behaviouralist and positivist concepts that Keohane and Nye use in their work are not able to account for technological development as a process and, as a result, the power to create soft power via technological design, with its necessarily historical elements, fall out of their analytical framework.

Shifting to the essentialist viewpoints, the work of optimistic technological determinists was briefly noted. This viewpoint is certainly not currently in favour, as events of the past decade have found out its primary arguments empirically. As important for our purposes, however, is the extremely underdeveloped theorization of optimist essentialists claims. In contrast pessimistic technological essentialists have placed their conception of technology within a significantly more-developed social theory. Work stressing the central role of speed in social life develops interesting insights into how our impression of social acceleration is altering the ability of political actors to react to events. However, despite the interesting insights, this work is unable to illustrate how this process is generated or why its effects are reproduced, or altered, as the case may be.

Finally, we noted how approaches in International Relations and Internet Studies that draw upon Social Construction of Technology (SCOT) approaches have moved beyond the (ultimately determinist) dichotomies of instrumentalism and essentialism. The SCOT literature is an important step forward in recognizing and rethinking the complex issues at play in the construction of technology. SCOT work stresses that technological artefacts are the product of specific political decisions made during the design process; no technical rationale of 'efficiency' exists outside of socially constructed processes. The argument presented here builds upon this work to present an account that stresses both the centrality of power politics and the manner in which technological reproduction is secured. SCOT work is often not clearly embedded within any wider theoretical perspective that explains: how actors come to gain the right or responsibility of technological development; how specific decisions may be biased towards larger political projects; or the role of discourse or ideology in closing down technological alternatives. Furthermore, power is not accorded centrality within this work, leaving out one of the core concepts of IR Theory.

Historical materialism and the international politics of technology

Chapter 3 then turned towards an historical-materialist conceptualization of power and technology in IR Theory. Reviewing the contested history of Marxist thought on technology, many strands of Marxism were found to replicate the problems of instrumentalist and essentialist determinisms. Instrumentalist Marxism was dealt with in the brevity it deserved. More substantively, both optimistic and pessimistic Marxist technological essentialists exhibited greater depth and sophistication in their argumentation. G.A. Cohen's Marxism outlined, with exceptional clarity, the case for technological determinism; with such a model, however, one could not analyse how technological objects are created. The work of the Frankfurt School presents the pessimistic alternative to Cohen's approach. Tracing the arguments of Frankfurt School Critical Theory from their classical Marxist origins prior to the Second World War to the abject pessimism of the *Dialectic of Enlightenment* revealed technological determinism as a central thread in Critical Theory. Noting their conception of a singular form of technological progress based upon an understanding of an inherently oppressive instrumental rationality, neither the work of Horkheimer and Adorno, nor Habermas's attempt at a reconstruction of the Frankfurt School project, provide adequate conceptual foundations within which to understand technological development and its power relations in global politics.

The argument of this book moves beyond the limits of classical Marxism and Critical Theory through an engagement with Andrew Feenberg's critical theory of technology. Feenberg's work provides the conceptual underpinnings for a consideration of the relationship between power and technology in International Relations. Feenberg overcomes the unnecessary dualism between instrumentalism and essentialism – or structure and agency – via his understanding of technological artefacts as 'biased but ambivalent'. This aphorism accepts that technological objects do play an important causal role in social life, as technological objects push social development in certain directions rather than others. Acknowledging the ambivalence in technical artefacts overcomes the spectre of determinism, as it foregrounds the contingent nature of technological institutions and the requirement that the bias of institutions is continually reproduced via social practice. This move reveals a need to place the development of technological objects within a broader account of social theory, in which certain structural and historical processes empower some actors to direct the design process – even if they ultimately choose not to exercise this capacity. It also provides a more detailed explanation of path dependency in which the reproduction of technological bias moves beyond a transaction cost perspective to consider the role of power, interests and identity.

With these building blocks in place, the book outlined an historical-materialist approach to information technology in International Relations. Technological institutions were delineated as a form of institutional power in global politics. Within an uneven and combined global political economy, certain actors possess greater power to direct technological development by virtue of their structural location. Technological artefacts thereby come to express the norms and values of dominant actors, structuring subordinate actors' political and economic decisions at a spatio-temporal distance. This power is enabled and supported by the values actors symbolically attach to a given technological configuration. This theoretical framework places design decisions within a wider context, stressing the central role of structural relations in generating innovation and pushing innovation in some directions rather than others. Rather than viewing the outcomes of ICT spread and development as the creation of a global civil society that functions as a counterweight to states and markets, this argument contributes to an increasingly critical literature which sees the formation of a global civil society as an extension of neo-liberal forms of regulation transnationally (Guilhot 2005; Comor 2001; Sending and Neumann 2006). Global civil society is created by and functions within the coordinates of political action set by dominant structural actors within the global political economy, detailed here through the creation and maintenance of the Internet as a particular kind of technology that makes information formally equal but substantively hierarchical.

The rules and norms of the network thereby shape and bound an electronic public sphere within particular parameters set by dominant social actors. What global civil society is – how we conceptualize this set of actors and their actions – cannot be adequately grasped without thinking through their technological preconditions and manifestations. This is an important corrective to perspectives that view the constitution of civil society as a zone of freedom from state and market imperatives. At the same time, it is also a crucial acknowledgement that, for civil society to grow and function, the process of transferring *power to* is crucial, and the Internet does indeed expand the *power to* of many actors – it simply does so in a manner which does not challenge other hierarchies within the global political economy.

In more concrete terms, the American state – an institution representing (and shaping) the interests of dominant social groups in American society – possesses greater structural power than other actors in the international system. As a result, the US government is able to push the development of the Internet in specific directions in an attempt to meet its foreign-policy aims, centred on opening markets and liberalizing other states. In turn, the Open Door approach is generated by the US structural position – the pursuit of the Open Door is understood by US officials as necessary for the reproduction of American society. The pursuit of technological closure by American foreign policy officials is the pursuit of a normative consensus around a technological configuration of the Internet that meets these aims.

Empirically illustrated via the study of American foreign policy discourse and practice regarding the politics and economics of the free flow of information Chapters 5 and 6, the discussion laid out the complex narrative of US foreign-policy officials in relation to Internet governance. American officials outline the pursuit of an Open Door Internet policy as supportive of the global spread of human rights and democracy. At the same time, the strong protection of intellectual property rights is noted as central for continued technological innovation and economic development, both for the United States and globally. These policies gain greater support from the attempt to securitize US policy aims, labelling violators of IPRs as a threat to American national security and global economic well-being more generally. The attempt to universalize and naturalize the specific US policy position is a clear articulation of a hegemonic discourse in pursuit of technological closure. The attempt has not, to date, been successful. While the US discourse has drawn upon various sources for the normative legitimacy of its arguments – from the UN to the OSCE to Jefferson and Lincoln – the legacy of colonialism loiters in the background for many developing states. This is not the first time Western officials have told China or Saudi Arabia or Iran or Russia or Vietnam or Indonesia what is in their best interests. These states stress the importance of state sovereignty and non-intervention in their own attempts to justify their Internet governance policies. The ability to suggest that the US is merely pursuing another phase in the project of Western imperialism should not be underestimated as a significant source of power internationally. It is at the intersection of these two positions, and the respective structural and productive power that each side can muster, that will guide the future of the Internet for the foreseeable future.

The future of US power after Snowden

The essential coordinates of US Internet-governance policy are fully articulated by the Bush and Obama administrations outlined in Chapters 5 and 6. The twin drives to liberalize other states via the extension of the 'free flow of information' combined with the attempt to ensure that private property rights are respected on the network are, and will remain, the generative dynamic behind specific US policy decisions. The long-term historical continuity in American foreign policy will not change in the medium term. This remains the case even in the wake of revelations by Edward Snowden in 2013 regarding the depth and extent of surveillance by the National Security Agency (NSA).

The foremost task in analysing the Snowden leaks at the moment is to place them in proper perspective; perspective was notably missing when the leaks were first made public. While they were rightly greeted by a significant furore, US government practice is not entirely historically novel nor entirely beyond the pale of our general understandings of global politics. This is not to suggest that the Snowden revelations regarding the NSA PRISM spying programme are unimportant or not rightly disturbing. However, some elements of the programme should not shock or surprise students of international relations – the spying on foreign leaders, including allies like Angela Merkel is not nearly as shocking or unexpected as suggested in some media accounts (Hillebrand 2013). Spying on allies may be a political embarrassment for the Obama administration and its European allies, but there is little to suggest that it will fundamentally alter either the US or the EU's stance towards Internet governance in general. In broader terms nothing in the NSA programme will affect the general symbiotic relationship between the United States and EU. Indeed, the proper point of comparison for the leaks may be the transatlantic rift that developed over the Iraq war in 2003. This demonstrated a serious breach in relations between France, Germany, and the United States, but a momentary breach nonetheless. The impact of the NSA leaks have not caused anywhere near the same level of tension and should be surmounted as easily.

In historical terms, this is not the first time that the United States government has tread too firmly on civil liberties in the United States. Post-9/11 critics of American policy would do well to remember the surveillance regimes of the first 'Red Scare', the second 'Red Scare', Japanese internment in the Second World War, and infiltration and COINTELPRO surveillance of domestic dissident groups in the 1960s (Williams 1981; Cunningham 2003; Lucas 2014: 35; Saito 2003). As noted in Chapter 3, the fear of the garrison state looms large in the American imagination; the NSA leaks may represent another moment in which the pendulum between security and liberty has been seen to swing too far towards the former. In this sense, the US government and the Obama administration have the chance to convince the public that equilibrium has been restored through the institution of appropriate checks and balances. At one level, of course, the PRISM programme exists, as Obama's speech on the topic outlined (Obama 2014) in order to meet American national security aims including the cybersecurity aims of US Internet policy. The NSA is spying upon cybercriminals, for example, in order to maintain secure property rights, not to undermine them. The lack of oversight and the potential for government abuse may rankle some actors, but if the generic aims of US policy were appealing to US citizens prior to the Snowden revelations, they should remain appealing afterwards.

The basic configuration of social forces outlined in the preceding analysis should also remain in place. There is no reason to assume that overreaching on the part of the NSA will alter the dominance of US high-technology capital or its dominance of the US state apparatus. The relationship between the US state and US high-technology capital was demonstrated by the leaks to be very close indeed. The initial protestations of Google, Facebook, and Apple that they were not aware of PRISM quickly faded as it was revealed that the corporations complied with NSA requests and that they were compensated for this compliance (MacAskill 2013; Whitehead 2014; Knight 2013). Corporations are legally required to comply with such requests from the government; however, there has been no indication of a significant push-back on these requests. It is a mistake to imagine that Internet companies do not have a stake in the US-led international order or that Google, Facebook, and the like, do not benefit from the security that the US government provides. These corporations are not being exploited by government, nor were they suffering any hardships prior to the NSA leaks emergence (or suffering much, beyond slightly tarnished reputations, at the moment). Capitalist corporations do not rely merely on markets to function; the political preconditions for their actions are as central as any other factor in their conduct, and some of these political preconditions are the ability to conduct their business absent the threat of physical violence – from any number of quarters – alongside the security of their property. Grasping this – the fundamentally 'political' foundations of economic agents in a capitalist economy – is essential to understanding how and why NSA surveillance has not been terribly troubling to those agents.

Similarly, nothing in the NSA leaks should push China or Russia or Iran or Saudi Arabia to alter their Internet-governance policies. If these states were not aware that the United States could spy, and was spying, on information that flowed across US fibre optics and settled in US-based servers they were either extremely naïve or badly uninformed. The back-and-forth accusations of spying between the United States and China exemplify persistent tension in a largely stable relationship, but this tension was already present prior to Snowden's actions. The United States will not stop trying to push China to allow for the creation of a liberal public sphere via the Internet, nor will it stop trying to enforce its intellectual property rights. China will not acquiesce and end its filtering programmes, nor will it fully enforce property rights if the benefit of technology transfer continues to outweigh the cost in lost foreign direct investment. The same set of calculations holds true for other states targeted by US rhetorical coercion in the past.

Yet, while these basic orientations should remain unaltered, the capacity of the US government to promote its Internet policies may be significantly diminished or, at the very least, open to question in a manner that they were not previously. While the drive for a free flow of information draws support from the norms of liberal international society, lurking behind this drive now looms the desire to tap these information flows for surveillance purposes. As an element of American policy, this is not new; as noted in Chapter 4, the US government has recognized for some time that the free flow of information provides the government with greater intelligence than shutting down or disrupting radical websites ever could. Nevertheless, the scale and scope of the surveillance has surely dented US credibility internationally. Monroe Price captures this dynamic perfectly:

> The global 'One Internet' concept was, momentarily, hoisted by its own petard. The United States and its allies had built much of the argument for the Internet – as they wished it – on the normative value of human rights in the struggle against alternative conceptions of the new technology. The Internet had been engineered for free flow: that was its bias. Now, cruelly, the very arguments for 'One Internet' and seamlessness could be turned against its most enthusiastic advocates. 'Technologies of freedom' became seen as engines of surveillance. International trust as a foundation of thousands of public and private arrangements became eroded, and the potential for closure around the Internet Freedom narrative declined, though there would be rapid efforts at repair. Internet governance became subject to the unsettled status of greater re-examination. (Price, forthcoming)

The very discourse of trust that the Obama administration repeatedly stressed throughout its policy narratives was now comprehensively undone. States and actors opposed to the American policy of promoting a liberal public sphere globally could now point to less noble US motives in order to undermine the American case with greater credence granted by their audiences. The universalism of the US message may appear to be little more than the self-interest of the national security state; openness may appear to be an instrumental rather than ethical end. The productive power of US discourse, the ability to suggest that the norms of the international community were the norms being promoted by American policy, has been damaged. And yet, while this is evident, this argument should also not be pushed too far. The structural power of the United States remains in place; its capital remains predominant, its extension via global civil social remains extensive, and – we should remember – its norms remain the dominant norms of international society. If the outer ditch of US hegemony has been taken, the extent of its earthworks should now be in clearer view (cf. Gramsci 1971: 238). It is simply too soon to suggest the eclipse of the American vision for the Internet, even if this vision has been tarnished.

Just as we should not rush to proclaim that the US ability to shape the politics of the Internet is in inexorable decline, reconsidering technology this way (as a form of institutional power in international politics) has significant relevance to contemporary debates over the decline of American power. The declinist thesis, fashionable in the aftermath of Vietnam, stagflation, and the malaise-laden presidency of Jimmy Carter has made a stunning comeback in the wake of failures in Iraq, Afghanistan, and the global economic recession of 2007 to 2009 (Berger 2009; Cox 2007, 2009; Nexon and Wright 2007; Brooks and Wohlforth 2008). The sudden re-emergence of these debates, following the no less-heated 'Empire' debates of the early part of this century, involves carefully considering the nature and scope of US power internationally. One element that these debates have largely neglected is a consideration of the nature of American power as expressed through global material culture. Beyond the arguments over 'Globalization as Americanization' fashionable among the 'No Logo' left in the late 1990s, which concerned primarily the role of American symbols and imagery in global society, there is a need to consider the manner in which an American-designed material culture is shaping the conduct of social relations within the domestic societies of countries across the globe. If the United States is in decline – this remains deeply uncertain – it is important to consider what kind of world it is declining into. Echoing the regime theorists' reply to the hegemonic stability arguments of the early 1980s, consideration of the power of material culture points towards the endurance of a liberal capitalist world order – in essence, an American world order – for some time to come. The ability to change the nature of social institutions is a difficult and lengthy process, as the transition from the Bretton Woods regime of the early post-war era to the neo-liberalism of the past 30 years has demonstrated. The ability to change the material bias of technological institutions may be more difficult to overcome. In the absence of any serious global challenge to the definition of material progress supplied by capitalist coordinates internationally, these values will remain in place.

International Relations and technology: future directions

Working outside the occasionally narrow confines of Internet governance studies, this book has sought to expand the scope of treatments of information technology and the Internet in International Relations. In the process the book has raised issues for future research. For example, further study into American policy officials' discursive construction of technological innovation as possible only via market-led processes could repay sustained attention. As noted briefly in Chapter 4, US officials have argued that part of the reason for the collapse of the Soviet Union may be attributed to the failure of socialist economies to innovate (Latham 2011: 186–190). While the broad course of US post-Cold

War policy and its expression of liberal capitalist values have been well charted (Smith 2007; Latham 2011: 186–219; Ekbladh 2010: 257–273), the specific employment of narratives around technological innovation in creating and sustaining an American order remains to be outlined. Post-Cold War policies promoting market-led practices in international development, establishment of strong intellectual property rights in the WTO, or democracy-promotion efforts globally, rely upon the promotion and acceptance of certain arguments about how technological innovation must occur based on understandings of incentives, planning, and human rationality. That is, investigating how US officials employ narratives surrounding the end of the Cold War in order to drive through US policies internationally points towards the politics of the construction and reproduction of US order. Such micro-processes and their relationship to macro-historical developments deserve further study.

Beyond this, the argument made here pushes for a reconsideration of some central aspects of International Relations Theory, again continuing processes of theoretical development that are emerging within the field on the centrality of science and technology to global politics. While drawing upon recent scholarship developing the theory of uneven and combined development (U&CD), the argument in the book points towards the potential supersession of these dynamics of the International. If, as argued here, technology functions as a form of institutional power altering the developmental trajectory of backward states, then this form of power may lead to the supersession of unevenness and the emergence of deeper forms of convergence in the social form of states throughout the international system. The geopolitical dynamics of the system may be overcome by technological developments, either through the increased complexity of military weaponry and its transnational production (Brooks 2005) or, as noted earlier, as a response to the fear of nuclear holocaust (Deudney 2008; Craig 2009). This suggests not only that technological artefacts alter the structure of international anarchy, but that certain forms of anarchy generate the very technological dynamics and development processes that will, in time, supersede this condition. Convergence, if it ever occurs, is then grasped, not as a natural working out of technological progress or historical momentum, but as the product of its active pursuit in the course of human material reproduction.

Grasping the socio-technical production of anarchy or hierarchy and the associated conditions of sovereignty requires a consideration of how particular artefacts are or are not altering the conduct of international relations, but also how dominant conceptions of anarchy and sovereignty create the space within which technological design occurs. This demands that we reflexively consider how our theoretical perspectives inform and shape technological development, as much as they are shaped by technological developments. Realist arguments about the unending condition of anarchy, liberal faith in historical progress and the mitigation of inter-state conflict, or Marxist scholarship emphasizing the politics of class conflict and the associated need for emancipation – these all help to produce, through their analyses, the social world within which technological innovation occurs. If anarchy and uncertainty can never be overcome, the politics of technological design looks significantly different than if the diffusion of technological progress generates greater wealth, prosperity, and international security. Outcomes of international technological development and standard setting structured by power asymmetries will possess significantly different values and legitimacy than institutions produced through genuine dialogue and cooperation. Whether the former or the latter process takes place is dependent, at least in part, on how international politics is understood.

For critical International Relations Theory, with its roots in the Marxist tradition, the task of engaging with the politics of technological development looms increasingly large. Turning away from the politics of language to the politics of production – considered broadly – requires that Critical IR Theory take physical materiality and the limits it places upon the development of democratic governance more seriously, a point rightly emphasized by Fluck (2012) in his discussion of Frankfurt School inspired discourse ethics. IR theorists grapple with the nature of hegemony in international politics through the division between primacy as material power and hegemony as legitimacy (Clark 2011), but the international politics of technology look beyond this dichotomy. Norms in international society are constituted, in part, by socio-technical practices that promote specific norms surrounding, for instance, warfare, human rights, sovereignty and non-intervention. If, as suggested throughout the book, the International is always internal to the development of technological artefacts, and this imposes a cost upon actors seeking to resist these values, the nature of international hegemony may need to be reconsidered as 'deeply saturating' the practices of everyday society across the international system (Williams 2005 [1980]: 37). The role of technological institutions, particularly exceptionally diffuse institutions such as the Internet, in sustaining practices that reflect the values of dominant actors suggests that the power of these institutions reach much further into the constitution of societies than traditionally credited in analyses of power in International Relations. In turn, the durability of these values – in this case, the durability of the values of liberal capitalism – is a product of their material substantiation within our lived environments. If global governance is not limited to the changing forms of regulation between states, or the growth of transnational regulatory bodies that sit above and below the state, but penetrates into the lived relations of individuals across the globe, then the endurance of this form of order may be much more substantial than either its proponents or opponents estimate. The task for any emancipatory movement thereby becomes significantly more complex, even as it becomes clearer.

Appendix: Discourse Analysis Guide

Step one – Location and context

1.1 What type of document is this? (policy statement, interview, comments to reports, congressional testimony, position paper, etc.)
1.2 Who is the author of the document? Does it represent the view of the United States government? Is it representative of personal opinion only? (If it has no personal author, does this make it seem more official/formal/authoritative?)
1.3 To whom is the author speaking? Is this document for a particular audience?
1.4 In relation to the other documents studied, does this document seem consistent with the others, or has the author specifically tailored their message to meet the approval of a given audience? (Consistency of message)

Step two – Representation of the Internet

2.1 What does the document say in a straightforward macro-reading? That is, who is doing what to whom in the article? What is it about?
2.2 Binary oppositions – what are people/actions/events/places defined in opposition to?
2.3 What are the verbs/adjectives attached to the Internet? (E.g. revolutionary, democratic, progressive, neutral?) What are the predicates and relations to other things and people? How, if at all, is the Internet related to other aspects of international society?
2.4 Is the Internet accorded a positive, negative, or neutral value overall? What are the metaphors employed? What other texts are referred to in the document?
2.5 Is the Internet deterministic, a neutral tool, a biased but ambivalent technology? Is any kind of causation implied?
2.6 Is the Internet described as an actor/agent? A state of being?
2.7 Are there any clear unquestioned assumptions about the Internet?

Appendix: Discourse Analysis Guide 163

Step three – Representations of markets, innovation and property rights

3.1 What are the verbs/adjectives attached to intellectual property rights? (Predicates/Relations)
3.2 Are property rights accorded a specific value? Are metaphors employed?
3.3 Relationship between intellectual property rights and the Internet?
3.4 What verbs/adjectives, if any, are attached to actors who violate intellectual property rights?
3.5 What role is accorded to markets in the article, if any? What predicates attach to markets? What values does this suggest adhere to markets, if any? What is the general relation to markets, intellectual property rights, innovation?
3.6 Does the narrative disclose any particular view or understanding of how innovation occurs?

Step four – United States foreign policy culture/practices

4.1 Does the document fit within a particular stain of American foreign policy culture? Is it Universalist/Exemplarist/Crusading/Isolationist/Realist? Does it suggest universal values or culturally specifically values?
4.2 Does the document refer to particular political values that resonate within American political culture? (E.g. freedom of speech/press)

Step five – Disjunctures

5.1 Are there any elements of the discourse that do not fit together, or do not fit with the wider discourse? What are the inconsistencies or contradictions?
5.2 Does the discourse significantly shift over time, e.g. with the change in administration from Bush to Obama?

Notes

1 Introduction

1. Schmidt (1998, 2002) has argued for an 'internalist' approach to the foundation of International Relations as a discipline. While this argument is helpful in preventing any claims to straightforward causal effects between the First World War and 'Idealist' thought claims, it misrepresents the nature of 'externalist' or contextualist approaches to the history of ideas (see Holden 2002). The cultural and intellectual climate engendered by the First World War should not be underestimated.
2. Please note that the discipline of International Relations (IR) will be capitalized, while the practise of international relations will remain in lower caps.
3. Please note that the focus here is on studies that actually engage with the politics of technological objects, as opposed to scholarship that emphasises the technology of politics. The latter examines how the political is treated technologically, engaging in a form of reification of technology that this book rejects. For an example of such approaches, see Reid (2009).
4. The approach taken here draws on both historical and sociological institutionalist approaches (Hall and Taylor 1996).
5. STS has acknowledged both the significance of technologies essential to the conduct of world politics, such as nuclear weapons (Mackenzie 1987; Spinardi 2013), and the importance of the transnational diffusion of technological objects (Van der Vleuten 2009), but not the relationship between states or political communities that form the distinctive terrain of IR.
6. Despite some shared emphasis on the important impact of technology, this book does not draw significantly on medium theory. This body of scholarship, while important in opening avenues for study, fails to outline in any depth how technology is created or maintained through social relations.
7. The debate over Internet politics has often been confined to a very narrow scope, such as the politics of the Internet Corporation for Assigned Names and Numbers (ICANN) or the relevance or obsolescence of the state. The decision to consider wider issue areas was partially driven by the United States officials interviewed for the book, who stressed debates around ICANN as a minor aspect in the overall structure of Internet governance.
8. On Actor-Network Theory, see Latour (2005) for a clear introduction. While an interesting approach to social theory which usefully provokes an engagement with difficult questions of methodology, ontology, agency and ethics, I find its enthnomethodological approach inconsistent, the inability to account for unequal power relations rooted in enduring social structures (or enduring networks) problematic, both analytically and politically, and the ontological agency attributed to non-human objects both deeply problematic and inconsistent with the Marxist historical materialism adopted here. For critiques of Actor Network Theory (ANT) consistent with my views, see Vandenberghe (2002), Castree (2002), and Hacking (1987).

2 Power and Information Technology: Determinism, Agency, and Constructivism

1. Please note that this chapter draws upon elements of McCarthy (2013).
2. Herrera (2006) notes the limitations of both Realist and Constructivist approaches to technology. The current discussion, in contrast to Herrera, distinguishes between instrumentalism and essentialism in IR theory, rather than discussing how different 'schools' conceptualize technology, in order to grasp the underlying concepts of power both types of determinism employ. As noted in the introduction, there is often as much variation within schools of IR theory as between them. For a discussion of the Realist approach to technology in general see Scheuerman (2009); for a discussion of Gramscian concepts of technology and materiality – one that also discusses Waltz's work – see McCarthy (2011b).
3. The literature on power in International Relations has tended to neglect considerations of technology: for example, Barnett and Duvall (2005) does not feature any consideration of technology or material culture in discussing forms of power.
4. Please note that this claim is distinct from claims surrounding 'cyberpower' as a new element of global politics (cf. Betz and Stevens 2010). The power referred to here, and developed further in Chapter 3, centres upon the 'ability to create abilities' expressed via the institution of ICTs, and not the actual abilities created, which belongs to the realm of recent theorizations of cyberpower.
5. The understanding of ICTs facilitating disaggregation is also highly contested: a large body of scholarship exists noting the ability of the state to assert its power in cyberspace. See, for example, Goldsmith and Wu (2006); Drezner (2004); Deibert, Palfrey, Rohozinski, and Zittrain (2008, 2010, 2012).
6. However, Rosenau does suggest that information technologies 'influence, contextualize, permit or inhibit courses of action' (Rosenau 2002: 276; 1990: passim), that they undermine state authority (1990: 90–100; 1992a: 3; 1992b: 256–265), and that they change learning patterns for world leaders and mass publics (1990: 321; 1992b: 262).
7. Hanson (2008: 6–7) describes Keohane and Nye as 'societal determinists.' This phrase is slightly awkward – it suggests that technology is not always already social – and cannot capture the technological determinism that underlies instrumentalist and essentialist viewpoints.
8. Nye's work builds on that of Peter Bachrach and Morton S. Baratz and their theorization of the 'second face' of power. See Nye (2004: 150, footnote 5). Bachrach and Baratz's understanding has been the subject of substantial criticism that has focused on their inability to break with behaviouralism. See Lukes (2005: 7, 19–27); Hay (1997: 45–52); Hayward (2000: 14–19). Nye has recently tried to integrate Lukes's 'third face' of power into his framework (Nye 2010c), but this effort does not grapple with the theoretical underpinnings that make such a move incompatible with the other aspects of his approach.
9. This form of power, outlined by Keohane and Nye, is sometimes attributed to them as 'institutional power': see, for example, Barnett and Duvall (2005: 48). I feel this usage is incorrect and confuses an institutional context with sociological institutionalism, particularly given Barnett and Duvall's understanding of institutional power as action at a distance, an understanding that Keohane

and Nye's behaviouralist model of power and causation seems to disallow. For Keohane and Nye, power does not lie in the institution: actor A acts on actor B within the institution, not through it, and thus the institution remains as a context rather than a form of power. On direct and indirect forms of power and their related concepts of causation, see Hay (1997: 51) and Ball (1975: 189–215, esp. 204).
10. These articles form the core of the 'power debate' in social science. The literature on the topic is massive: for critical summaries see Hayward (2000: 11–39); Wartenburg (1990: 53–70).
11. I thank Matthew Fluck for reminding me of this point.
12. Williams's argument was directed against similar understandings of causation in Marxist accounts of the 'base–superstructure' relationship.
13. On 'problem-solving theory' and 'critical theory', see Cox (1981).
14. The roots of these ideas may lie in the rudimentary political theory of the actual engineers of the Internet, many of whom expressed – and continue to express – adherence to relatively simplistic right-wing libertarian ideologies (Murray 2007: 6–8; Goldsmith and Wu 2006: 23; Cerf 2012).
15. I will not be dealing with poststructuralist literature that focuses on the 'technology of politics', as opposed to the politics of technology. These works rarely actually focus upon non-human objects as such, and instead relate thought about technology to thought about the social world, a useful project but one removed from our concerns here. For examples of such work, see Dillon (1996: 75–76, 85–86) and Reid (2009: 607–623). Reid considers how the idea of connectivity is made political, not how technological objects either do or do not foster forms of connectivity, and is concerned only with discourse, not materiality.
16. Kitching (2008) offers an excellent account of how this style of writing obscures human agency and lends itself to metaphysical arguments. I thank Richard Rathbone for bringing this source to my attention.
17. This point touches upon several difficult theoretical and conceptual issues around the agent–structure problem. Space does not permit a full consideration of these issues.
18. Please note that this viewpoint does not contradict a Realist ontology: technological artefacts, produced by human beings, are not natural objects, and thus have a different ontological status to entities like electrons.
19. Arguments outlining technological path dependence are prevalent in economic history, with the example of the QWERTY keyboard featuring prominently. For surveys of this literature see Mahoney (2000: 515, passim), Pierson (2000: 254, passim), and Djelic and Quack (2007: 162–163, passim).
20. See Bijker (1995: 276–277); Pinch and Bijker (1987) 28–40.
21. This phenomenon is present in the complex construction of a liberal global political order more generally; see Duffield (2005); Hurrell (2005); Guilhot (2005).

3 A Historical Materialist Approach to Technological Power in International Relations

1. Germain (2007) has highlighted the need to acknowledge that there are several 'historical materialisms' in social theory. While I recognize that there

are many 'historical materialisms', I will refer to Marxism as historical materialism throughout in keeping with conventional usage in IR.
2. The main chapters of *Capital* that deal with technology and machinery – Part IV, chapters 14 and 15 – alone provide the material for several different and contradictory readings of Marx's conception of technology. See Marx (1867: 455–636). For excellent summations of the variety of Marxist approaches to technology, see Feenberg (1991) and Dyer-Whitherford (2000: 38–61). For a recent analysis of Marx's view of technology see Wendling (2009).
3. Callinicos's work is developed as a defence of a classic understanding of the conflict between the forces and relations of production which, while sympathetic to Cohen, recognizes some weaknesses in his argument. This is deployed to criticize the work of 'Political Marxists' such as Ellen Meiksins Wood and Robert Brenner, arguing that they provide no account of how structural crises occur, while a focus on the conflict between forces and relations of production does allow for such an account. This criticism is misplaced, and relies on an exogenous and teleological understanding of technological development. For Wood's reply, see Wood (1990: 122–128). Chibber (2011) provides an excellent survey and discussion of 'canonical' historical materialism and the limitations of Cohen's approach.
4. The number of scholars rejecting the 'technologist' interpretation of Marx is substantial. For a small sample, see Postone (1993), Ollman (1976: 7–8, 25), Harvey (2006 [1982]: 98–104), Sayer (1987: 1–49), Wood (1981: 72).
5. While this work has been influential in International Relations, for the most part such scholarship has focused upon a critique of positivism or the ethical dilemmas of international politics (Neufeld 1995; Linklater 1998; Diez and Steans 2005), rather than the Frankfurt School's materialist heritage, although there are a few notable exceptions (Wyn Jones 1999; Peoples 2009; Fluck 2012).
6. *Dialectic of Enlightenment* relies upon an untenable historical narrative, one which, for this author, weakens its critical purchase entirely. On the rhetorical strategies of the book and their critical intent, see Honneth (2000).
7. In his historical analysis of the rise and fall of rational communication in the public sphere, Habermas leans on his differentiation of knowledge constitutive interests to argue for the insulation of the public sphere from the rationalization of instrumental thought. This historical argument has been subject to critique within the media and communications literature – see Thompson (1995: 71–76) and Curran (2002: 45).
8. This problem is the product of SCOT's and ANT's ontological commitments.
9. Gramscian scholarship in International Relations is informed by this functionalist portrayal of technology. See, for example, Cox (1987: 11–12, 21, 314–315). Criticism of this position is offered in McCarthy (2011b).
10. While cultural values are important, we need to be careful about reifying a particular set of national cultural values, claiming cohesion where none exists. For our purposes, the assumption is that the cultural values embedded in technological objects are those of dominant social actors – those of capital and fractions of capital. These values are not automatically produced by the structural location of capital, but interact with the pressures of material reproduction, previous historical experience, religious values, and so forth. Chibber (2013: 209–248) provides an interesting account of the interaction between capital and cultural factors.

11. Functionalist explanations of technological development are widespread in Marxist thought and in International Relations. For examples, see Brenner (1990; 2006) and Waltz (1979).
12. Please note that this understanding of structural power is distinct from that offered by Ward (1987) or Gill and Law (1989), in which social structures themselves are conceived as powerful. Such interpretations tend to be overly structuralist, with human agents as mere bearers of structures. I agree with Lukes (2005) and Morriss (2002) that to speak of structural power as the power of social structures is to blur the concept of social power. Within International Relations this approach is primarily associated with Gramscian scholarship (Rupert 2005; Gill and Law 1989), although it is characteristic of Marxist approaches in the field more generally.
13. On these different forms of social relations, see Wight (2006: 163–176).
14. On internal relations, see Sayer (2000) and Ollman (1976).
15. These formulations avoid the metaphysical conception of power common to Foucauldian approaches. On the problem of Foucault's formulation, see Hayward (2000: 6–7), Wartenberg (1990: 135–140) and Lukes (2005: 88–98).
16. For a sample of work examining the relationship between capitalism and the states system see Chase-Dunn (1980), Rosenberg (1994, 2006), Teschke (2003), Lacher (2006), Wood (2002: 166–181), and the essays collected in Anievas (2011).
17. The 'capitalist peace' has generated a wide literature, with differing claims as to the reason why capitalist states do not fight – see Brooks (2005), Gartzke (2007), Mousseau, Hegre and O'Neal (2003), and J. Mueller (2010), among others.
18. This passage will necessarily skate over the intricacies of state theory in order to proceed with the argument. In brief, I find the Realist concept of the state and its suggestion that states act like units does not adequately capture the texture of the International and the varied goals states pursue due to their domestic social form, a critique levelled by both liberal and Marxist scholars (Moravcsik 1997; Teschke 2003). 'Relative' autonomy – favoured by many Marxists – is a formulation that only makes sense in the context of the 'base-superstructure' metaphor, which I reject, in which the state is 'relatively' autonomous from the economic base, suggesting an untenable reductionism. For clearly written criticisms of the 'relative' autonomy position see Giddens (1985: 214–218) and Jessop (1982: 226–227). My approach draws on Jessop (1982, 2002, 2007). As Jessop notes, 'class power depends less on the class background of those nominally in charge of the state or their subjective class identities and projects than on the differential class relevance of the effects of the exercise of state capacities in a complex and changing conjuncture' (Jessop 2007: 31).
19. For example, the Vice Chairman of the ACICIP, Richard Wiley, is chairman of influential law firm Wiley Rein LLP. Wiley Rein is (according to its own website) the largest telecoms legal firm in the country, and had three partners on the ACICIP. Richard Wiley, the founder of the firm, was a former chair of the Federal Communications Commission responsible for pushing forward deregulation and liberalization of the telecoms industry. The firm was the destination of choice for former US Ambassador for Information Policy under the Bush administration, David A. Gross, and his senior deputy,

Richard C. Beaird, who both joined Wiley Rein on completion of their time in government. See Wiley Rein (2013).
20. Consulting the biographies of any of the top information and telecommunications officials in either the Bush or Obama administrations illustrates this principle clearly – individuals shift between the private sector and government and back to the private sector with regularity. Nevertheless, Jessop's point noted above still applies to the argument overall.
21. DeNardis (2012) makes the important point that the literature on Internet governance is often focused upon the institutions of Internet governance – ICANN, RIRs, and so forth – to the exclusion of a focus upon the power of the Internet architecture. Interestingly, US foreign policy officials seem to share this view: see the Introduction.
22. This requires attending to counterfactual possibilities, as noted throughout the literature on social power. See, for a sample, Dowding (1996), Guzinni (1993), Morriss (2002). The classic political-science definition is based upon such an understanding: power, as the ability to get B to do what B *would not otherwise do*.

4   US Foreign Relations and the Institutional Power of the Internet

1. For alternative approaches emphasizing national security, the military-industrial complex, and identity politics, see, among others, Gaddis (1983); Craig and Logevall (2009); Campbell (1998) and Hixson (2009).
2. This formulation attempts to overcome the differentiation between material interests or identity as drivers of social action. This approach is perhaps best captured by Raymond Williams's notion of 'structures of feeling' (1962) in which material reproduction is recognized as the product of 'material' interests that are, jointly, the pursuit of norms of identity that are deeply embodied.
3. Williams's work inspired a number of historians of American diplomacy, sometimes labelled the 'Wisconsin School', and was influential on 'New Left' or revisionist historians generally. See LaFeber (1980), McCormick (1995), Gardner (1976). In International Relations, see Bacevich (2004), Colas (2008), Jahn (2007).
4. This is not to suggest that Williams, or the Open Door approach in general, ignored the salience of American political ideas. On the contrary, and in marked contrast to charges of economism levelled by Michael Hunt (among others), Williams sought to outline American expansionism as a cultural phenomenon. Hunt criticizes Williams for suggesting that 'Ideology was functional, a tool used by the grandees of American capitalism to maintain their economic power and with it their socio-political control' (1989: 9). In *The Contours of American History*, the concept of *weltanschauung* is foregrounded in analysis, with Williams noting that it 'cuts across and subsumes personal motives, group interests, and class ideologies' (1966: 20). Critics of Williams at times argue that his explanation was both 'fundamentally economic' and ideational in the same paper – see J. Thompson (1973: 94, 97). Williams's approach attempted to avoid these binaries and sought to define

an expansionist foreign policy as a 'way of life': 'a way of life is the combination of patterns of thought and action that, as it becomes habitual and institutionalized, defines the thrust and character of a culture and society' (Williams 1980: 4). To characterize Williams as a contradictory thinker because he is both a determinist and a voluntarist, as Melanson (1978) does, is to misunderstand the nature of these claims.
5. For a recent overview of self-determination in US policy, see Simpson (2012).
6. This policy is now enshrined in international trade law in the World Trade Organization's Most Favoured Nation (MFN) provision. See Chapter 6.
7. Williams's work is sometimes characterized by critics as Leninist (Gaddis 1983: 172), but such claims fail to grasp the substantial differences between Lenin's theorization of inter-imperialist rivalry and Williams's theorization of neo-imperial domination, badly misreading both authors. Williams saw US policy as opening markets in a non-exclusionary manner in direct contrast to Lenin's theorization of inter-imperialist rivalry via territorial control, derived from the conjuncture of the First World War. This basic divide remains salient in critical work on US conduct in international relations. For example, Harvey (2003) emphasizes territorial control in explaining US foreign policy, as does Callinicos's essentially Leninist interpretation (2009), while Hardt and Negri (2000) and Wood (2003) stress that imperialism under capitalism does not require territorial control. The approach taken here is sympathetic to the latter position, while not ascribing to all aspects of it.
8. This is in contrast to positions that stress state policies as driven by 'Realpolitik' (Manijikian 2010), a formulation that lacks any clear content.
9. I thank James Vaughan for reminding me of this necessary corrective to Mearsheimer's view.
10. The International Covenant on Civil and Political Rights (ICCPR), for example, was only ratified by the United States in 1992, after its initial creation at the UN in 1966 – with such significant amendments that its actual force was effectively nullified.
11. I thank John Dumbrell for pressing me to clarify this point.
12. This analysis has been challenged by other Marxists for its focus upon the horizontal competition among capitals, rather than upon the central role of class struggle and increased wages as the cause of decreased profit rates. For a sample of the extensive debate on this issue, see *Historical Materialism: Research in Critical Marxist Theory* 4(1) 1999.
13. Importantly, Howard notes that civil-society organizations are at least as prominent as radical and violent political groups in such societies. This stands in stark contrast to literature about terrorism and the Internet in general.

5 Pursuing Technological Closure: Symbolic Politics, Legitimacy, and Internet Filtering

1. Please note this is an updated and revised version of McCarthy (2011a).
2. On free speech and free expression, generally, see Marx (1975: 132–181), Mill (1974), Keane (1991) and Lee (1990). For an excellent analysis of the place of free speech in liberal political thought, see Peters (2005).

Notes   171

3. That this regime is legitimate does not make any claims about how this legitimacy was generated. For an interesting recent account that challenges conventional wisdom about the US role in promoting human rights – including that which informs the present analysis – see Reus-Smit (2013).
4. Article 19: 'Everyone has the right to freedom of opinion and expression; this right includes freedom to hold opinions without interference and to seek, receive and impart information and ideas through any media and regardless of frontiers' (UN 1948).
5. Article 29: '(1) Everyone has duties to the community in which alone the free and full development of his personality is possible; (2) In the exercise of his rights and freedoms, everyone shall be subject only to such limitations as are determined by law solely for the purpose of securing due recognition and respect for the rights and freedoms of others and of meeting the just requirements of morality, public order and the general welfare in a democratic society; (3) These rights and freedoms may in no case be exercised contrary to the purposes and principles of the United Nations' (UN 1948).
6. The deep tensions between this belief in universal natural rights and the nationalist belief in American exceptionalism cannot be explored here. For discussion of these issues, see Hoff (2008), Lyons (2006), McCrisken (2003), and Hixson (2009).
7. GIFT was re-launched by Secretary Clinton in 2010 as the NetFreedom Task Force.
8. This comment echoes a classic formulation of technological instrumentalism: 'Guns don't kill people, people kill people'. See McCarthy (2013: 474).
9. This understanding of transparency is reliant on a problematic theory of knowledge and sidesteps often difficult issues of political conflict. For a critique of such approaches to information in IR that share characteristics of US foreign policy officials' discourse, see Hurrell (2005).
10. 'The participating countries include: Austria, Canada, Costa Rica, Czech Republic, Finland, France, Estonia, Georgia, Germany, Ghana, Ireland, Kenya, Latvia, the Republic of Maldives, Mexico, Mongolia, The Netherlands, Tunisia, the United Kingdom, the United States, and Sweden' (Freedom Online Coalition 2013).
11. DDoS mitigation allows targeted network sites to pass on the high levels of information flooding their networks to higher-capacity networks.
12. Please note, again, that I am not taking a stand in relation to these ethical debates, and this discussion should not be taken as an ethical criticism of US policy.

6 The Narration of Innovation in US Internet Policy

1. Nevertheless, this is definitely preferable to a decision to charge users for different levels of access and speed over the network, a proposal forwarded by American telecommunications companies The debate over these issues has been labelled the 'Net Neutrality' debate. The difference between formal equality and substantive inequality is central to grasping the nature of the Internet. On the difference between these concepts and the tendency to

obscure them see Marx (1974 [1867]: 280, 621; 1875), Corrigan and Sayer (1981: 21–53).
2. Explicitly Marxist scholarship has been slow to recognize this. See Vaden and Suoranta (2009) and Moore and Taylor (2009).
3. The focus of this discussion is directed primarily at the innovative activities that take place in the applications and content layer of the network rather than at the level of control protocols that are the primary responsibility of the Internet Corporation for Assigned Names and Numbers (ICANN). The end-to-end principle ensures that the innovation largely occurs here, at the edges of the network, rather than at the lower levels of hardware and control protocols. The key point to grasp is that, while users may have equal access to application (but not content due to pay walls around academic journals, *The New York Times*, and so forth), suppliers of applications benefit from structural power.
4. The GNU-General Public License is a 'copyleft' free software license that ensures that software produced under this license is freely available to copy or alter.
5. The need for a World Summit on the Information Society (WSIS) was agreed by the International Telecommunications Union (ITU) in 1998, and carried forward in two phases, with summits in Tunisia in 2003 and Geneva in 2005. The WSIS was designed to address how the information society was affecting development outcomes and global governance in general, with a specific focus upon the problems posed by the 'digital divide'. However, in practice discussion also turned to issues surrounding Internet governance. See Mueller (2010: 64–80).
6. These formulations are consistent with US policies from the Clinton Administration – see the *Framework for Global Electronic Commerce* (1997).
7. At the 2012 World Conference on International Telecommunications, hosted by the International Telecommunications Union, the US proposal to the conference centred precisely upon the need to create a stable, market-based regulatory environment to ensure the growth of ICT developed globally (United States of America 2012). The failure of the ITU to agree to US proposals led to US inability to sign the agreement, a move supported by the United Kingdom, Canada, and Australia, among others (Goldstein 2012).
8. The Lockean perspective is usefully contrasted with Hegelian understandings of labour that view it as a process of self-actualization which overcomes alienation and is thereby necessary for ethical development. See May (2000: 16–44).
9. The literature on the motivations of FOSS developers highlights the prevalence of motives other than financial benefit. See Bitzer, Schrettl, and Schröder (2007), Oreg and Nov (2008), Wu, Gerlach and Young (2007), and Moore and Taylor (2009).
10. On the construction of relation and subject positions, see Fairclough (2001: 39–41) and Milliken (1999: 229).
11. This rests upon an understanding of 'consumer sovereignty' in which consumers exercise a guiding hand over the process of technological development (Chadwick 2006: 290). The notion of 'consumer sovereignty' has been criticized by a number of perspectives – see Manning (2001) and Barry (2003) for examples.

12. This position – the general stance of the United States government toward greater state regulation and ITU involvement in the governance of the Internet – is articulated by the private sector as well. For instance, the Software & Information Industry Alliance 'applauded' both the House and the Senate's opposition to 'control by intergovernmental bodies that could threaten Internet freedom. Expanding the control of [i]ntergovernmental bodies could undermine international trade and access to the Internet for people around the globe' (SIIA 2012a). The SIIA includes among its 500 members Adobe, Google, Oracle, and Qualcomm. The organization notes its close ties with government as a central benefit for members.
13. For treatments of strategic rhetoric that have informed this analysis, see Barnett (1999) and Krebs and Jackson (2007).
14. For an account that notes similar disagreements between the United States and EU over the structure of global financial regulation, see Abdelal (2010).
15. The IIPA stated: 'While the US has apparently inserted into the documents commendable references to the need for "cyber-security," this term is usually understood to refer to prohibitions against hacking or other unauthorized intrusions into computer or other telecommunications systems. References to cyber-security should be accompanied by references to the dangers to the information society resulting from unchecked commercial piracy or other infringements that occur regularly on the Internet' (IIPA 2003: 3). On securitization, see Buzan, Waever, and de Wilde (1998). These representations do not achieve full securitization, lacking any expression in emergency measures.
16. Garnsey notes Lincoln's approval of Jefferson: '[T]he Jefferson party formed upon the supposed superior devotion to the personal rights of man, holding the rights of property to be secondary only and greatly inferior,' quoting *Lincoln, Collected Works*, Basler (ed) 374–376.
17. In an example of the value the US private sector places on the Open Door, the Business Software Alliance (BSA) honoured US Trade Representative Ron Kirk 'in recognition of his leadership in promoting the growth of digital commerce by pressing for robust intellectual property protections and greater access to overseas markets for software and other IT products and services' (BSA 2012a).
18. M. Mueller (2010: 135) suggests – against 'leftists' – that 'in reality, both the policy objectives and the effects of market liberalism in telecommunications were directly opposed to those supporting the globalization of IP protection'. Mueller conflates the drive to undermine *some* monopolies – state telecommunications monopolies in the developing world – with the drive to undermine *all* monopolies, such as those of large Western corporations secured through the TRIPs agreement.
19. The 'Special 301' is a trade policy initiated in 1986 that threatens to exclude trade violators from the American market entirely. Each year the United States Trade Representative conducts a review of trade violations, with particularly heinous violators placed on a priority watch list.
20. See Drahos (2002), Matthews (2002), and May (2007: 27–33), on the road to the TRIPs agreement and the benefit secured by developing states. Mueller (2010: 131) notes the agenda-setting power of the United States in its ability to keep issues of intellectual property off the agenda of the IGF.

21. Advocacy such as Mackinnon's (2012) or Lee, Liu, and Li's (2011) is laudable. However, I feel that it overestimates the moral potential of corporations, tending towards an idealistic reading of corporate social responsibility policies and the ability of corporations to promote human rights (which is, in any case, not their legal remit or purpose).

Bibliography

Abbate, J. (2000) *Inventing the Internet* (Boston: The MIT Press).
Abdelal, R. (2009) *Capital Rules: The Construction of Global Finance* (Cambridge, MA: Harvard University Press).
Abrahamsen, R. (2000) *Disciplining Democracy: Development Discourse and Good Governance in Africa* (London: Zed Books).
Adas, M. (1989) *Machines as the Measure of Men: Science, Technology, and Ideologies of Western Dominance* (Ithaca, NY: Cornell University Press).
Adas, M. (2006) *Dominance by Design: Technological Imperatives and America's Civilizing Mission* (Cambridge, MA: The Belknap Press of Harvard University Press).
Adler, E. and Bernstein, S. (2005) 'Knowledge in Power: The Epistemic Construction of Global Governance' in M. Barnett and R. Duvall (eds) *Power in Global Governance* (Cambridge: Cambridge University Press).
Ali, T. (2010) *The Obama Syndrome: Surrender at Home, War Abroad* (London: Verso).
Allinson, J. and Anievas, A. (2009) 'The Uses and Misuses of Uneven and Combined Development: An Anatomy of a Concept' *Cambridge Review of International Affairs* 22, 47–67.
Allinson, J. and Anievas, A. (2011) 'Approaching "the International": Beyond Political Marxism' in A. Anievas (ed) *Marxism and World Politics: Contesting Global Capitalism* (London: Routledge).
Althusser, L. (1969) *On Ideology* (London: Verso).
Ambrosius, L. (2006) 'Woodrow Wilson and George W. Bush: Historical Comparisons of Ends and Means in their Foreign Policies' *Diplomatic History* 30, 509–543.
Anderson, C. (2009) *Free: The Future of A Radical Price* (New York: Hyperion).
Anderson, M.S. (1993) *The Rise of Modern Diplomacy, 1415–1990* (London: Longman).
Anderson, P. (1983) *In the Tracks of Historical Materialism* (London: Verso).
Anderson, W. and Adams, V. (2008) 'Pramoedya's Chickens: Postcolonial Studies of Technoscience' in E.J. Hackett, O. Amsterdamska, M. Lynch, and J. Wacjman (eds) *The Handbook of Science and Technology Studies, Third Edition* (London: The MIT Press).
Anievas, A. (2011) (ed) *Marxism and World Politics: Contesting Global Capitalism* (London: Routledge).
Arndt, R.T. (2005) *The First Resort of Kings: American Cultural Diplomacy in the Twentieth Century* (Virginia: Potomac Books).
Arquilla, J. and Ronfeldt, D. (1999) *The Emergence of Noopolitik: Toward an American Information Strategy*. http://www.rand.org/pubs/monograph_reports/MR1033/. Accessed September 3, 2010.
Arrighi, G. (2005) 'Hegemony Unravelling I' *New Left Review* II/32, 23–80.
Augelli, E. and Murphy, C.N. (1988) *America's Quest for Supremacy and the Third World* (London: Pinter Publishers).

Bailes, K.E. (1981) 'The American Connection: Ideology and the Transfer of American Technology to the Soviet Union, 1917–1941' *Comparative Studies in Society and History* 23, 421–448.
Baldwin, D. (1989) *Paradoxes of Power* (Oxford: Basil Blackwell).
Ball, T. (1975) 'Power, Causation & Explanation' *Polity* 8, 189–215.
Bachrach, P. and Baratz, M. (1962) 'Two Faces of Power' *The American Political Scientist Review* 56, 947–952.
Bao, B. (2013) 'How Internet Censorship is Curbing Innovation in China' *The Atlantic* April 22 2013, http://www.theatlantic.com/china/archive/2013/04/how-internet-censorship-is-curbing-innovation-in-china/275188/. Accessed November 19, 2013.
Barbour, I. (1992) *Ethics in an Age of Technology* (London: SCM Press).
Barboza, D. (2008) 'Chinese Court Convicts 11 in Microsoft Piracy Case' *The New York Times* December 31, 2008, http://www.nytimes.com/2009/01/01/business/worldbusiness/01soft.html. Accessed March 25, 2010.
Barnbrook, R. and Cameron, A. (1996) 'The Californian Ideology' *Science as Culture* 6, 44–72.
Barnett, M. (1997) 'Bringing in the New World Order: Liberalism, Legitimacy and the United Nations' *World Politics* 49, 526–551.
Barnett, M. (1999) 'Culture, Strategy, and Foreign Policy Change: Israel's Road to Oslo' *European Journal of International Relations* 5, 5–36.
Barnett, M. and Duvall, R. (2005) 'Power in International Politics' *International Organization* 59, 39–75.
Barrett, E.W. (1983) 'American Values and the Ideological Struggle: Truth is Our Weapon' in Thompson, K.W. (ed) *Institutions for Projecting American Values Abroad*, vol. III (Boston: University Press of America).
Becker, L.C. (1977) *Property Rights: Philosophic Foundations* (London: Routledge & Keegan Paul).
Beitz, C. (2001) 'Human Rights as a Common Concern' *American Political Science Review* 95, 269–282.
Bell, D. (2009) 'Writing the World: Disciplinary History and Beyond' *International Affairs* 85, 3–22.
Bendrath, R., Eriksson, J. and Giacomello, G. (2007) 'From "Cyberterrorism" to "Cyberwar", Back and Forth: How the United States Securitized Cyberspace' in J. Eriksson and G. Giacomello (eds) *International Relations and Security in the Digital Age* (London: Routledge).
Benkler, Y. (2003) 'Freedom in the Commons: Towards a Political Economy for Information' *Duke Law Journal* 52, 1245–1276.
Berger, M.T. (2009) 'From *Pax Romana* to *Pax Americana*? The History and Future of the New American Empire' *International Politics* 46, 140–156.
Berman, M. (1982) *All That Is Solid Melts into Air: The Experience of Modernity* (London: Verso).
Bernstein, S. (2002) 'Liberal Environmentalism and Global Environmental Governance' *Global Environmental Politics* 2, 1–16.
Betz, D. and Stevens, T. (2010) *Cyberspace and the State: Towards a Strategy for Cyberpower* (London: Routledge).
Bieler, A. and Morton, A.D. (2008) 'The Deficits of Discourse in IPE: Turning Base Metal into Gold?' *International Studies Quarterly* 52, 103–128.
Bijker, W.E., Hughes, T.P. and Pinch, T. (1987) (eds) *The Social Construction of Technological Systems* (Cambridge, MA: The MIT Press).

Bijker, W.E. and Law, J. (1992) (eds) *Shaping Technology/Building Society* (Cambridge, MA: The MIT Press).
Bijker, W.E. (1995) *Of Bicycles, Bakelites, and Bulbs: Toward a theory of sociotechnical change* (Cambridge, MA: The MIT Press).
Bitzer, J., Schrettl, W. and Schröder, P.J.H. (2007) 'Intrinsic Motivation in Open Source Software Development' *Journal of Comparative Economics* 35, 160–169.
Bloor, D. (1976) *Knowledge and Social Imagery* (London: Routledge).
Boffey, P.M. (1971) 'Science Policy: An Insider's View of LBJ, DuBridge, and the Budget' *Science* 171, 874–876.
Booth, K. and Wheeler, N. (2007) *The Security Dilemma: Fear, Cooperation and Trust in World Politics* (Basingstoke: Palgrave).
Bouchet, N. (2013) 'The Democracy Tradition in US Foreign Policy and the Obama Presidency' *International Affairs* 89, 31–51.
Bourdieu, P. (1991) *Language and Symbolic Power* (Cambridge: Polity Press).
Bousquet, A. (2009) *The Scientific Way of Warfare: Order and Chaos on the Battlefields of Modernity* (London: Hurst).
Braverman, H. (1974) *Labour and Monopoly Capital: The Degradation of Work in the Twentieth Century* (New York: Monthly Review Press).
Bremmer, I. (2010) 'Democracy in Cyberspace: What Information Technology Can and Cannot Do' *Foreign Affairs* 89, 86–92.
Brenner, R. (1976) 'Agrarian Class Structure and Economic Development in Pre-Industrial Europe' *Past and Present* 70, 30–75.
Brenner, R. (1977) 'The Origins of Capitalist Development: a Critique of Neo-Smithian Marxism' *New Left Review* I/104, 25–92.
Brenner, R. (1982) 'The Agrarian Roots of European Capitalism' *Past and Present* 97, 16–113.
Brenner, R. (1986) 'The Social Basis of Economic Development' in J. Roemer (ed) *Analytical Marxism* (Cambridge: Cambridge University Press).
Brenner, R. (1998) 'The Economics of Global Turbulence' *New Left Review* I/229.
Brenner, R. (2002) *The Boom and the Bubble: The US in the World Economy* (London: Verso).
Brenner, R. (2006) 'What Is and What Is Not Imperialism?' *Historical Materialism: Research in Critical Marxist Theory* 14, 79–105.
Brenner, R. and Glick, M. (1990) 'The Regulation Approach: Theory and History' *New Left Review* I/188, 45–119.
Bromley, S. (2008) *American Power and the Prospects for International Order* (Cambridge: Polity).
Brooks, S.G. (2005) *Producing Security: Multinational Corporations, Globalization, and the Changing Calculus of Conflict* (Princeton: Princeton University Press).
Brooks, S.G. and Wohlforth, W.C. (2008) *World Out of Balance: International Relations and the Challenge of American Primacy* (Princeton: Princeton University Press).
Bruff, I. (2009) 'The Totalisation of Human Social Practice: Open Marxists and Capitalist Social Relations, Foucauldians and Power Relations' *The British Journal of Politics & International Relations* 11, 332–351.
Buinicki, M.T. (2008) *Negotiating Copyright: Authorship and the Discourse of Literary Property Rights in Nineteenth Century America* (London: Routledge).
Bush, V. (1950) *Modern Arms and Free Men: A Discussion of the Role of Science in Preserving Democracy* (London: William Heinemann Ltd.)

Buzan, B., Waever, O., and de Wilde, J. (1998) *Security: A New Framework for Analysis* (Boulder: Lynne Rienner).
Buzan, B. and Little, R. (2000) *International Systems in World History: Remaking the Study of International Relations* (Oxford: Oxford University Press).
Buzan, D. and Albert, M. (2010) 'Differentiation: A Sociological Approach to International Relations Theory' *European Journal of International Relations* 16, 315–337.
Business Week. The Infotech 100. http://bwnt.businessweek.com/interactive_reports/lt100_2009/?chan=magazine+channel_in+depth. Accessed June 25, 2009.
Calinoff, J. (2010) 'Beijing's Foreign Internet Purge' *Foreign Policy* January 15, 2010. http://www.foreignpolicy.com/articles/2010/01/14/chinas_foreign_internet_purge. Accessed April 10, 2010.
Callieres, F. (1919 [1713]) *The Practice of Diplomacy* (London: Constable and Company).
Callinicos, A. (1990) "The Limits of Political Marxism' *New Left Review* I/184, 110–115.
Callinicos, A. (2004) *Making History: Agency, Structure and Change in Social Theory* (Leiden: Brill).
Callinicos, A. (2006) 'G.A. Cohen and the Critique of Political Economy' *Science & Society* 70, 252–274.
Callinicos, A. (2009) *Imperialism and the Global Political Economy* (Cambridge: Polity).
Callinicos, A. (2011) 'Does Capitalism Need the State System?' in A. Anievas (ed) *Marxism and World Politics: Contesting Global Capitalism* (London: Routledge).
Campbell, D. (1998) *Writing Security: United States Foreign Policy and the Politics of Identity, Second Edition* (Manchester: Manchester University Press).
Carlson, W.B. (1992) 'Artifacts and Frames of Meaning: Thomas A. Edison, His Managers, and the Cultural Construction of Motion Pictures' in W. Bijker and J. Law (eds) *Shaping Technology/Building Society* (Cambridge, MA: The MIT Press).
Carr, M. (2012) 'The Political History of the Internet: A Theoretical Approach to the Implications for US Power' in S.S. Costigan and J. Perry (eds) *Information Technology and International Affairs* (Surrey: Ashgate).
Carruthers, S. (2001) 'New Media, New War' *International Affairs* 3, 671–689.
Castells, M. (1996) *The Rise of the Network Society: The Information Age: Economy, Society, and Culture*, vol. I (Oxford: Blackwell).
Castree, N. (2002) 'False Antithesis? Marxism, Nature and Actor-Networks' *Antipode* 34, 111–146.
Centre for Democracy and Technology. http://opt-out.cdt.org/speech/net-neutrality/. Accessed March 25, 2010.
Chadwick, A. (2006) *Internet Politics: States, Citizens, and New Communication Technologies* (Oxford: Oxford University Press).
Chase-Dunne, C. (1980) 'Interstate System and Capitalist World-Economy: One Logic or Two?' *International Studies Quarterly* 25, 19–42.
Chibber, V. (2011) 'What is Living and What is Dead in the Marxist Theory of History' *Historical Materialism: Research in Critical Marxist Theory* 19, 60–91.
Chibber, V. (2013) *Postcolonial Theory and the Specter of Capital* (London: Verso).
Choucri, N. (2000) 'Introduction: CyberPolitics in International Relations' *International Political Science Review* 21, 243–263.

Chowdhury, A. and Krebs, R. (2010) 'Talking About Terror: Counterterrorist Campaigns and the Logic of Representation' *European Journal of International Relations* 16, 25–50.

Clark, D. (1988) 'The Design Philosophy of the DARPA Internet Protocols' *ACM SIGCOMM Computer Communications Review* 18, 106–114.

Clark, I. (2007) *International Legitimacy and World Society* (Oxford: Oxford University Press).

Clark, I. (2009) 'Democracy in International Society: Promotion or Exclusion?' *Millennium Journal of International Studies* 37, 563–581.

Cogburn, D.L., Mueller, M., McKnight, L., Klein, H. and Mathiason, J. (2005) 'The U.S. Role in Global Internet Governance' *IEEE Communications Magazine* 43, 12–14.

Cohen, G.A. (1978) *Karl Marx's Theory of History: A Defence* (Oxford: Clarendon Press).

Cohen, G.A. (1982) 'Reply to Elster on Marxism, Functionalism and Game Theory' *Theory and Society* 11, 483–495.

Cohen, G.A. (2000) *Karl Marx's Theory of History: A Defence, Expanded Edition* (Oxford: Clarendon Press).

Colas, A. (2008) 'Open Doors and Closed Frontiers: The Limits of American Empire' *European Journal of International Relations* 14, 619–643.

Columbia Journalism Review. 'Who Owns What' http://www.cjr.org/resources/index.php. Accessed August 25, 2010.

Comninel, G. (1987) *Rethinking the French Revolution* (London: Verso).

Comor, E. (2001) 'The Role of Communication in Global Civil Society: Forces, Processes, Prospects' *International Studies Quarterly* 45, 389–408.

Comor, E. and Bean, H. (2012) 'America's "Engagement" Delusion: Critiquing a Public Diplomacy Consensus' *International Communication Gazette* 74, 203–220.

Connolly, W.E. (1983) *The Terms of Political Discourse, Second Edition* (Princeton: Princeton University Press).

Connolly, W.E. (2000) 'Speed, Concentric Circles and Cosmopolitanism' *Political Theory* 28, 596–613.

Corrales, J. and Westhoff, F. (2006) 'Information Technology Adoption and Political Regimes' *International Studies Quarterly* 50, 911–933.

Corrigan, P. and Sayer, D. (1981) 'How the Law Rules: Variations on Some Themes in Karl Marx' in B. Fryer, A. Hunt, D. McBarnet, and B. Moorehose (eds) *Law, State and Society* (London: Croom Helm).

Cowhey, P.F. (1990) 'The International Telecommunications Regime: The Political Roots of Regimes for High Technology' *International Organization* 42, 169–199.

Cowhey, P.F., Aronson, J.D., and Richards, J. (2009) 'Shaping the Architecture of the U.S. Information and Communication Technology Architecture: A Political Economic Analysis' *Review of Policy Research* 26, 105–125.

Cowhey, P.F., Aronson, J.D., and Abelson, D. (2012) *Transforming Global Information and Communication Markets: The Political Economy of Innovation* (Cambridge, MA: The MIT Press).

Cox, M. (2007a) 'Still the American Empire' *Political Studies Review* 5, 1–10.

Cox, M. (2007b) 'Is the United States in Decline – Again?' *International Affairs* 83, 643–653.

Cox, R.W. (1981) 'Social Forces, States and World Orders: Beyond International Relations Theory' *Millennium: Journal of International Affairs* 10, 126–156.

Cox, R.W. (1987) *Production, Power and World Order: Social Forces in the Making of History* (New York: Columbia University Press).
Cox, R.W. (1996 [1983]) 'Gramsci, Hegemony, and International Relations: An Essay in Method' in R.W. Cox and T.J. Sinclair (eds) *Approaches to World Order* (Cambridge: Cambridge University Press).
Cox R.W. (1996 [1992]) 'Multilateralism and World Order' in R.W. Cox and T.J. Sinclair (eds) *Approaches to World Order* (Cambridge: Cambridge University Press).
Cox, R.W. (1996 [1993]) 'Production and Security' in R.W. Cox and T.J. Sinclair (eds) *Approaches to World Order* (Cambridge: Cambridge University Press).
Craig, C. (2003) *Glimmer of a New Leviathan: Total War in the Realism of Niebuhr, Morgenthau and Waltz* (New York: Columbia University Press).
Craig, C. (2009) 'American Power Preponderance and the Nuclear Revolution' *Review of International Studies* 35, 27–44.
Craig, C. and F. Logevall (2009) *America's Cold War: The Politics of Insecurity* (Cambridge, MA: The Belknap Press of Harvard University Press).
Croft, S. (2006) *Culture, Crisis, and America's War on Terror* (Cambridge: Cambridge University Press).
Cull, N.J. (2008) *The Cold War and the United States Information Agency: American Propaganda and Public Diplomacy, 1945–1989* (Cambridge: Cambridge University Press).
Cunningham, D. (2003) 'The Patterning of Repression: FBI Counterintelligence and the New Left' *Social Forces* 82, 209–240.
Curran, J. (2002) *Media and Power* (London: Routledge).
Curran, J., Fenton, N., and Freedman, D. (2012) *Misunderstanding the Internet* (London: Routledge).
Daalder, I. and Lindsay, J.M. (2003) *America Unbound: The Bush Revolution in Foreign Policy* (Washington, DC: The Brookings Institution).
Dahl, R. (1957) 'The Concept of Power' *Behavioural Science* 2, 201–215.
Dahlberg, L. (2007) 'Rethinking the Fragmentation of the Cyberpublic: From Consensus to Contestation' *New Media & Society* 9, 827–847.
Dann, G.E. and Haddow, N. (2008) 'Just Doing Business or Doing Just Business: Google, Microsoft, Yahoo! and the Business of Censoring China's Internet' *Journal of Business Ethics* 79, 219–234.
Davidson, N. (2005) 'How Revolutionary Were the Bourgeois Revolutions? (contd.)' *Historical Materialism: Research in Critical Marxist Theory* 13, 3–54.
Debrix, F. (2008) *Tabloid Terror: War, Culture and Geopolitics* (London: Routledge).
de Goede, M. (2003) 'Beyond Economism in International Political Economy' *Review of International Studies* 29, 79–97.
Deibel, T.L. (2007) *Foreign Affairs Strategy: Logic for American Statecraft* (Cambridge: Cambridge University Press).
Deibert, R.J. (1997) *Parchment, Printing and Hypermedia: Communication in World Order Transformation* (New York: Columbia University Press).
Deibert, R.J. (1999) 'Harold Innis and the Empire of Speed' *Review of International Studies* 25, 273–289.
Deibert, R.J. (2008) 'Black Code Redux: Censorship, Surveillance, and the Militarization of Cyberspace' in M. Boler (ed) *Digital Media and Democracy: Tactics in Hard Times* (Boston: The MIT Press).

Deibert R.J. and Villeneuve, N. (2005) 'Firewalls and Power: An Overview of Global State Censorship of the Internet' in M. Kling and A. Murray (eds) *Human Rights in the Digital Age* (London: Glasshouse Press).
Deibert, R.J., Palfrey, J., Rohozinski, R., and Zittrain, J. (2008) (eds) *Access Denied: The Practice and Policy of Global Internet Filtering* (Cambridge, MA: The MIT Press).
Deibert, R.J. (2010) 'China's Cyberspace Control Strategy: An Overview and Considerations of Issues for Canadian Policy' China Papers No. 7 2010. University of British Columbia: Canadian International Council.
Deibert, R.J. and Rohozinski, R. (2010) 'Undercover of the Net' in A. Clunan and H. Trinkunas (eds) *Ungoverned Spaces? Alternatives to State Authority in an Era of Softened Sovereignty* (Stanford: Stanford University Press).
Delbourgo, J. and Dew, N. (2008) (eds) *Science and Empire in the Atlantic World* (New York: Routledge).
DeNardis, L. (2009) *Protocol Politics: The Globalization of Internet Governance* (Cambridge, MA: The MIT Press).
DeNardis, L. (2012) 'Hidden Levers of Internet Control' *Information, Communication & Society* 15, 720–738.
Der Derian, J. (1987) *On Diplomacy: A Genealogy of Western Estrangement* (Oxford: Basil Blackwell).
Der Derian, J. (1990) 'The (S)pace of International Relations: Simulation, Surveillance, and Speed' *International Studies Quarterly* 34, 95–310.
Der Derian, J. (1992) (ed) *The Virilio Reader* (Oxford: Basil Blackwell).
Der Derian, J. (2001) *Virtuous War* (Boulder: Westview Press).
Der Derian, J. (2003) 'The Question of Information Technology in International Relations' *Millennium: Journal of International Studies* 32, 441–456.
De Toqueville, A. (1994 [1835]) *Democracy in America* (London: Everyman's Library).
Deudney, D.H. (2008) *Bounding Power: Republican Security Theory from the Polis to the Global Village* (Princeton: Princeton University Press).
Diamond, L. (2010) 'Liberation Technology' *Journal of Democracy* 21, 69–83.
Diez, T. and Steans, J. (2005) 'A Useful Dialogue? Habermas and International Relations' *Review of International Studies* 31, 127–140.
Dillon, M. (1996) *Politics of Security: Toward a Political Philosophy of Continental Thought* (London: Routledge).
Dizard Jr., W.P. (2004) *Inventing Public Diplomacy: The Story of the U.S. Information Agency* (Boulder, Colorado: Lynne Rienner Publishers).
Djelic, M-L. and Quack, S. (2007) 'Overcoming Path Dependency: Path Generation in Open Systems' *Theory and Society* 36, 161–186.
Donnelly, J. (2003) *Universal Human Rights in Theory and Practice, Second Edition* (Ithaca, NY: Cornell University Press).
Donnelly, J. (2007) 'The Relative Universality of Human Rights' *Human Rights Quarterly* 29, 81–306.
Dowding, K. (1996) *Power* (Milton Keynes: Open University Press).
Dowding, K. (2008) 'Power, Capability and Ableness: The Fallacy of the Vehicle Fallacy' *Contemporary Political Theory* 7, 238–258.
Drahos, P. (2002) 'Developing Countries and Intellectual Property Standard-Setting' *The Journal of World Intellectual Property* 5, 765–789.

Drahos, P. with Braithwaite, J. (2002) *Information Feudalism: Who Owns the Knowledge Economy?* (London: Earthscan Publications).
Drezner, D. (2007) *All Politics is Global: Explaining International Regulatory Regimes* (Princeton: Princeton University Press).
Drezner, D. and Farrell, H. (2004) 'Web of Influence' *Foreign Policy* November/December, 32–41.
Dueck, C. (2006) *Reluctant Crusaders: Power, Culture, and Change in American Grand Strategy* (Princeton: Princeton University Press).
Dunn, D.H. (2005) 'Isolationism Revisited: Seven Persistent Myths in the Contemporary American Foreign Policy Debate' *Review of International Studies* 31, 237–261.
Dunn, M., Krishna-Hensel, S.F., and Mauer, V. (2007) (eds) *The Resurgence of the State: Trends and Processes in Cyberspace Governance* (Aldershot: Ashgate).
Dunn Cavelty, M., Mauer, V., and Krishna-Hensel, S.F. (2007) (eds) *Power and Security in the Information Age* (London: Ashgate).
Dyer-Witherford, N. (1999) *Cyber-Marx: Cycles and Circuits of Struggle in High-Technology Capitalism* (Chicago: University of Illinois Press).
Eagleton, T. (1991) *Ideology: A Critical Introduction* (London: Verso).
Edelstein, D.M. and Krebs, R.R. (2005) 'Washington's Troubling Obsession with Public Diplomacy' *Survival* 47, 89–104.
Edwards, P.N. (1996) *The Closed World: Computers and the Politics of Discourse in Cold War America* (London: The MIT Press).
Ekbladh, D. (2010) *The Great American Mission: Modernization and the Construction of an American World Order* (Princeton: Princeton University Press).
Elder-Vass, D. (2008) 'Searching for Realism, Structure and Agency in Actor-Network Theory' *The British Journal of Sociology* 59, 455–473.
Elster, J. (1982) 'The Case for Methodological Individualism' *Theory and Society* 11, 453–482.
Elster, J. (1989) *Nuts and Bolts for the Social Sciences* (Cambridge: Cambridge University Press).
Engerman, D.C. (2007) 'American Knowledge and Global Power' *Diplomatic History* 31, 599–622.
Eriksson, J. and Giacomello, G. (2009) 'The Forum: Who Controls the Internet? Beyond the Obstinacy or Obsolescence of the State' *International Studies Review* 11, 205–210.
Evans, R.J. (2005) *The Third Reich in Power* (London: Penguin).
Fairclough, N. (1995) *Critical Discourse Analysis: The Critical Study of Language* (London: Longman).
Fairclough, N. (2001) *Language and Power, 2nd Edition* (London: Longman).
Fairclough, N. (2003) *Analyzing Discourse: Textual Analysis for Social Research* (London: Routledge).
Faris, R. and Etling, B. (2008) 'Madison and the Smart Mob: The Promise and Limitations of the Internet for Democracy' *The Fletcher Forum of World Affairs* 32, 65–85.
Farrell, H. (2012) 'The Consequences of the Internet for Politics' *Annual Review of Political Science* 15, 35–52.
Fearon, J. (1995) 'Rationalist Explanations for War' *International Organization* 49, 379–414.

Feenberg, A. (1991) *Critical Theory of Technology* (Oxford: Oxford University Press).
Feenberg, A. (1994) 'The Technocracy Thesis Revisited: On *The Critique of Power*' *Inquiry* 37, 85–102.
Feenberg, A. (1995) 'Subversive Rationalization: Technology, Power and Democracy' in A. Feenberg and A. Hannay (eds) *Technology and the Politics of Knowledge* (Bloomington: Indiana University Press).
Feenberg, A. (1999) *Questioning Technology* (London: Routledge).
Feenberg, A. (2002) *Transforming Technology: A Critical Theory Revisited* (Oxford: Oxford University Press).
Feldman, S.M. (2008) *Free Expression and Democracy in America: A History* (Chicago: University of Chicago Press).
Finnemore, M. (1993) 'International Organizations as Teachers of Norms: The United Nations Educational, Scientific, and Cultural Organization and Science Policy' *International Organization* 47, 565–597.
Fluck, M. (2012) 'The Best There Is? Communication, Objectivity and the Future of Critical International Relations Theory' *European Journal of International Relations* 20, 56–79.
Foley, M. (2007) *American Credo: The Place of Ideas in US Politics* (Oxford: Oxford University Press).
Free Software Foundation. http://www.fsf.org. Accessed March 25, 2010.
Freeman, C. (1995) 'The 'National System of Innovation' in historical perspective' *Cambridge Journal of Economics* 19, 5–24.
Friedman, T.L. (2005) *The World is Flat: The Globalized World in the Twenty-First Century* (London: Penguin).
Fritsch, S. (2011) 'Technology and Global Affairs' *International Studies Perspectives* 12, 27–45.
Fukuyama, F. (1992) *The End of History and the Last Man* (New York: Penguin).
Fukuyama, F. (2004) 'The Neoconservative Moment' *The National Interest* 76 Summer, 57–68.
Gaddis, J.L. (1983) 'The Emerging Post-Revisionist Synthesis on the Origins of the Cold War' *Diplomatic History* 7, 171–190.
Gamble, A. (2009) *The Spectre at the Feast: Capitalist Crisis and the Politics of Recession* (London: Palgrave).
Gardner, L.C. (1976) *Imperial America: American Foreign Policy Since 1898* (New York: Harcourt Brace).
Garnsey, P. (2007) *Thinking About Property: From Antiquity to the Age of Revolution* (Cambridge: Cambridge University Press).
Gartzke, E. (2007) 'The Capitalist Peace' *American Journal of Political Science* 51, 166–191.
Gerges, F. (2013) 'The Obama Approach to the Middle East: The End of America's Moment?' *International Affairs* 89, 299–323.
Germain, R.D. (2007) 'Critical Political Economy, Historical Materialism and Adam Morton' *Politics* 27, 127–131.
Gerschenkron, A. (1962) *Economic Backwardness in Historical Perspective* (Cambridge, MA: Harvard University Press).
Giacomello, G. (2005) *National Governments and Control of the Internet: A Digital Challenge* (London: Routledge).

Gill, S. and Law, D. (1989) 'Global Hegemony and the Structural Power of Capital' *International Studies Quarterly* 33, 475–499.
Gilman, N. (2003) *Mandarins of the Future: Modernization Theory in Cold War America* (Baltimore: The Johns Hopkins University Press).
Glezos, S. (2011) 'The Ticking Bomb: Speed, Liberalism, and *Ressentiment* Against the Future' *Contemporary Political Theory* 10, 147–165.
Glezos, S. (2013) *The Politics of Speed: Capitalism, the State and War in an Accelerating World* (London: Routledge).
Godin, B. (2006) 'The Linear Model of Innovation: The Historical Construction of an Analytical Framework' *Science, Technology & Human Values* 31, 639–667.
Goldsmith, J. and Wu, T. (2006) *Who Controls the Internet? Illusions of a Borderless World* (Oxford: Oxford University Press).
Goldstein, D. (2012) 'Predictable WCIT Outcome Sees US Lead Objections to ITU's Internet Governance Changes' *Domain Pulse*, http://www.domainpulse.com/2012/12/14/preditable-wcit-outcome-sees-us-lead-objections-to-itus-internet-governance-changes/. Accessed November 19, 2013.
Graber, D. (2003) 'The Media and Democracy: Beyond Myths and Stereotypes' *Annual Review of Political Science* 6, 39–160.
Gramsci, A. (1971) *Selections from the Prison Notebooks* (London: Lawrence and Wishart).
Gramsci, A. (1995) *Further Selections from the Prison Notebooks* (London: Lawrence and Wishart).
Guilhot, N. (2005) *The Democracy Makers: Human Rights and International Order* (New York: Columbia University Press).
Guzzini, S. (1993) 'Structural Power: The Limits of Neorealist Analysis' *International Organization* 47, 443–478.
Guzzini, S. (2005) 'The Concept of Power: A Constructivist Analysis' *Millennium: Journal of International Studies* 33, 495–521.
Habermas, J. (1989 [1962]) *The Structural Transformation of the Public Sphere* (Cambridge: Polity Press).
Habermas, J. (1971 [1968]) *Knowledge and Human Interests* (Boston: Beacon Press).
Habermas, J. (1987) *The Theory of Communicative Action*, vol. 2: *The Critique of Functionalist Reason* (Cambridge: Polity Press).
Habermas, J. (1992) *The Philosophical Discourse of Modernity* (Cambridge: Polity).
Hacking, I. (1988) 'The Participant Irrealist at Large in the Laboratory' *The British Journal for the Philosophy of Science* 39, 277–294.
Hacking, I. (1999) *The Social Construction of What?* (Cambridge, MA: Harvard University Press).
Hafner-Burton, E.M., Tsutsui, K. and Meyer, J.W. (2008) 'International Human Rights Law and the Politics of Legitimation: Repressive States and Human Rights Treaties' *International Sociology* 23, 115–141.
Hall, S. (1985) 'Signification, Representation, Ideology: Althusser and the Post-Structuralist Debates' *Critical Studies in Mass Communication* 2, 94–114.
Hall, P. and Taylor, R. (1996) 'Political Science and the Three New Institutionalisms' *Political Studies* 44, 936–957.
Hansen, L. (2006) *Security as Practice: Discourse Analysis and the Bosnian War* (London: Routledge).
Hansen, L. and Nissenbaum, H. (2009) 'Digital Disaster, Cyber Security and the Copenhagen School' *International Studies Quarterly* 53, 1155–1175.

Hanson, E.C. (2008) *The Information Revolution and World Politics* (London: Rowman & Littlefield).
Hardt, M. and Negri, A. (2001) *Empire* (Cambridge, MA: Harvard University Press).
Harman, C. (2006 [2004]) 'The Origins of Capitalism' *International Socialism* 111, http://www.isj.org.uk/index.php4?id=219&issue=111. Accessed May 17 2014.
Hartz, L. (1955) *The Liberal Tradition in America: An Interpretation of American Political Thought Since the Revolution* (New York: Harcourt, Brace & World).
Harvey, D. (2006 [1982]) *The Limits to Capital* (London: Verso).
Harvey, D. (2003) *The New Imperialism* (Oxford: Oxford University Press).
Harvey, D. (2005) *A Brief History of Neoliberalism* (Oxford: Oxford University Press).
Haugaard, M. (2010) 'Power: A "Family Resemblance Concept"' *European Journal of Cultural Studies* 13, 419–438.
Hay, C. (1997) 'Divided by a Common Language: Political Theory and the Concept of Power' *Politics* 17, 45–52.
Hayward, C.R. (2000) *De-Facing Power* (Cambridge: Cambridge University Press).
Held, D. and McGrew, A., Goldblatt, D., and Perraton, J. (1999) *Global Transformations: Politics, Economics, Culture* (Cambridge: Polity).
Herrera, G.L. (2002) 'The Politics of Bandwidth: International Political Implications of a Global Digital Information Network' *Review of International Studies* 28, 93–122.
Herrera. G.L. (2003) 'Technology and International Systems' *Millennium: Journal of International Studies* 32, 559–593.
Herrera, G.L. (2006) *Technology and International Transformation: The Railroad, the Atom Bomb, and the Politics of Technological Change* (Albany: State University of New York Press).
Herrera, Y.M. and Braumoeller, B.F. (2004) 'Symposium: Discourse and Content Analysis' *Qualitative Methods* 2, http://www.prio.no/upload/3598/QMspring2004vol2no1.pdf. Accessed May 25, 2010.
Herz, J. (1950) 'Idealist Internationalism and the Security Dilemma' *World Politics* 2, 157–180.
Hillebrand, C. (2013) 'Merklephone Scandal Shocks but Spies Remain Unmoved' *The Conversation* October 26, 2013, http://theconversation.com/merkelphone-scandal-shocks-europe-but-spies-are-unmoved-19567. Accessed May 16, 2014.
Hills, J. (2007) *Telecommunications and Empire* (Chicago: University of Illinois Press).
Hixson, W. (2009) *The Myth of American Diplomacy: National Identity and U.S. Foreign Policy* (New Haven: Yale University Press).
Hobson, C. (2008) 'Democracy as Civilisation' *Global Society* 22, 75–95.
Hobson, C. (2009) 'Beyond the End of History: The Need for a "Radical Historicisation" of Democracy in International Relations' *Millennium Journal of International Studies* 37, 631–657.
Hoff, J. (2008) *A Faustian Foreign Policy from Woodrow Wilson to George W. Bush: Dreams of Perfectability* (Cambridge: Cambridge University Press).
Holden, G. (2002) 'Who Contextualizes the Contextualizers? Disciplinary History and the Discourse About IR Discourse' *Review of International Studies* 28, 253–270.
Holmqvist, C. (2013) 'Undoing War: War Ontologies and the Materiality of Drone Warfare' *Millennium: Journal of International Affairs* 41, 535–522.

Horkheimer, M. (1974 [1947]) *Eclipse of Reason* (New York: Continuum).
Horkheimer, M. (1992) *Critical Theory: Selected Essays* (New York: Continuum).
Horkheimer, M. and Adorno, T. (1997 [1944]) *The Dialectic of Enlightenment* (London: Verso).
Howard, P.N. (2010) *The Digital Origins of Dictatorship and Democracy: Information Technology and Political Islam* (Oxford: Oxford University Press).
Howarth, D. (2006) 'Space, Subjectivity, and Politics' *Alternatives: Global, Local, Political* 31, 105–134.
Hughes, T.P. (1983) *Networks of Power: Electrification in Western Society 1880–1930* (Cambridge, MA: The MIT Press).
Hughes, T.P. (1994) 'Technological Momentum' in M.R. Smith and L. Marx (eds) *Does Technology Drive History? The Dilemma of Technological Determinism* (Cambridge, MA: The MIT Press).
Hunt, M.H. (1987) *Ideology and U.S. Foreign Policy* (New Haven: Yale University Press).
Hurrell, A. (2005) 'Power, Institutions and the Production of Inequality' in M. Barnett and R. Duvall (eds) *Power in Global Governance* (Cambridge: Cambridge University Press).
Hurst, S. (2005) 'Myths of Neoconservatism: George W. Bush's "Neo-Conservative" Foreign Policy Revisited' *International Politics* 42, 75–96.
Hurst, S. (2009) 'Is the Bush Revolution Over?' *International Politics* 46, 157–176.
Huth, P.K. and Allee, T.L. (2002) *The Democratic Peace and Territorial Conflict in the Twentieth Century* (Cambridge: Cambridge University Press).
Ikenberry, G.J. (1998–1999) 'Institutions, Strategic Restraint, and the Persistence of American Postwar Order' *International Security* 23, 43–78.
Ikenberry, G.J. (2000) 'America's Liberal Grand Strategy: Democracy and National Security in the Post-War Era' in M. Cox, G.J. Ikenberry, and T. Inoguchi, (eds) *American Democracy Promotion: Impulses, Strategies and Impacts* (Oxford: Oxford University Press).
Ikenberry, G.J. (2006) *Liberal Order and Imperial Ambition* (Cambridge: Polity).
Indyk, M.S., Liberthal, K.G., and O'Hanlon, M.E. (2012) 'Scoring Obama's Foreign Policy: A Progressive Pragmatist Tries to Bend History' *Foreign Affairs* 91, 29–43.
Innis, H. (1972) *Empire and Communications* (Toronto: University of Toronto Press).
Isaac, J.C. (1987) *Power and Marxist Theory: A Realist Approach* (Ithaca, NY, and London: Cornell University Press).
Jackson, R. (2005) *Writing the War on Terrorism: Language, Politics and Counter-Terrorism* (Manchester: Manchester University Press).
Jahn, B. (2007) 'The Tragedy of Liberal Diplomacy: Democratization, Intervention, Statebuilding (Part I)' *Journal of Intervention and Statebuilding* 1, 87–106.
Jameson, F. (2011) *Representing Capital: A Reading of Volume One* (London: Verso)
Jay, M. (1973) *The Dialectical Imagination: A History of the Frankfurt School and the Institute for Social Research 1923–1950* (Berkley: University of California Press).
Jervis, R. (1978) 'Cooperation Under the Security Dilemma' *World Politics* 30, 167–214.
Jessop, B. (1982) *The Capitalist State: Marxist Theories and Methods* (Oxford: Blackwell).
Jessop, B. (2002) *The Future of the Capitalist State* (Cambridge: Polity).

Jessop, B. (2007) *State Power* (Cambridge: Polity).
Joseph, J. (2010) 'The Problem with Networks Theory' *Labor History* 51, 127–144.
Josephson, P.R. (1995) 'Projects of the Century in Soviet History: Large-Scale Technologies from Lenin to Gorbachev' *Technology and Culture* 36, 519–559.
Kalathil, S. and Boas, T. (2003) *Open Networks, Closed Regimes: The Impact of the Internet on Authoritarian Rule* (New York: The Carnegie Endowment for International Peace).
Kautsky, K. (1964 [1918]) *The Dictatorship of the Proletariat* (Ann Arbor: University of Michigan Press).
Keane, J. (1991) *The Media and Democracy* (Cambridge: Polity Press).
Keane, J. (2009) *The Life and Death of Democracy* (London: Simon & Schuster).
Kellner, D. (1975) 'The Frankfurt School Revisited: A Critique of Martin Jay's *The Dialectical Imagination*' *New German Critique* 4, 131–152.
Kennedy, L. and Lucas, S. (2005) 'Enduring Freedom: Public Diplomacy and U.S. Foreign Policy' *American Quarterly* 57, 309–333.
Keohane, R.O. (1984) *After Hegemony: Cooperation and Discord in the World Political Economy* (Princeton: Princeton University Press).
Keohane, R.O. (1989) *International Institutions and State Power: Essays in International Relations* (London: Westview Press).
Keohane, R.O. (2002) *Power and Governance in a Partially Globalized World* (London: Routledge).
Keohane R.O. and Nye, J.S. (1989) *Power and Interdependence, Second Edition* (Boston: HarperCollins Publishers).
Khatib, L., Dutton, W. and Thelwall, M. (2011) 'Public Diplomacy 2.0: An Exploratory Case Study of the U.S. Digital Outreach Team' *The Middle East Journal* 66, 453–472.
King, G., Keohane, R., and Verba, S. (1994) *Designing Social Inquiry* (Princeton: Princeton University Press).
Kitching, G. (2008) *The Trouble with Theory: The Educational Costs of Postmodernism* (London: Allen & Unwin).
Klien, H. (2002) 'ICANN and Internet Governance: Leveraging Technical Coordination to Realize Global Public Policy' *The Information Society* 18, 193–207.
Klein, H. and Klienman, D.L. (2002) 'The Social Construction of Technology: Structural Considerations' *Science, Technology & Human Values* 27, 28–52.
Knei-Paz, B. (1978) *The Social and Political Thought of Leon Trotsky* (Oxford: Clarendon Press).
Knight, B. (2013) 'How Telcos "Collude" with the NSA and GCHQ' *DW* August 11 2013, http://www.dw.de/how-telcos-collude-with-the-nsa-and-gchq/a-17213850. Accessed May 18, 2014.
Kossler, R. and Muchie, M. (1990) 'American Dreams and Soviet Realities: Socialism and Taylorism A Reply to Chris Nyland' *Capital & Class* 14, 61–88.
Kotz, D.M. (2002) 'Socialism and Innovation' *Science and Society* 66, 94–108.
Krasner, S.D. (1991) 'Global Communications and National Power: Life on the Pareto Frontier' *World Politics* 43, 336–366.
Kranser, S.D. (2004) 'Globalization, Power, and Authority' in E.D. Mansfield and R. Sisson (eds) *The Evolution of Political Knowledge: Democracy, Autonomy, and Conflict in Comparative and International Politics* (Columbus: Ohio State University Press).

Krebs, R.R. and Jackson, P.T. (2007) 'Twisting Tongues and Twisting Arms: The Power of Political Rhetoric' *European Journal of International Relations* 13, 35–66.
Krige, J. (2006) *American Hegemony and the Postwar Reconstruction of Science in Europe* (Cambridge, MA: The MIT Press).
Kristal, T. (2013) 'The Capitalist Machine: Computerization, Workers' Power, and the Decline in Labor's Share within U.S. Industries' *American Sociological Review* 78, 361–399.
Kshetri, N. (2009) 'Institutionalization of Intellectual Property Rights in China' *European Management Journal* 27(3) 2009: 155–164.
Kuklick, B. (2007) 'A Pact with the Devil: Washington's Bid for World Supremacy and the Betrayal of the American Promise – Roundtable Review' H-Diplo November 7, 2007, http://www.h-net.org/~diplo/roundtables/PDF/APactWithTheDevil-Kuklick.pdf. Accessed June 8, 2009.
Kurki, M. (2008) *Causation in International Relations: Reclaiming Causal Analysis* (Cambridge: Cambridge University Press).
Lacher, H. (2002) 'Making Sense of the International System' in M. Rupert and H. Smith (eds) *Historical Materialism and Globalization* (London: Routledge).
Lacher, H. (2006) *Beyond Globalization: Capitalism, Territoriality, and the International Relations of Modernity* (London: Routledge).
LaFeber, W. (1980) *America, Russia, and the Cold War, 1945–1980* (New York: John Wiley and Sons).
LaFeber, W. (2000) 'Technology and U.S. Foreign Relations' *Diplomatic History* 24, 1–19.
Latham, M.E. (2011) *The Right Kind of Revolution: Modernization, Development, and U.S. Foreign Policy from the Cold War to the Present* (Ithaca, NY: Cornell University Press).
Latour, B. and Woolgar, S. (1987) *Laboratory Life: The Construction of Scientific Facts* (Princeton: Princeton University Press).
Latour, B. (2005) *Reassembling the Social: An Introduction to Actor-Network-Theory* (Oxford: Oxford University Press).
Layne, C. (2006) *The Peace of Illusions: American Grand Strategy from 1940 to the Present* (Ithaca, NY: Cornell University Press).
Lee, S. (1990) *The Cost of Free Speech* (London: Faber & Faber).
Leffler, M.P. (2004) 'Bush's Foreign Policy' *Foreign Policy* 144 September–October, 22–28.
Leffler, M.P. (2011) 'September 11 in Retrospect: George W. Bush's Grand Strategy, Reconsidered' *Foreign Affairs* 90, 33–44.
Leiner, B.M., Cerf, V.G., Clark, D.D., Kahn, R.C., Kleinrock, L., Lynch, D.C., Postel, J., Roberts, L.G., and Wolf, S. *A Brief History of the Internet*. http://www.isoc.org/internet/history/brief.shtml. Accessed March 25, 2010.
Lessig, L. (2004) *Free Culture: How Big Media Uses Technology and the Law to Lock Down Culture and Control Creativity* (New York: The Penguin Press).
Lessig, L. (2006) *Code: Version 2.0* (New York: Basic Books).
Leye, V. (2009) 'Information and Communication Technologies for Development: A Critical Perspective' *Global Governance* 15, 29–35.
Li, X. (2010) 'The Agreement on Trade-Related Aspects of Intellectual Property Rights Flexibilities on Intellectual Property Enforcement: The World Trade Organization Panel Interpretation of China-Intellectual Property Enforcement

of Criminal Measures and Its Implications' *The Journal of World Intellectual Property* 13, 639–659.
Lieber, K. (2000) 'Grasping the Technological Peace: The Offense-Defense Balance and International Security' *International Security* 25, 71–104.
Lieber, R.J. (2005) *The American Era: Power and Strategy for the 21st Century* (Cambridge: Cambridge University Press).
Lieber, R.J. (2009) 'Persistent Primacy and the Future of the American Era' *International Politics* 46, 119–139.
Linday, J.M. (2011) 'George W. Bush, Barack Obama and the Future of US Global Leadership' *International Affairs* 87, 2–16.
Linklater, A. (1982) *Men and Citizens in the Theory of International Relations* (Basingstoke: Palgrave Macmillan).
Linklater, A. (1998) *The Transformation of Political Community: Ethical Foundations of the Post-Westphalian Era* (Cambridge: Polity).
Liu, C. (2011) 'Internet Censorship as a Trade Barrier: A Look at the WTO Consistency of the Great Firewall in the Wake of the China-Google Dispute' *Georgetown Journal of International Law* 42, 1199–1240.
Lowenheim, O. and Steele, B.J. (2010) 'Institutions of Violence, Great Power Authority, and the War on Terror' *International Political Science Review* 31, 23–39.
Lu, J. and Weber, I. (2008) 'Chinese Government and Software Copyright: Manipulating the Boundaries Between Public and Private' *International Journal of Communication* 1, 81–99.
Lucas, Jr., G.R. (2014) 'NSA Management Directive #424: Secrecy and Privacy in the Aftermath of Edward Snowden' *Ethics & International Affairs* 28, 29–38.
Lukes, S. (2005) *Power: A Radical View, Second Edition* (London: Palgrave Macmillan).
Lum, T. (2006) 'Internet Development and Information Control in the People's Republic of China' Congressional Research Service http://assets.opencrs.com/rpts/RL33167_20051122.pdf. Accessed November 30, 2013.
Lum, T., Moloney Figliola, P., and Weed, M. (2012) 'China, Internet Freedom and U.S. Policy' Congressional Research Service https://www.fas.org/sgp/crs/row/R42601.pdf. Accessed November 30, 2013.
Lynch, W.T. and Fuhrnam, E. (1991) 'Recovering and Expanding the Normative: Marx and the New Sociology of Scientific Knowledge' *Science, Technology and Human Values* 16, 233–248.
Lyon, D. (2010) 'Liquid Surveillance: The Contribution of Zygmunt Bauman to Surveillance Studies' *International Political Sociology* 4, 325–338.
Lyons, P. (2006) 'George W. Bush's City on a Hill' *The Journal of the Historical Society* 6, 119–131.
Ma, Z. and Gao, W. (2012) 'Impact of the "Tomato Garden" Software Case on Combating Copyright Infringement in China' *Journal of Intellectual Property Rights* 17, 27–36.
MacAskill, E. (2013) 'NSA Paid Millions to Cover Prism Compliance Costs for Tech Companies' *The Guardian* August 23, 2013, http://www.theguardian.com/world/2013/aug/23/nsa-prism-costs-tech-companies-paid. Accessed May 18, 2014.
MacDonald, P.K. and Parent, J. (2011) 'Graceful Decline? The Surprising Success of Great Power Retrenchment' *International Security* 35, 7–44.

MacKinnon, R. (2012) *Consent of the Networked: The Worldwide Struggle for Internet Freedom* (New York: Basic Books).
MacKenzie, D. (1984) 'Marx and the Machine' *Technology and Culture* 25, 473–502.
MacKenzie, D. (1987) 'Missile Accuracy: A Case Study in the Social Processes of Technological Change' in W. Bijker, T.P. Hughes, and T. Pinch (eds) *The Social Construction of Technological Systems: New Directions in the Sociology and History of Technology* (Cambridge, MA: The MIT Press).
Mahoney, J. (2000) 'Path Dependence in Historical Sociology' *Theory and Society* 29, 507–540.
Mann, M. (1986) *The Sources of Social Power*, vol. I: *A History of Power from the Beginning to A.D. 1760* (Cambridge: Cambridge University Press).
Mann, M. (1993) *The Sources of Social Power*, vol. II: *The Rise of Classes and Nation-States, 1760–1914* (Cambridge: Cambridge University Press).
Manning, P. (2001) *News and News Sources: A Critical Introduction* (London: Sage Publications).
Mansell, R. (2011) 'New Visions, Old Practices: Policy and Regulation in the Internet Era' *Continuum: Journal of Media & Cultural Studies* 25, 19–32.
Marcuse, H. (1964) *One Dimensional Man: The Ideology of Industrial Society* (London: Sphere Books).
Marlin-Bennett, R. (2013) 'Embodied Information, Knowing Bodies, and Power' *Millennium: Journal of International Studies* 41, 601–622.
Marx, K. (1975 [1842]) 'Debates on Freedom of the Press' in *Karl Marx and Frederick Engels Collected Works:* vol. 1 (London: Lawrence and Wishart)
Marx, K. (1971 [1857–1858]) *Grundrisse: Foundations of the Critique of Political Economy* (London: Penguin Books).
Marx, K. (1976 [1867]) *Capital: A Critique of Political Economy*, vol. 1 (London: Penguin Books).
Marx, Karl. *Critque of the Gotha Programme.* http://www.marxists.org/archive/marx/works/1875/gotha/ch01.htm. Accessed March 10, 2010.
Marx, Karl and F. Engels (1976 [1845]) 'The German Ideology' in *Karl Marx and Frederick Engels Collected Works:* vol. 5 (London: Lawrence & Wishart) 19–539.
Mathews, J.T. (1997) 'Power Shift' *Foreign Affairs* 76, 50–66.
Mattern, J.B. (2005) 'Why "Soft Power" Isn't So Soft: Representational Force and the Sociolinguistic Construction of Attraction in World Politics' *Millennium: Journal of International Studies* 33, 583–561.
May, C. (2000) *A Global Political Economy of Intellectual Property Rights: The New Enclosures?* (London: Routledge).
May, C. and Sell, S.K. (2006) *Intellectual Property Rights: A Critical History* (London: Lynne Rienner).
May, C. (2007) 'The Hypocrisy of Forgetfulness: The Contemporary Significance of Early Innovations in Intellectual Property' *Review of International Political Economy* 14, 1–25.
May, C. (2007) *Digital Rights Management: The Problem of Expanding Ownership Rights* (Oxford: Chandos Publishing).
McCarthy, D.R. (2011a) 'Open Networks and the Open Door: American Foreign Policy and the Narration of the Internet' *Foreign Policy Analysis* 7, 89–111.
McCarthy, D.R. (2011b) 'The Meaning of Materiality: Rethinking the Materialism of Gramscian IR' *Review of International Studies* 37, 1215–1234.

McCarthy, D.R. (2013) 'Technology and "the International": Or, How I Learned to Stop Worrying and Love Determinism' *Millennium: Journal of International Studies* 41, 470–490.
McCarthy, T. (1981) *The Critical Theory of Jurgen Habermas* (Cambridge, MA: The MIT Press).
McCormick, T.J. (1995) *America's Half-Century: United States Foreign Policy in the Cold War and After, Second Edition* (Baltimore: The Johns Hopkins University Press).
McCrisken, T.B. (2003) *American Exceptionalism and the Legacy of Vietnam: US Foreign Policy since 1974* (Basingstoke: Palgrave MacMillan).
McEvoy Manjikian, M. (2010) 'From Global Village to Virtual Battlespace: The Colonizing of the Internet and the Extension of Realpolitik' *International Studies Quarterly* 54, 381–401.
McFaul, M. (2004–2005) 'Democracy Promotion as a World Value' *The Washington Quarterly* 28, 147–163.
McLaughlin, P. (2001) *What Functions Explain: Functional Explanations and Self-Reproducing Systems* (Cambridge: Cambridge University Press).
McLuhan, M. (1997 [1964]) *Understanding Media: The Extensions of Man* (London: Routledge).
McNair, B. (1998) *The Sociology of Journalism* (London: Hodder).
Mearsheimer, J. (2001) *The Tragedy of Great Power Politics* (New York: W.W. Norton & Company).
Mearshimer, J. (2005) 'Hans Morgenthau and the Iraq War: Realism Versus Neo-Conservatism' *Open Democracy* May 18, 2005. http://www.opendemocracy.net/democracy-americanpower/morgenthau_2522.jsp. Accessed April 18, 2010.
Mill, J.S. (1974) *On Liberty* (London: Penguin Books).
Milliken, J. (1999) 'The Study of Discourse in International Relations: A Critique of Research and Methods' *European Journal of International Relations* 5, 225–254.
Milner, H.V. (2006) 'The Digital Divide: The Role of Institutions in Technology Diffusion' *Comparative Political Studies* 39, 176–199.
Moloney Figliola, P. (2013) 'Promoting Global Internet Freedom: Policy and Technology' Congressional Research Service, http://www.fas.org/sgp/crs/row/R41837.pdf. Accessed December 6, 2013.
Monten, J. (2005) 'The Roots of the Bush Doctrine: Power, Nationalism and Democracy Promotion in U.S. Strategy' *International Security* 29, 112–156.
Moore, P. and Taylor, P.A. (2009) 'Exploitation of the Self in Community-Based Software Production: Workers' Freedoms or Firm Foundations?' *Capital & Class* 97, 99–119.
Mor, B.D. (2006) 'Public Diplomacy in Grand Strategy' *Foreign Policy Analysis* 2, 157–176.
Morgenthau, H. (1946) *Scientific Man vs. Power Politics* (Chicago: University of Chicago Press).
Morozov, E. (2011) *The Net Delusion: The Dark Side of Internet Freedom* (London: Penguin).
Morriss, P. (2002) *Power: A Philosophical Analysis* (Manchester: Manchester University Press).
Morton, A.D. (2005) 'The Age of Absolutism: Capitalism, the Modern States-System and International Relations' *Review of International Studies* 31, 501–515.

Morton, A.D. (2007) *Unravelling Gramsci: Hegemony and Passive Revolution in the Global Political Economy* (London: Pluto Press).

Mousseau, M., Hegre, H., and O'Neal, J.R. (2003) 'How the Wealth of Nations Conditions the Liberal Peace' *European Journal of International Relations* 9, 277–314.

Mowrey, D.C. and Rosenberg, N. (1999) *Paths of Innovation: Technological Change in 20th-Century America* (Cambridge: Cambridge University Press).

Mowrey, D.C. and Simcoe, T. (2002) 'Is the Internet a U.S. invention? An Economic and Technological History of Computer Networking' *Research Policy* 31, 1369–1387.

Mueller, J. (2010) 'Capitalism, Peace and the Historical Movement of Ideas' *International Interactions* 36, 169–184.

Mueller, M. (2010) *Networks and States: The Global Politics of Internet Governance* (Cambridge, MA: The MIT Press).

Mueller, M. (2012) 'China and Global Internet Governance: A Tiger by the Tail' in R. Deibert, J. Palfrey, R. Rohozinski, and J. Zittrain (eds) *Access Contested: Security, Identity and Resistance in Asian Cyberspace* (Cambridge, MA: The MIT Press).

Mukunda, G. (2010) 'We Cannot Go On: Disruptive Innovation and the First World War Royal Navy' *Security Studies* 19, 124–159.

Murdoch, S.J. and Anderson, R. (2008) 'Tools and Technology of Internet Filtering' in R. Deibert, J. Palfrey, R. Rohozinski, and J. Zittrain (eds) *Access Denied: The Practice and Policy of Global Internet Filtering* (Cambridge, MA: The MIT Press).

Murray, A.D. (2007) *The Regulation of Cyberspace: Control in the Online Environment* (London: Routledge).

Murray, D. (2013) 'Military Action but Not as We Know It: Libya, Syria, and the Making of an Obama Doctrine' *Contemporary Politics* 19, 146–166.

Muzaka, V. (2011) 'Linkages, Contests and Overlaps in the Global Intellectual Property Rights Regime' *European Journal of International Relations* 17, 755–776.

Myres, S.L. (2011) 'Plan for Online Freedoms Stalls at European Meeting' *The New York Times* December 6, 2011, http://www.nytimes.com/2011/12/07/world/europe/a-proposal-for-freedoms-in-cyberspace-meets-resistance.html?_r=0. Accessed November 19, 2013.

Nelson, R.R. (1993) (ed) *National Innovation Systems: A Comparative Analysis* (Oxford: Oxford University Press).

Neufeld, M.A. (1995) *The Restructuring of International Relations Theory* (Cambridge: Cambridge University Press).

Nexon, D.H. and Wright, T. (2007) 'What's at Stake in the Empire Debate?' *The American Political Science Review* 101, 253–271.

Noam, E.M. (2005) 'Why the Internet is Bad for Democracy' *Communications of the ACM* 48, 57–58.

Noam, E. (2006) 'Fundamental Instability: Why Telecom Is Becoming a Cyclical and Oligopolistic Industry' *Information Economics and Policy* 18, 272–284.

Noam, E. (2009) *Media Concentration and Ownership in America* (Oxford: Oxford University Press).

Noble, D.F. (1979) *America by Design: Science, Technology, and the Rise of Corporate Capitalism* (New York: Alfred A. Knopf).

Nye, J.S. (1990) *Bound to Lead: The Changing Nature of American Power* (New York: Basic Books).

Nye, J.S. (2002) *The Paradox of American Power: Why the World's Only Superpower Can't Go It Alone* (Oxford: Oxford University Press).
Nye, J.S. (2002) 'Information Technology and Democratic Governance' in E.C. Kamarck and J.S. Nye (eds) *Governance.com: Democracy in the Information Age* (Washington, DC: Brookings Institution Press).
Nye, J.S. (2004) *Soft Power: The Means to Success in World Politics* (New York: Public Affairs).
Nye, J.S. (2008) *The Powers to Lead* (Oxford: Oxford University Press).
Nye, J.S. (2010a) *The Future of Power* (New York: Public Affairs).
Nye, J.S. (2010b) 'The Future of American Power: Dominance and Decline in Perspective' *Foreign Affairs* 89, 2–12.
Nye, J.S. (2010c) 'Cyberpower' Belfer Centre for Science and International Affairs, Harvard Kennedy School http://belfercenter.ksg.harvard.edu/files/cyber-power.pdf. Accessed November 30, 2013.
Nye, J.S. and Owens, W. (1996) 'America's Information Edge' *Foreign Affairs* 75, 20–36.
Nyland, C. (1987) 'Scientific Management and Planning' *Capital & Class* 11, 53–85.
Ollman, B. (1976) *Alienation: Marx's Conception of Man in Capitalist Society, Second Edition* (Cambridge: Cambridge University Press).
Ollman, B. (1993) *Dialectical Investigations* (London, Routledge).
Open Net Initiative (2009) 'Country Profiles: Iran' http://opennet.net/research/profiles/iran. Accessed November 10, 2013.
OpenNetInitiative(2012)'NeitherHereNorThere:Turkmenistan'sDigitalDoldrums' https://opennet.net/neither-here-nor-there-turkmenistan%E2%80%99s-digital-doldrums. Accessed November 19, 2013.
Oreg, S. and Nov, O. (2008) 'Exploring Motivations for Contributing to Open Source Initiatives: The Roles of Contribution Context and Personal Values' *Computers in Human Behavior* 24, 2055–2073.
Osiander, A. (1998) 'Re-reading Early Twentieth-Century IR: Idealism Revisited' *International Studies Quarterly* 42, 409–432.
Padovani, C. (2005) 'Debating Communication Imbalances from the MacBride Report to the World Summit on the Information Society: An Analysis of a Changing Discourse' *Global Media and Communication* 1, 316–338.
Palacin, M. and Oliver, M., Infante, J., Oechsner, S., and Bikflavi, A. (2013) 'The Impact of Content Delivery Networks on the Internet Ecosystem' *Journal of Information Policy* 3, 304–330.
Parmar, I. (2009) 'Foreign Policy Fusion: Liberal Interventionists, Conservative Nationalists and Neoconservatives – The New Alliance Dominating the US Foreign Policy Establishment' *International Politics* 46, 177–209.
Paul, D.E. (2007) 'The Siren Song of Geopolitics: Towards A Gramscian Account of the Iraq War' *Millennium: Journal of International Studies* 36, 51–76.
Peoples, C. (2009) *Justifying Ballistic Missile Defence: Technology, Security and Culture* (Cambridge: Cambridge University Press).
Peters, J.D. (2005) *Courting the Abyss: Free Speech and the Liberal Tradition* (Chicago: University of Chicago Press).
Phillips, N. (2007) 'The Limits of 'Securitization': Power, Politics and Process in US Foreign Economic Policy' *Government and Opposition* 42, 158–189.
Pierson, P. (2000) 'Increasing Returns, Path Dependence, and the Study of Politics' *American Political Science Review* 94, 251–267.

Pinch, T. and Bijker, W.E. (1984) 'The Social Construction of Facts and Artefacts: Or How the Sociology of Science and the Sociology of Technology Might Benefit Each Other' *Social Studies of Science* 14, 399–441.
Pollard, S. (1981) *Peaceful Conquest: The Industrialization of Europe 1760–1970* (Oxford: Oxford University Press).
Post, C. (1995) 'The Agrarian Origins of US Capitalism: The Transformation of the Northern Countryside Before the Civil War' *Journal of Peasant Studies* 22, 389–445.
Post, C. (2011) *The American Road to Capitalism* (Leiden: Brill).
Postone, M. (1993) *Time, Labour, and Social Domination: A Reinterpretation of Marx's Critical Theory* (Cambridge: Cambridge University Press).
Poulantzas, N. (1978) *State, Power, Socialism* (London: New Left Books).
Price, M. (forthcoming) *Free Expression, Globalism, and the New Strategic Communication* (Cambridge: Cambridge University Press).
Quinn, A. (2007) 'The Great Illusion: Chimeras of Isolationism and Realism in Post-Iraq U.S. Foreign Policy' *Politics and Policy* 35, 522–547.
Quinn, A. (2008) '"The Deal": The Balance of Power, Military Strength, and Liberal Internationalism in the Bush National Security Strategy' *International Studies Perspectives* 9, 40–56.
Quinn, A. and Cox, M. (2007) 'For Better, for Worse: How America's Foreign Policy Became Wedded to Liberal Universalism' *Global Society* 21, 499–519.
Ramasoota, P. (2012) 'Internet Politics in Thailand after the 2006 Coup: Regulation by Code and a Contested Ideological Terrain' in R. Deibert, J. Palfrey, R. Rohozinski, and J. Zittrain (eds) *Accessed Contested: Security, Identity and Resistance in Asian Cyberspace* (Cambridge, MA: The MIT Press).
Reid, J. (2009) 'Politicizing Connectivity: Beyond the Biopolitics of Information Technology in International Relations' *Cambridge Review of International Affairs* 22, 607–623.
Reporters without Borders. http://www.rsf.org/en-ennemi26134-China.html. Accessed July 11, 2009.
Reus-Smit, C. (2013) *Individual Rights and the Making of the International System* (Cambridge: Cambridge University Press).
Richards, D.G. (2004) *Intellectual Property Rights and Global Capitalism: The Political Economy of the TRIPS Agreement* (New York: M.E. Sharpe).
Rid, Thomas (2013) *Why Cyberwar Will Not Take Place* (London: Hurst).
Robinson, R. (2005) 'How to Build Market Societies: The Paradoxes of the Neoliberal Revolution' *New Political Economy* 10, 247–257.
Robinson, W.I. (1996) *Promoting Polyarchy: Globalization, US Intervention, and Hegemony* (Cambridge: Cambridge University Press).
Rohlinger, D.A. and Brown, J. (2009) 'Democracy, Action, and the Internet after 9/11' *American Behavioural Scientist* 53, 133–150.
Rosenau. J.N. (1986) 'Before Cooperation: Hegemons, Regimes, and Habit-Driven Actors in World Politics' *International Organization* 40, 849–872.
Rosenau, J.N. (1990) *Turbulence in World Politics: A Theory of Change and Continuity* (Princeton: Princeton University Press).
Rosenau, J.N. (1992a) 'Governance, Order, and Change in World Politics' in J.N Rosenau and E.O. Czempiel (eds) *Governance without Government: Order and Change in World Politics* (Cambridge: Cambridge University Press).

Rosenau, J.N. (1992b) 'The Relocation of Authority in a Shrinking World' *Comparative Politics* 24, 253–272.
Rosenau, J.N. (1995) 'Governance in the Twenty-First Century' *Global Governance* 1, 13–43.
Rosenau, J.N. (2002a) 'Governance in a New Global Order' in D. Held and A. McGrew (eds) *Governing Globalization: Power, Authority and Global Governance* (Cambridge: Polity).
Rosenau, J.N. (2002b) 'Information Technologies and the Skills, Networks, and Structures that Sustain World Affairs' in J.N. Rosenau and J.P. Singh (eds) *Information Technologies and Global Politics: The Changing Scope of Power and Governance* (Albany: State University of New York Press).
Rosenau, J.N. (2005) 'Illusions of Power and Empire?' *History and Theory* 44, 73–87.
Rosenberg, J. (1994) *The Empire of Civil Society* (London: Verso).
Rosenberg, J. (2000) *The Follies of Globalization Theory* (London: Verso).
Rosenberg, J. (2005) 'Globalization Theory: A Post Mortem' *International Politics* 42, 2–74.
Rosenberg, J. (2006) 'Why Is There No International Historical Sociology?' *European Journal of International Relations* 12, 307–340.
Rosenberg, J. (2013) 'Anarchy in the Mirror of Uneven and Combined Development: An Open Letter to Kenneth Waltz' *International Politics* 50, 183–230.
Rosenberg, N. (1970) 'Economic Development and the Transfer of Technology: Some Historical Perspectives' *Technology and Culture* 11, 550–575.
Rostow, W.W. (1990) *The Stages of Economic Growth: A Non-Communist Manifesto, Third Edition* (Cambridge: Cambridge University Press).
Rotter, A.J. (2011) 'Empire of the Senses: How Seeing, Hearing, Smelling, Tasting, and Touching Shaped Imperial Encounters' *Diplomatic History* 35, 3–19.
Ruggie, J.G. (1983) 'Continuity and Transformation in the World Polity: Toward a Neorealist Synthesis' *International Organization* 35, 261–285.
Ruggie, J.G. (1997) 'The Past as Prologue? Interests, Identity, and American Foreign Policy' *International Security* 21, 89–125.
Rupert, M. (1995) *Producing Hegemony: The Politics of Mass Production and American Global Power* (Cambridge: Cambridge University Press).
Rupert, M. (2005) 'Class Power and the Politics of Global Governance' in M. Barnett and R. Duvall (eds) *Power In Global Governance* (Cambridge: Cambridge University Press).
Saito, N.T. (2003) 'Whose Liberty? Whose Security? The USA PATRIOT Act in the Context of COINTELPRO and the Unlawful Repression of Political Dissent' *Oregon Law Review* 81, 1051–1132.
Salter, M. (2004) 'Passports, Mobility, and Security: How Secure Can the Border Be?' *International Studies Perspectives* 5, 71–91.
Saraswati, J. (2008) 'The Indian ICT Industry and Neoliberalism: The Irony of a Mythology' *Third World Quarterly* 29, 1139–1152.
Sauer, F. and Schornig, N. (2012) 'Killer Drones: The "Silver Bullet" of Democratic Warfare?' *Security Dialogue* 43, 363–380.
Sayer, A. (2000) *Method in Social Science: A Realist Approach, 2nd Edition* (London: Routledge).

Sayer, D. (1987) *The Violence of Abstraction: The Analytic Foundations of Historical Materialism* (Oxford: Basil Blackwell).
Scheel, S. (2013) 'Autonomy of Migration Despite Its Securitisation? Facing the Terms and Conditions of Biometric Rebordering' *Millennium: Journal of International Studies* 41, 575–600.
Scheuerman, W. (2001) 'Liberal Democracy and the Empire of Speed' *Polity* 34, 41–67.
Scheuerman, W. (2009) 'Realism and the Critique of Technology' *Cambridge Review of International Affairs* 14, 564–584.
Schiller, D. (1999) *Digital Capitalism: Networking the Global Market System* (Cambridge, MA: The MIT Press).
Schmidt, B. (1998) *The Political Discourse of Anarchy: A Disciplinary History of International Relations* (Albany: State University of New York Press).
Schmidt, B. (2002) 'Anarchy, World Politics and the Birth of a Discipline: American International Relations, Pluralist Theory and the Myth of Interwar Idealism' *International Relations* 16, 9–31.
Schmidt, B. (2005) 'Competing Realist Conceptions of Power' *Millennium: Journal of International Studies* 33, 523–549.
Scholte, J.A. (2005) *Globalization: A Critical Introduction, Second Edition* (Basingstoke: Palgrave).
Scholte, J.A. (2008) 'Defining Globalisation' *The World Economy* 31, 1471–1502.
Segal, A. (2010) 'The Chinese Internet Century' *Foreign Policy* January 26, 2010, http://www.foreignpolicy.com/articles/2010/01/26the_chinese_internet_century. Accessed April 10, 2010.
Segal, A. (2012) 'The Cyber Trade War' *Foreign Policy* October 25, 2012, http://www.foreignpolicy.com/articles/2012/10/25/the_cyber_trade_war. Accessed December 6, 2013.
Sell, S.K. (2003) *Private Power, Public Law: The Globalization of Intellectual Property Rights* (Cambridge: Cambridge University Press).
Sell. S.K. (2013) 'Revenge of the "Nerds": Collective Action against Intellectual Property Maximalism in the Information Age' *International Studies Review* 15, 67–85.
Selwyn, B. (2011) 'Trotsky, Gerschenkron and the Political Economy of Late Capitalist Development' *Economy and Society* 40, 421–450.
Sending, O.J. and Neumann, I. (2006) 'Governance to Governmentality: Analyzing NGOs, States and Power' *International Studies Quarterly* 50, 651–672.
Shadlen, K.C., Schrack, A. and Kurtz, M.J. (2005) 'The Political Economy of Intellectual Property Protection: The Case of Software' *International Studies Quarterly* 49, 45–71.
Shavitt, Y. and Weinsberg, U. (2012) 'Topological Trends of Internet Content Providers' *Simplex* 12, 13–18.
Shaw, W. (1978) *Marx's Theory of History* (Stanford: Stanford University Press).
Shilliam, R. (2009) *German Thought and International Relations* (London: Palgrave).
Shirky, C. (2010) 'The Political Power of Social Media' *Foreign Affairs* 90, 28–41.
Shultz, G. (1984–1985) 'New Realities and New Ways of Thinking' *Foreign Affairs* 63, 705–721.
Sims, B. and Henke, C.R. (2012) 'Repairing Credibility: Repositioning Nuclear Weapons Knowledge after the Cold War' *Social Studies of Science* 42, 324–347.

Simmons, C. (2010) 'Weaving a Web within the Web: Corporate Consolidations of the Web, 1999–2008' *The Communication Review* 13, 105–119.

Simpson, B. (2012) 'The United States and the Curious History of Self-Determination' *Diplomatic History* 36, 675–694.

Singh, J.P. (2008) *Negotiation and the Global Information Economy* (Cambridge: Cambridge University Press).

Singh, J.P. (2009) 'What is Being Controlled on the Internet?' *International Studies Review* 11, 218–221.

Singh, J.P. (2013) 'Information Technologies, Meta-power, and Transformations in Global Politics' *International Studies Review* 15, 5–29.

Singh, R. and Lynch, T.J. (2008) *After Bush: The Case for Continuity in American Foreign Policy* (Cambridge: Cambridge University Press).

Sismondi, S. (2008) 'Science and Technology Studies and an Engaged Program' in E.J. Hackett, O. Amsterdamska, M. Lynch and J. Wacjman (eds) *The Handbook of Science and Technology Studies, Third Edition* (London: The MIT Press).

Skidmore, D. (2012) 'The Obama Presidency and US Foreign Policy: Where's the Multilateralism?' *International Studies Perspectives* 13, 43–64.

Slaughter, A.M. (2004) *A New World Order* (Princeton: Princeton University Press).

Slotten, H.R. (2013) 'The International Telecommunications Union, Space Radio Communications, and U.S. Cold War Diplomacy, 1957–1963' *Diplomatic History* 37, 313–371.

Smith, N. (1990 [1984]) *Uneven Development: Nature, Capital and the Production of Space* (London: Wiley-Blackwell).

Smith, T. (2000) 'National Security Liberalism and American Foreign Policy' in M. Cox, G.J. Ikenberry, and T. Inoguchi (eds) *American Democracy Promotion: Impulses, Strategies and Impacts* (Oxford: Oxford University Press).

Smith, T. (2007) *A Pact with the Devil: Washington's Bid for World Supremacy and the Betrayal of the American Promise* (London: Routledge).

Spinardi, G. (2013) 'Technical Controversy and Ballistic Missile Defence: Disputing Epistemic Authority in the Development of Hit-to-Kill Technology' *Science as Culture*/online first.

Spinello, R.A. (2003) 'The Future of Intellectual Property' *Ethics and Information Technology* 5, 1–16.

Stevens, T. (2012) 'A Cyberwar of Ideas? Deterrence and Norms in Cyberspace' *Contemporary Security Policy* 33, 148–170.

Stockman, F. (2009) 'US Set to Hike Aid Aimed at Iranians: Funding for Cyber-Resistance' *The Boston Globe*, July 26, 2009. http://www.boston.com/news/nation/washington/articles/2009/07/26/us_to_increase_funding_for_hackivists_aiding_iranians/. Accessed September 29, 2009.

Stokes, D. (2005) *America's Other War: Terrorizing Colombia* (London: Zed Books).

Sylvest, C. (2013) 'Technology and Global Politics: The Modern Experiences of Bertrand Russell and John H. Herz' *The International History Review* 35, 121–142.

Taylor, P.M. (1997) *Global Communications, International Affairs and the Media since 1945* (London: Routledge).

Taylor, M.Z. (2004) 'Empirical Evidence Against Varieties of Capitalism's Theory of Technological Innovation' *International Organization* 58, 601–631.

Teschke, B. (2003) *The Myth of 1648* (London: Verso).

The Economist (2012) 'Survival of the Biggest' December 1–7, 2012.
Thierer, A. and Crews Jr., C.W. (2003) (eds) *Who Rules the Net? Internet Governance and Jurisdiction* (Washington, DC: Cato Institute).
Thompson, E.P. (1967) 'Time, Work-Discipline and Industrial Capitalism' *Past & Present* 38, 56–98.
Thompson, E.P. (1978) *The Poverty of Theory and Other Essays* (London: The Merlin Press).
Thompson, J.A. (1973) 'William Appleman Williams and the "American Empire"' *Journal of American Studies* 7, 91–104.
Thompson, J.B. (1995) *The Media and Modernity: A Social Theory* (Cambridge: Polity Press).
Thorpe, C. (2008) 'Political Theory in Science and Technology Studies' in E.J. Hackett, O. Amsterdamska, M. Lynch, and J. Wacjman (eds) *The Handbook of Science and Technology Studies, Third Edition* (London: The MIT Press).
Tilly, C. (2007) *Democracy* (Cambridge: Cambridge University Press).
Ting, M. (2011) 'The Role of the WTO in Limiting China's Censorship Policies' *Hong Kong Journal of Law* 41, 285–316.
Townes, M. (2012) 'The Spread of TCP/IP: How the Internet Became the Internet' *Millennium: Journal of International Affairs* 41, 43–64.
Vaden T. and Suoranta, J. (2009) 'A Definition and Criticism of Cybercommunism' *Capital & Class* 97, 159–177.
Vandenberghe, F. (2002) 'Reconstructing Humants: A Humanist Critique of Actant-Network Theory' *Theory, Culture & Society* 19, 51–67.
Van der Vleuten, E. (2009) 'Toward a Transnational History of Technology: Meanings, Promises, Pitfalls' *Technology and Culture* 49, 974–994.
Van der Pijl, K. (2007) 'Capital and the State System: A Class Act' *Cambridge Review of International Affairs* 20, 619–637.
Van Eeten, M.J.G. and Mueller, M. (2013) 'Where Is the Governance in Internet Governance?' *New Media & Society* 15, 720–736.
Vogel, S. (1995) 'New Science, New Nature: The Habermas-Marcuse Debate Revisited' in A. Feenberg and A. Hannay (eds) *Technology and the Politics of Knowledge* (Bloomington: Indiana University Press).
Wade, R.H. (2002) 'Bridging the Digital Divide: New Route to Development or New Form of Dependency?' *Global Governance* 8, 443–451.
Walker III, W.O. (2009) *National Security and Core Values in American History* (Cambridge: Cambridge University Press).
Waltz, K.N. (1979) *Theory of International Politics* (New York: McGraw-Hill Inc.).
Ward, H. (1987) 'Structural Power – A Contradiction in Terms?' *Political Studies* 35, 593–610.
Wartenberg, T.E. (1990) *The Forms of Power: From Domination to Transformation* (Philadelphia: Temple University Press).
Weiser, P.J. (2003) 'The Internet, Innovation, and Intellectual Property Policy' *Columbia Law Review* 103, 534–613.
Wendling, A.E. (2009) *Karl Marx on Technology and Alienation* (London: Routledge).
Westad, O.A. (2000) 'The New International History of the Cold War: Three (Possible) Perspectives' *Diplomatic History* 24, 551–565.
Whitehead, J.W. (2014) 'Orwell's Nightmare: The NSA and Google – Big Brother Meets Big Business' *The Huffington Post* May 13, 2014, http://www.huffingtonpost.com/john-w-whitehead/orwells-nightmare-the-nsa_b_5310171.html. Accessed May 18, 2014.

Wiggershaus, R. (1995) *The Frankfurt School: Its History, Theories and Political Significance* (Cambridge, MA: The MIT Press).
Wight, C. (2006) *Agents, Structures and International Relations: Politics as Ontology* (Cambridge: Cambridge University Press).
Wight, C. and Patomaki, H. (2000) 'After Postpositivism? The Promises of Critical Realism' *International Studies Quarterly* 44, 213–237.
Williams, D. (1981) 'The Bureau of Investigation and Its Critics, 1919–1921: The Origins of Federal Political Surveillance' *The Journal of American History* 68, 560–579.
Williams, E. (1944) *Capitalism and Slavery* (London: Andre Deutsch).
Williams, M.C. (2003) 'Words, Enemies, Images: Securitization and International Politics' *International Studies Quarterly* 47, 511–531.
Williams, M.C. (2007) *Culture and Security: Symbolic Power and the Politics of International Security* (London: Routledge).
Williams, M.C. and Schmidt, B. (2008) 'The Bush Doctrine and the Iraq War: Neoconservatives Versus Realists' *Security Studies* 17, 191–220.
Williams, R. (1961) *The Long Revolution* (London: Chatto & Windus).
Williams, R. (2005 [1980]) *Culture and Materialism: Selected Essays* (London: Verso).
Williams, W.A. (1966) *The Contours of American History* (Chicago: Quadrangle Books).
Williams, W.A. (1972 [1959]) *The Tragedy of American Diplomacy, New Edition* (New York: W.W. Norton).
Williams, W.A. (1980) *Empire as a Way of Life* (Oxford: Oxford University Press).
Winner, L. (1977) *Autonomous Technology: Technics-out-of-Control as a Theme in Political Thought* (Cambridge, MA: The MIT Press).
Wolf, E.R. (1982) *Europe and the People without History* (Berkeley: University of California Press).
Wolf, E.R. (1999) *Envisioning Power: Ideologies of Dominance and Crisis* (Berkeley: University of California Press).
Wood, E.M. (1981) 'The Separation of the Economic and the Political in Capitalism' *New Left Review* I/127, 66–95.
Wood, E.M. (1990) 'Explaining Everything or Nothing?' *New Left Review* I/184, 116–128.
Wood, E.M. (1995) *Democracy against Capitalism: Renewing Historical Materialism* (Cambridge: Cambridge University Press).
Wood, E.M. (2002a) *The Origin of Capitalism: A Longer View* (London: Verso).
Wood, E.M. (2002b) 'Global Capital, National States' in M. Rupert and H. Smith (eds) *Historical Materialism and Globalization* (London: Routledge).
Wood, E.M. (2003) *Empire of Capital* (London: Verso).
Wriston, W.B. (1997) 'Bits, Bytes, and Diplomacy' *Foreign Affairs* 76, 172–182.
Wu, C.G., Gerlach, J.H., and Young, C.E. (2007) 'An Empirical Analysis of Open Source Software Developers' Motivations and Continuance Intentions' *Information & Management* 44, 253–262.
Wu, T. (2006–2007) 'The World Trade Law of Censorship and Internet Filtering' *Chicago Journal of International Law* 7, 263–287.
Wyn Jones, R. (1999) *Security, Strategy and Critical Theory* (Boulder: Lynne Rienner).
Yu, P.K. (2000) 'From Pirates to Partners: Protecting Intellectual Property in China in the Twenty-First Century' *American University Law Review* 55, 131–244.

Yu, P.K. (2005) 'From Pirates to Partners (Episode II): Protecting Intellectual Property in Post-WTO China' *American University Law Review* 55, 101–195.
Zakaria, F. (1997) 'The Rise of Illiberal Democracy' *Foreign Affairs* 76, 22–43.
Zenithoptimedia (2013) 'Google Takes Top Position in Global Media Owner Rankings' http://www.zenithoptimedia.com/wp-content/uploads/2013/05/Top-30-Global-Media-Owners-2013-press-release.pdf. Accessed November 30, 2013.
Zhu, L. and Liu, J. (2008) 'Sino-US Intellectual Property Dispute: A New Chapter in WTO History' *Journal of Intellectual Property Law and Practice* 3, 194–200.
Zimmern, A. (1928) 'The Prospects for Democracy' *International Affairs* 7, 153–191.
Zittrain, J. (2004) 'Normative Principles for Evaluating Free and Proprietary Software' *The University of Chicago Law Review* 71, 265–287.
Zittrain, J. (2006) 'The Generative Internet' *Harvard Law Review* 119, 1975–2040.
Zittrain, J. and Palfrey, J. (2008) 'Reluctant Gatekeepers: Corporate Ethics on a Filtered Internet' in R. Deibert, J. Palfrey, R. Rohozinski and J. Zittrain (eds) *Access Denied: The Practice and Policy of Global Internet Filtering* (Cambridge, MA: The MIT Press).

Primary Source Documents

Baer, D. (2011a) 'Media Availability in Hanoi, Vietnam' Hanoi, February 23, 2011, http://state.gov/j/drl/rls/rm/2011/157197.htm. Accessed November 19, 2013.
Baer, D. (2011b) 'LiveAtState: Internet Freedom and U.S. Foreign Policy' Washington, DC, December 13, 2011, http://www.state.gov/r/pa/ime/178707.htm. Accessed November 19, 2013.
Baer, D. (2012) 'Keynote Address to the U.S.–ASEAN Symposium on the ASEAN Human Rights Declaration' Washington, DC, November 28, 2012, http://www.state.gov/j/drl/rls/rm/2012/201210.htm. Accessed November 30, 2013.
Beaird, R. (2002) 'Remarks at the Pan European Regional Ministerial Conference' November 7, 2002, http://2001-2009.state.gov/e/eeb/rls/rm/2002/16527.htm. Accessed March 25, 2010.
Beaird, R. (2003) 'US Priorities for the World Summit on the Information Society' January 14, 2003, http://2001-2009.state.gov/e/eeb/rls/rm/2003/16762.htm. Accessed June 10, 2008.
Beaird, R. (2008a) 'The Internet Economy' Remarks to American Bar Association Section of Business Law, Annual Meeting, New York, August 9, 2008, http://2001-2009.state.gov/e/eeb/rls/rm/2008/108180.htm. Accessed March 25, 2010.
Beaird, R. (2008b) 'Perspectives on Internet Governance – What Might the Future Hold?' Remarks to the American Bar Association Business Law Meeting, Texas, April 11 2008, http://www.gov/e/eeb/rls/rm/2008/103764/htm. Accessed November 4, 2008.
Beaird, R. (2008c) Remarks at the Third Internet Governance Forum. Hyderabad, India. December 5, 2008, http://www.state.gov/e/eeb/rls/rm/2008/113363.htm. Accessed January 6, 2009.
Beers, C. (2001) 'The Role of Public Diplomacy in Support of the Anti-terrorism Campaign' Hearing Before the Committee on International Relations, U.S. House of Representatives, Washington, DC, October 10, 2001, http://

commdocs.house.gov/committees/intlrel/hfa75634.000/hfa75634_0.HTM. Accessed August 30, 2010.

Biden, J. (2011) Remarks to The London Conference on Cyberspace, London, November 1, 2011, http://www.whitehouse.gov/photos-and-video/video/2011/11/01/vice-president-biden-delivers-remarks-london-conference-cyberspace#transcript. Accessed November 19, 2013.

Broadcasting Board of Governors (2002) *Marrying the Mission to the Market: Strategic Plan 2002-2007*, http://www.bbg.gov/reports/BBG_Strategic_Plan.pdf. Accessed August 30, 2010.

Broadcasting Board of Governors (2008) *BBG 2008 Annual Report*, http://www.bbg.gov/reports/documents/2008_BBGAnnualReport_LoRes.pdf. Accessed July 20, 2009.

Broadcasting Board of Governors (2010) *2010 Budget Report*, http://www.bbg.gov/reports/budget/bbg_fy10_budget_request.pdf. Accessed September 11, 2010.

Bush, G.W. (2003) 'Remarks to the National Endowment for Democracy' November 6, 2003, http://ics.leeds.ac.uk/papers/vp01.cfm?outfit=pmt&folder=339&paper=939. Accessed April 18, 2010.

Bush, G.W. (2005) State of the Union Address, February 2, 2005, http://news.bbc.co.uk/go/pr/fr/-/1/hi/world/americas/4231571.stm. Accessed April 10, 2009.

Bush, G.W. (2008a) 'Statement by the President on World Press Freedom Day' Washington, DC, May 1, 2008, http://georgewbush-whitehouse.archives.gov/news/releases/2008/05/20080501-9.html. Accessed August 11, 2009.

Bush, G.W. (2008b) Speech During Visit to Thailand, August 7, 2008, http://georgewbush-whitehouse.archives.gov/news/releases/2008/08/print/20080807-8.html. Accessed October 1, 2009.

Business Software Alliance (2012a) 'BSA Honors US Trade Representative Ron Kirk with Cyber Champion Award' November 28, 2012, http://www.bsa.org/news-and-events/news/news-archive/2012/en-11282012-kirk. Accessed May 18, 2014.

Business Software Alliance (2012b) *Lockout: Lockout How a New Wave of Trade Protectionism Is Spreading through the World's Fastest-Growing IT Markets – and What to Do about It*, http://www.bsa.org/~/media/Files/Policy/Trade/BSA_MarketAccess_Report_FINAL_WEB_062012.pdf. Accessed May 18, 2014.

Clinton, H. (2009) 'Human Rights Agenda for the 21st Century' Remarks at Georgetown University, December 14, 2009, http://www.state.gov/secretary/rm/2009a/12/133544.htm. Accessed November 19, 2013.

Clinton, H. (2010a) 'Remarks on Internet Freedom' Washington, DC, July 21, 2010, http://www.state.gov/secretary/20092013clinton/rm/2010/01/135519.htm. Accessed November 19, 2013.

Clinton, H. (2010b) 'Leading through Civilian Power: Redefining American Diplomacy and Development' *Foreign Affairs* 89, 13–24.

Clinton, H. (2011a) 'Internet Rights and Wrongs: Choices and Challenges in a Networked World' Remarks at George Washington University, February 15, 2011, http://www.state.gov/secretary/rm/2011/02/156619.htm. Accessed November 19, 2013.

Clinton, H. (2011b) 'Remarks at the Civil Society Meet and Greet' Vilnius, December 6, 2011, http://www.state.gov/secretary/20092013clinton/rm/2011/12/178313.htm. Accessed November 19, 2013.

Clinton, H. (2011c) Remarks at Hague Conference on Internet Freedom, December 8, 2011, http://www.state.gov/secretary/rm/2011/12/178511.htm. Accessed November 19, 2013.

Denny, D. (2007) 'Internet Censorship Concern for Businesses as Well as Activists' *USINFO* May 11, 2007, http://www.america.gov/st/washfile-english/2007/May/20070511111320adynned0.99461.html. Accessed June 10, 2008.

Dudas, J.W. (2005) 'Issues Before the U.S.-China Joint Commission on Commerce and Trade' Remarks Before the Committee on Energy and Commerce Subcommittee on Commerce, Trade, and Consumer Protection, United States House of Representatives, June 9, 2005, http://www.uspto.gov/web/offices/com/speeches/2005jun09.pdf. Accessed August 30, 2010.

Freedom House (2006) *Annual Report 2006: Reinvigorating the Advance of Freedom*. http://www.freedomhouse.org/uploads/special_report/49.pdf. Accessed September 3, 2010.

Freedom House (2007) *Annual Report 2007:A Catalyst for Freedom and Democracy*. http://www.freedomhouse.org/uploads/special_report/89.pdf. Accessed September 3, 2010.

Gallagher, M. (2005) 'Governing the Internet' Remarks to Foreign Press Roundtable, Washington, DC, October 6, 2005, http://2001-2009.state.gov/e/eeb/rls/rm/2005/54794.htm. Accessed March 25, 2010.

Glassman, J.K. (2008a) 'Public Diplomacy 2.0: A New Approach to Global Engagement' Remarks to the New America Foundation, December 1, 2008, http://2001-2009.state.gov/r/us/2008/112605.htm. Accessed July 20, 2009.

Glassman, J.K. (2008b) 'Briefing on US Public Diplomacy and the War of Ideas' Washington, DC, October 28, 2008, http://2001-2009.state.gov/r/us/2008/111372.htm. Accessed July 10, 2009.

Global Internet Freedom Consortium (2013) http://www.internetfreedom.org/ (home page). Accessed November 29, 2013.

Gross, D.A. (2002) 'Information and Communication Technologies for Development' Remarks at the United Nations General Assembly, June 17, 2002, http://2001-2009.state.gov/e/eeb/rls/rm/2002/11239.htm. Accessed March 25, 2010.

Gross, D.A. (2003) 'ICT, WSIS and the Future of Freedom' WSIS High Level Dialogue, Geneva, Switzerland, December 9, 2003, http://geneva.usmission.gov/press2003/1209GrossSpeech.htm. Accessed April 11, 2008.

Gross, D.A. (2004) 'ICANN Oversight and Security of Internet Root Servers and Domain Name System' Testimony before the Senate Committee on Commerce, Science, and Transportation Subcommittee on Communications September 30, 2004, http://www.state.gov/e/eeb/rls/rm/36700.htm. Accessed June 10, 2008.

Gross, D.A. (2005a) Remarks at the 6th APEC Ministerial Meeting on Telecommunications and Information Industry, June 8, 2005, http://2001-2009.state.gov/e/eeb/rls/rm/2005/47803.htm. Accessed April 18, 2010.

Gross, D.A. (2005b) 'Freedom of Choice: US Communications and Foreign Policy' Remarks at GIIC Commissioner Conference, Washington, DC, March 2, 2005, http://2001-2009.state.gov/e/eeb/rls/rm/2005/42960.htm. Accessed June 10, 2008.

Gross, D.A. (2005c) 'Governing the Internet' Remarks at Media Roundtable, October 6, 2005, http://www.state.gov/e/eeb/rls/rm/2005/54794.htm. Accessed April 11, 2008.

Gross, D.A. (2006a) 'New Technologies and the Rise of Political Liberty' 2006 Grafstein Lecture, University of Toronto Faculty of Law February 7, 2006, http://www.state.gov/e/eeb/rls/rm/2006/61085.htm. Accessed June 20, 2009.

Gross, D.A. (2006b) 'Global Internet Freedom Task Force Strategy Announcement' Washington, DC, December 20, 2006, http://www.state.gov/e/eeb/rls/rm/2006/78145.htm. Accessed June 10, 2008.

Gross, D.A. (2007a) 'Global Trends and Converging Expectations' Distinguished Infocomm Speaker Event, Singapore, February 6, 2007, http://2001-2009.state.gov/e/eeb/rls/rm/2007/80481.htm. Accessed August 30, 2010.

Gross, D.A. (2007b) 'Trends in Global Communications: Navigating Uncharted Waters' International Institute of Communications Conference 2007, Chatham House, London, October 22, 2007, http://www.state.gov/e/eeb/rls/rm/2007/95694.htm. Accessed June 10, 2008.

Gross, D.A. (2007c) 'Open for Business' The Financial Express, December 31, 2007, http://2001-2009.state.gov/e/eeb/rls/rm/2007/99317.htm. Accessed March 25, 2010.

Gross, D.A. (2008a) 'Fighting for Worldwide Internet Freedom' *Real Clear World*, Washington, DC, August 14, 2008, http://www.state.gov/e/eeb/rls/rm/2008/108764.htm. Accessed January 6, 2009.

Gross, D.A. (2008b) 'Building on Success and Expanding Opportunities' Remarks at the Pike & Fischer Broadband Policy Summit IV, Washington, DC, June 13, 2008, http://2001-2009.state.gov/e/eeb/rls/rm/2008/105925.htm. Accessed November 30, 2013.

Gross, D.A. (2008c) 'Bridging Gaps With Information and Communication Technologies and the Internet' Remarks at the International Telecommunication Union's Global Standardization Symposium, Johannesburg, South Africa, October 22, 2008, http://www.state.gov/e/eeb/rls/rm/2008/111543.htm. Accessed January 6, 2009.

Gross, D.A. (2008d) 'Securing the Future of a Safe and Free Internet' Remarks at the High Level Segement of the 2008 International Telecommunication Union Council, Geneva, Switerzland, November 12, 2008, http://www.state.gov/e/eeb/rls/rm/2008/11814.htm. Accessed January 6, 2009.

Holmes, K. (2003) 'International Organization and Press Freedom' Remarks to the World Press Freedom Committee and Communications Media Committee of the Association of the Bar of the City of New York's Conference on Press Freedom on the Internet, New York, June 27, 2003, http://2001-2009.state.gov/p/io/rls/rm/2003/22115.htm. Accessed November 30, 2013.

Hughes, K. (2005) 'America's Dialogue with the World' Testimony before the Committee on International Relations, United States House of Representatives, November 10, 2005, http://2001-2009.state.gov/r/us/2005/56926.htm. Accessed September 3, 2010.

Hughes, K. (2007a) Presentation to U.S. House of Representatives Committee on Appropriations Subcommittee on State, Foreign Operations, and Related Programs, April 2007, http://uscpublicdiplomacy.org/pdfs/070703_hughes.pdf. Accessed November 30, 2013.

Hughes, K. (2007b) 'New Strategic Initiatives and Multimedia Tools to Help Better Tell America's Story Around the World' Foreign Press Briefing Centre, New York, December 10, 2007, http://2002-2009-fpc.state.gov/97861.htm. Accessed July 20, 2009.

International Intellectual Property Alliance (2003) Letter to U.S. Department of State Undersecretaries Larson and Grossman, May 1, 2003.
International Intellectual Property Alliance (2008) *2008 Special 301 Report: Copyright Protection and Enforcement Around the World*, February 11, 2008, http://www.iipa.com/2008_SPEC301_TOC.htm. Accessed August 30, 2010.
International Intellectual Property Alliance (2011) 'IIPA Applauds USTR Notorious Market Piracy List' Washington, DC, December 20, 2011, http://www.iipa.com/pressrel.html. Accessed May 18, 2014.
Internet Engineering Notes (1980) DoD Protocol Standardization, http://www.rfc-editor.org/ien/ien152.txt. Accessed November 30, 2013.
Internet Engineering Task Force (1981) Request for Comment 793, http://www.rfc-editor.org/rfc/rfc793.txt. Accessed November 19, 2013.
Internet Engineering Task Force (1985) Request for Comment 945, http://www.rfc-editor.org/rfc/rfc945.txt. Accessed November 19, 2013.
Kaufman, S. (2007) 'Free Speech on the Internet a Basic Human Right, United States Says' USINFO, February 22, 2007, http://www.america.gov/st/democracyhr-english/2007/February/20070222153604esnamfuak0.2887384.html. Accessed January 10, 2009.
Kaufman, S. (2008) 'Private Sector Should Resist Internet Censorship, Official Says: State's Dobriansky Says Incentives Can Help Block Authoritarian Pressure' USINFO, September 15, 2008, http://www.america.gov/st/democracyhrenglish/2008/September/20080915175335esnamfuak0.8041956.html. Accessed July 20, 2009.
Kirk, R. (2011) 'Remarks in Recognition of World Intellectual Property Day' Washington, DC, May 5, 2011, http://www.ustr.gov/about-us/press-office/speeches/transcripts/2011/may/remarks-ambassador-ron-kirk-recognition-world-in. Accessed November 30, 2013.
Locke, G. (2010a) 'Remarks at Copyright Policy in the Internet Economy Symposium' July 1, 2010, http://www.commerce.gov/news/secretary-speeches/2010/07/01/remarks-copyright-policy-internet-economy-symposium. Accessed November 30, 2013.
Locke, G. (2010b) 'Remarks at Cybersecurity Forum' Georgetown University Washington, DC, September 23, 2010, http://www.ntia.doc.gov/print/speechtestimony/2010/remarks-cybersecurity-forum-georgetown-university. Accessed November 30, 2013.
Locke, G. (2011) 'Remarks at U.S. Chamber of Commerce on Global Flow of Information on the Internet' Washington, DC, June 16, 2011, http://www.ntia.doc/speechtestimony/2011/remarks-us-chamber-commerce-global-flow-information-internet. Accessed November 30, 2013.
Marburger, J. (2003a) Remarks at the World Summit on the Information Society, December 11, 2003, http://www.itu.int/wsis/geneva/coverage/statements/usa/us.pdf. Accessed November 30, 2013.
Marburger, J. (2003b) CEBIT America Opening Night Dinner Address, New York. June 17, 2003.
Marburger, J. (2004a) Discriminators Defining Development of High Technology – U.S. Experience. Centre for Strategic and International Studies, Washington, DC, September 21, 2004.
Marburger, J. (2004b) Remarks, Council on Competitiveness First Annual High Performance Computing Users Conference, Washington, DC, July 13, 2004.

Marburger, J. (2004c) Congressional Economic Leadership Institute, Washington, DC, July 15, 2004.
Marburger, J. (2005a) *Science and Technology Policy Towards the Islamic World*, Brooking Institute Workshop, Washington, DC, January 4, 2005.
Marburger, J. (2005b) U.S. Statement in the WSIS Plenary, Remarks to the World Summit on the Information Society, Tunis, Tunisia, November 18, 2005, http://2001-2009.state.gov/e/eeb/rls/rm/2005/57996.htm. Accessed August 30, 2010.
Marburger, J. (2008) 'Adjusting Policy to New Dimensions in Science, Technology, and Innovation' Keynote Address to OECD High Level Meeting of the Committee for Scientific and Technological Policy, Norway, March 4, 2008, http://www.eirma.org/eiq/014/pages/eiq-2008-014-0002.html. Accessed November 30, 2013.
McConnell, K. (2007) 'New Approach to Development Embraces Information Technology' USINFO November 30, 2007, http://usinfo.state.gov/xarchices/display/display.html?p=washfile-english&y=2007&m=November&x=200711301407712AKllennoCcM0.6883509. Accessed June 10, 2008.
McHale, J. (2009a) 'Public Diplomacy: A National Security Imperative' Washington, DC, June 11, 2009, http://www.state.gov/r/remarks/2009/124640.htm. Accessed November 30, 2013.
McHale, J. (2009b) 'Remarks to Vilnius University' Vilnius, Lithuania, December 11, 2009, http://www.state.gov/r/remarks/209/2009/133438.htm. Accessed November 30, 2013.
McHale, J. (2010a) 'Future of U.S. Public Diplomacy' Washington, DC, March 10, 2010, http://www.state.gov.r/remarks/2010/138283.htm. Accessed November 30, 2013.
McHale, J. (2010b) 'Enduring Leadership: Marshall's Legacy for American Public Diplomacy in the 21st Century' Lexington, Virginia, October 7, 2010, http://www.state.gov/r/remarks/2010/149208.htm. Accessed November 30, 2013.
McHale, J. (2010c) 'Opening Plenary of the U.S. Summit and Initiative for Global Citizen Diplomacy' November 17, 2010, http://www.state.gov/r/remarks/2010/151053.htm. Accessed November 30, 2013.
McHale, J. (2010d) 'Remarks at the Bali Democracy Forum' Bali, Indonesia, December 9, 2010, http://www.state.gov.r/remarks/2010/152589.htm. Accessed November 30, 2013.
McHale, J. (2011a) 'Remarks at the Global Technology Symposium' Menlo Park California March 24, 2011, http://www.state.gov/r/remarks/159141.htm. Accessed November 30, 2013.
McHale, J. (2011b) 'The Exchange 2.0 Summit' Washington, DC, April 27, 2011, http://www.state.gov/r/remarks/2011/161854.htm. Accessed November 30, 2013.
McHale J. (2011c) 'Strengthening U.S. Engagement with the World: A Review of U.S. Public Diplomacy' New York, June 21, 2011, http://www.state.gov/r/remarks/2011/166596.htm. Accessed November 30, 2013.
Melia, T.O. (2010) 'OSCE Session on Press Freedom' Astana Kazakhstan November 26, 2010, http://www.state.gov/j/drl/rls/rm/2010/152627.htm. Accessed November 19, 2013.
Melia, T.O. (2011) 'U.S. Policy on Supporting Human Rights and the Rule of Law in Russia' Washington, DC, December 14, 2011, http://www.state.gov/j/drl/rls/rm/2011/178843.htm. Accessed November 19, 2013.

National Information Technology Labratory (2011) 'Internet Policy Task Force Cybersecurity Green Paper: Comments Received' http://www.nist.gov/itl/greenpapercomments.cfm. Accessed November 19, 2013.

Pinkos, S. (2005) 'Piracy of Intellectual Property' Remarks before the Committee on the Judiciary Subcommittee on Intellectual Property, United States Senate, May 25, 2005, http://www.uspto.gov/news/speeches/2005/2005may25_pinkos.jsp. Accessed March 25, 2010.

Pinkos, S. (2006) 'Stop!: A Progress Report on Protecting and Enforcing Intellectual Property Here and Abroad' July 26, 2006, http://www.hsgac.senate.gov/subcommittees/oversight-of-government-management/hearings/stop-a-progress-report-on-protecting-and-enforcing-intellectual-property-rights-here-and-abroad. Accessed November 30, 2013.

Posner, M. (2010) 'Global Internet Freedom and the Rule of Law Part II' Statement before the Senate Judiciary Human Rights and the Law Subcommittee, March 2, 2010, http://www.state.gov/j/drl/rls/rm/2010/134307.htm. Accessed November 30, 2013.

Posner, M. (2011a) 'Internet Freedom: Promoting Human Rights in the Digital Age' Remarks to Press, Conference on Internet Freedom, Geneva, March 4, 2011, http://www.state.gob/j/drl/rls/rm/2011/162496.htm. Accessed November 30, 2013.

Posner, M. (2011b) 'The Four Freedoms Turn 70' Address to American Society of International Law March 24, 2011, http://www.state.gov/drl/rls/rm/2011/159195.htm. Accessed November 30, 2013.

Posner, M. (2011c) 'Press Availability at U.S. Embassy Beijing' Beijing, April 28, 2011, http://www.state.gov/j/drl/rls/rm/2011/162414.htm. Accessed November 19, 2013.

Posner, M. (2011d) 'Defending Press Freedom in the 21st Century' World Press Freedom Day Washington, DC, May 3, 2011, http://www.state.gov/j/drl/rls/rm/2011/162572.htm, November 19, 2013.

Posner, M. (2011e) 'Human Rights and Democratic Reform in Iran' Washington, DC, May 11, 2011, http://www.state.gov/j/drl/rls/rm/2011/163123.htm. Accessed November 19, 2013.

Posner, M. (2011f) 'Internet Freedom and Human Rights: The Obama Administration's Perspective' Remarks to the New American Foundation 'Future Tense' Conference, July 13, 2011, http://www.state.gov/j/drl/rls/rm/2011/168475.htm. Accessed November 30, 2013.

Posner, M. (2011g) 'U.S. Human Rights Policy toward Iran and Syria' Washington, DC, July 27, 2011, http://www.state.gov/j/drl/rls/rm/2011/169180.htm. Accessed November 19, 2013.

Posner, M. (2011h) 'Free Speech in the Digital Age' Los Angeles, October 24, 2011, http://www.state.gov/j/drl/rls/rm/2011/176075.htm. Accessed November 19, 2013.

Posner, M. (2011i) 'Remarks on Internet Freedom and Responsibility' Silicon Valley Human Rights Conference October 25, 2011, http://www.state.gov/j/drl/rls/rm/2011/176144.htm. Accessed November 19, 2013.

Posner, M. (2012a) 'Internet Freedom and the Digital Earthquake of 2011' Washington, DC, January 17, 2012, http://www.state.gov/j/drl/rls/rm/2012/180958.htm. Accessed November 19, 2013.

Posner, M. (2012b) 'Briefing on the 17th U.S.-China Human Rights Dialogue, Washington, DC, July 25, 2012, http://www.state.gov/j/drl/rls/rm/2012/195498.htm. Accessed November 19, 2013.

Posner, M. (2012c) 'Remarks to the "Freedom Online" Conference' Nairobi, Kenya September 5, 2012, http://www.state.gov/j/rl/rls/rm/197590.htm. Accessed November 19, 2013.

Posner, M. and Ross, A. (2010) 'Briefing on Internet Freedom and 21st Century Statecraft' Washington, DC, January 22, 2010, http://www.state.gov/j/drl/rls/rm/2010/134306.htm. Accessed November 19, 2013.

Posner, M. and Crowley, P. (2011) 'Conversations with America: The State Department's Internet Freedom Strategy' Washington, DC, February 18, 2011, http://www.state.gov.j/drl/rls/rm/157089.htm. Accessed November 19, 2013.

Posner, M. and Dibble, P.L. (2011) 'Human Rights and Democratic Reform in Iran' Statement before the Senate Foreign Relations Committee, Subcommittee on Near Eastern and South and Central Asian Affairs, Washington, DC, May 11, 2011, http://www.state.gov/j/drl/rls/rm/2011/163123.htm. Accessed November 19, 2013.

Posner, M. and Feltman, J.D. (2011) 'U.S. Human Rights Policy Towards Iran and Syria' Statement Before the House Foreign Affairs Committee, Subcommittee on the Middle East and South Asia Washington, DC, July 27, 2011, http://www.state.gov/j/drl/rls/rm/2011/169180.htm. Accessed November 19, 2013.

Posner, M. and Chamberlain Donahoe, E. (2011) 'Internet Freedom: Promoting Human Rights in the Digital Age' Press Conference Geneva Switzerland March 4, 2011, http://www.state.gov/j/drl/rls/rm/2011/162496.htm. Accessed November 19, 2013.

Powell, C. (2001) Confirmation Hearing Remarks, January 17, 2001, http://2001-2009.state.gov/secretary/former/powell/remarks/2001/443.htm. Accessed September 3, 2010.

Powell, C. (2005) 'No Country Left Behind' *Foreign Policy* January 5, 2005 http://www.foreignpolicy.com/articles/2005/01/05/no_country_left_behind?page=0,3. Accessed March 25, 2010.

OECD Ministerial Meeting (2008) *The Seoul Declaration for the Future of the Internet Economy*, June 17–18, 2008, http://www.oecd.org/dataoecd/49/28/40839436.pdf. Accessed March 25, 2010.

Obama, B. (2014) 'Remarks by the President on the Review of Signal Intelligence' Washington, DC, January 17, 2014, http://www.whitehouse.gov/the-press-office/2014/01/17/remarks-president-review-signals-intelligence. Accessed May 18, 2014.

Rice, C. (2005a) 'The Promise of Democratic Peace: Why Promoting Is the Only Realistic Path to Security' *Washington Post*, December 11, 2005: B07.

Rice, C. (2005b) Letter to Jack Straw, November 7, 2005 http://www.theregister.co.uk/2005/12/02/rice_eu_letter/. Accessed March 25, 2010.

Rice, C. (2008a) 'Rethinking the National Interest: American Realism for a New World' *Foreign Affairs* 87(4) July/August 2008, 2–26.

Rice, C. (2008b) 'New Media vs New Censorship: The Authoritarian Assault on Information' quoted in Paula Dobriansky, Remarks to Broadcasting Board of Governors, Washington, DC, September 10, 2008, http://www.state.gov/g/rls/rm/109509/htm. Accessed September 1, 2009.

Rumsfeld, D. (2005) 'Central Party School: Remarks as Prepared for Delivery by Secretary of Defense Donald H. Rumsfeld' Beijing, October 19, 2005, http://www.defenselink.mil/speeches/speech.aspx?speechid=233. Accessed July 20, 2009.

Russell, R. (2004) 'A Year Later: R&D Issues to Ensure Trustworthiness in Telecommunications and Information Systems that Directly or Indirectly Impact National Security and Emergency Preparedness' October 28, 2004.

Schwartz, A. (2011) 'Protecting Our Electronic Main Street' June 8, 2011 http://www.ntia.doc.gov/other-publication/2011/protecting-our-electronic-main-street. Accessed November 30, 2013.

Shiner, J. (2006) 'Why Global Internet Freedom Matters' *Financial Times* Op-Ed, May 5, 2006 http://www.state.gov/e/rls/rm/2006/65977.htm. Accessed October 21, 2007.

Software & Information Industry Association (2012a) 'SIIA Hails Passage of House Resolution Opposing International Internet Regulation' Washington, DC, August 2, 2012, https://www.siia.net/index.php?option=com_content&view=article&id=1109:siia-hails-unanimous-passage-of-house-resolution-opposing-international-internet-regulation-&catid=62:press-room-overview&Itemid. Accessed May 18, 2014.

Software & Information Industry Association (2012b) 'SIIA Applauds Senate Resolution Against International Internet Regulation' Washington, DC, September 19, 2012 https://www.siia.net/index.php?option=com_content&view=article&id=1129:siia-applauds-senate-resolution-against-international-internet-regulation&catid=62:press-room-overview&Itemid=1177. Accessed May 18, 2014.

Sonenshine, T. (2012a) 'Remarks at the Capstone Dinner' Washington, DC, May 17, 2012, http://www.stat.gov/r/remarks/2012/195927.htm. Accessed November 30, 2013.

Sonenshine, T. (2012b) 'The State of American Public Diplomacy' Washington, DC, June 28, 2012, http://state/gov/r/remarks/2012/195947.htm. Accessed November 30, 2013.

Sonenshine, T. and Posner, M. (2012) 'Free the Press Campaign' Washington, DC, April 18, 2012, http://fpc.state.gov/188075.htm. Accessed November 30, 2013.

Specht, M. (2006) 'State Official Calls for Flexible Telecommunications Policies: Gross Also Stresses Intellectual Property Protection, Freedom of Expression' USINFO November 21, 2006, http://usinfo.state.gov/xarchives/display.html?p=washfile-english&y=2006&m=November&x200611211817531mthceps0.3995783. Accessed June 10, 2008.

Strickling, L. (2010a) 'Remarks at the Media Institute' Washington, DC, February 24, 2010, http://www.ntia.doc.gov/speechtestimony/2010/remarks-assistant-secretary-strickling-media-institute. Accessed November 30, 2013.

Strickling, L. (2010b) 'Remarks at the Internet Society's INET Series' Washington, DC, April 29, 2010, http://www.ntia.doc.gov/print/speechtestimony.2010/remarks-assistant-secretary-strickling-internet-societys-inet-series. Accessed November 30, 2013.

Strickling, L. (2011a) 'Keynote Remarks at 40th Meeting of ICANN' San Francisco March 14, 2011, http://www.ntia.doc.gov/speechestestimony/2011/keynote-remarks-lawrence-e-strickling-assistant-secretary-commerce-communicat. Accessed November 30, 2013.

Strickling, L. (2011b) Remarks at American University's GigaNET Conference Washington, DC, May 5, 2011, http://www.ntia.doc.gov/speechtestimony/2011/remarks-assistant-secretary-strickling-american-universitys-giganet-conference. Accessed November 30, 2013.

Strickling, L. (2011c) Remarks at Internet Society's INET Conference New York June 14, 2011, http://www.ntia.doc.gov/speechtestimony/2011/keynote-remarks-assistant-secretary-strickling-internet-societys-inet-conference. Accessed November 30, 2013.

Strickling, L. (2011d) Remarks at the OECD High Level Meeting on the Internet Economy Paris June 29, 2011, http://www.ntia.doc.gov/speechtestimony/2011/keynote-remarks-assistant-secretary-strickling-oecd-high-level-meeting-internet-economy. Accessed November 30, 2013.

Strickling, L. (2011e) Remarks at the Danish Internet Governance Forum Copenhagen August 23, 2011, http://www.ntia.doc.gov/speechtestimony/2011/remarks-assistant-secretary-strickling-danish-internet-governance-forum. Accessed November 30, 2013.

Strickling, L. (2012a) Keynote Address at Silicon Flatirons Center Conference Boulder Colorado February 12, 2012, http://www.ntia.doc.gov/speechtestimony/2012/keynote-address-assistatn-secretary-strickling-silicon-flatirons-center-conference. Accessed November 30, 2013.

Strickling, L. (2012b) Keynote Speech at U.S. Chamber of Commerce Telecommunications and E-Commerce Committee Washington, DC, June 15, 2012, http://www.ntia.doc.gov/speechtestimony/2012/keynote-speech-lawrence-e-strickling-assistant-secretary-commerce-communication. Accessed November 30, 2013.

Strickling, L. (2012c) Remarks at Columbia Institute for Tele-Information New York September 26, 2012, http://www.ntia.doc.gov/speechtestimony/2012/remarks-assistant-secretary-strickling-columbia-institute-tele-information. Accessed November 30, 2013.

Strickling, L. (2012d) Remarks at Internet Governance Forum Baku Azerbaijan November 6, 2012, http://www.ntia.doc.gov/speechtestimony/2012/remarks-assistant-secretary-strickling-internet-governance-forum. Accessed November 30, 2013.

Strickling, L. (2012e) Remarks at the PLI/FCBA Telecommunications Policy & Regulation Institute Washington, DC, December 14, 2012, http://www.ntia.doc.gov/Remarks_by_Assistant_Secretary_Strickling_at_PLI/FCBA. Accessed November 30, 2013.

Sullivan, D. (2008) 'Protecting Innovation in the Global Knowledge Economy' Remarks to Software and Information Industry Association, January 31, 2008, http://2001-2009.state.gov/e/eeb/rls/rm/2008/105868.htm. Accessed March 25, 2010.

The 9/11 Commission (2004) *Recommendations on Public Diplomacy: Defending Ideals and Defining the Message*, Hearing Before the Subcommittee on National Security, Emerging Threats and International Relations of the Committee on Government Reform, House of Representatives, August 22, 2004, http://www.access.gpo.gov/congress/house/pdf/108hrg/98211.pdf. Accessed August 30, 2010.

United Nations Economic and Social Council, Commission on Science for Technology and Development (2004) *Promoting the application of science and* technology to meet the Development Goals contained in the Millennium Declaration, April 2, 2004, http://www.unctad.org/en/docs//ecn162004d2_en.pdf. Accessed March 25, 2010.

United Nations Working Group on Internet Governance. (2005) *Report of the Working Group on Internet Governance, June 2005*, http://www.wgig.org/docs/WGIGREPORT.pdf. Accessed August 29, 2008.

United Nations World Summit on the Information Society (2003) Declaration of Principles: Building the Information Society: a global challenge in the new Millennium, December 12, 2003, http://www.itu.int/wsis/docs/geneva/official/dop.html. Accessed August 30, 2010.

United Nations World Summit on the Information Societ (2005) *WSIS: Tunis Agenda for the Information Society*. November 18, 2005, http://www.itu.int/wsis/docs2/tunis/off/6rev1.html. Accessed August 29, 2010.

United States of America (2003) 'Comments on March 21st Version of the WSIS Draft Declaration and Action Plan, May 29, 2003' http://www.itu.int/dms_pub/itu-s/md/03/wsispc3/c/S03-WSISPC3-C-0047!!PDF-E.pdf. Accessed November 30, 2013.

United States of America (2003) Press Release on Outcome of WSIS, Geneva, Switzerland, December 10, 2003, http://geneva.usmission.gov/press2003/1210USWSIS.html. Accessed April 11, 2008.

United States of America (2004a) Approach to the Internet: Guiding Principles for the UN Working Group on Internet Governance, September 14, 2004, http://2001-2009.state.gov/e/eeb/cip/wsis2005/c12677.htm. Accessed March 25, 2010.

United States of America (2004b) Initial Views of the United States of America in Preparation for Phase II of the World Summit on the Information Society, Contribution to the second meeting of the Group of Friends of the Chair, http://2001-2009.state.gov/e/eeb/rls/othr/40799.htm. Accessed August 30, 2010.

United States of America (2005) Comments of the United States of America on Internet Governance, August 15, 2005, http://2001-2009.state.gov/e/eeb/rls/othr/2005/51063.htm. Accessed June 10, 2008.

United States of America (2006) Approach to the Internet: Guiding Principles for the UN Working Group on Internet Governance, May 4, 2006, www.wgig.org/docs/usa.doc. Accessed August 30, 2010.

United States of America (2012) Additional Proposals for the World Conference on International Telecommunications, October 31, 2012.

U.S. Copyright Office, *Copyright Registration for Online Works*, http://www.copyright.gov/circs/circ66.pdf. Accessed November 30, 2013.

U.S. Department of Commerce (2004) *Strategic Plan FY 2004–2009: Our Mission, Vision, Strategic Goals, and Objectives*, http://www.osec.doc.gov/bmi/budget/strategic04-1002.htm. Accessed August 30, 2010.

U.S. Department of Commerce (2011) *Cybersecurity, Innovation and the Internet Economy*, http://www.nist.gov/itl/upload/Cybersecurity_Green-Paper_Final-Version.pdf. Accessed November 19, 2013.

U.S. Department of Commerce (2012) *The Competitiveness and Innovation Capacity of the United States*, http://www.commerce.gov/sites/default/files/documents/2012/january/competes_010511_0.pdf. Accessed November 19, 2013.

U.S. Department of Commerce National Telecommunications and Information Administration (1998) Management of Internet Names and Addresses, July 1998, http://www.ecommerce.gov. Accessed August 30, 2010.

U.S. Department of Commerce National Telecommunications and Information Administration (2006) Technical and Economic Assessment of Internet Protocol Version 6 (IPv6), January 2006, http://www.ntia.doc.gov/ntiahome/ntiageneral/ipv6/final/ipv6finalTOC.htm. Accessed September 3, 2010.

U.S. Department of Defense (2004) *Report of the Defense Science Board on Strategic Communications 2004*, http://www.fas.org/irp/agency/dod/dsb/commun.pdf. Accessed August 30, 2010.

U.S. Department of Defense (2008) *Report of the Defense Science Board on Strategic Communications 2008*, http://www.businessfordiplomaticaction.org/action/2008_01_strategic_co_1c55f0.pdf. Accessed August 30, 2010.

U.S. Department of Homeland Security (2003) *The National Strategy to Secure Cyberspace*, February 2003, http://www.dhs.gov/xlibrary/assets/National_Cyberspace_Strategy.pdf. Accessed August 30, 2010.

U.S. Department of Homeland Security. National Security Telecommunications Advisory Committee. *NSTAC Report to the President on International Communications*. August 16, 2007, http://www.ncs.gov/nstac/reports/2007/NSTAC%20International%20Report.pdf. Accessed August 30, 2010.

U.S. Department of Justice (2006) *Progress Report on the Department of Justice's Task Force on Intellectual Property*, http://www.justice.gov/criminal/cybercrime/2006IPTFProgressReport%286-19-06%29.pdf. Accessed March 25, 2010.

U.S. Department of State Advisory Commission on Public Diplomacy (2003) *The New Diplomacy: Utilizing Innovative Concepts that Recognize Resource Restraints*, http://www.state.gov/documents/organization/22956.pdf. Accessed August 30, 2010.

U.S. Department of State (2004–2005) *Digital Freedom Initiative Annual Report, 2004–2005*, http://www.volunteersforprosperity.gov/news/2004-2005_DFI_Annual_Report_3-23-05.pdf. Accessed March 25, 2010.

U.S. Department of State (2005) Advisory Commission on Public Diplomacy, *2005 Report of the Advisory Commission on Public Diplomacy*. http://www.state.gov/documents/organization/55989.pdf. Accessed August 30, 2010.

U.S. Department of State (2006a) *2005 Country Reports on Human Rights: Introduction*, http://www.state.gov/g/drl/rls/hrrpt/2005/61550.htm. Accessed October 1, 2009.

U.S. Department of State (2006b) Bureau of International Information Programs *Global Issues: Media Emerging*, http://www.america.gov/media/pdf/ejs/0306ej.pdf. Accessed August 30, 2010.

U.S. Department of State (2006c) 'Global Internet Freedom Task Force (GIFT): A Blueprint for Action' http://2001-2009.state.gov/g/drl/rls/78340.htm. Accessed July 20, 2009.

U.S. Department of State (2006d) Summary of Global Internet Freedom Task Force Fact Sheet, http://usinfo.state.gov/xarchives/display.html?p=texttrans-englsh&y=2006&m=December&x=20061220173640xjsnommis0.7082331. Accessed June 10, 2008.

U.S. Department of State (2007a) *2006 Country Reports on Human Rights Practices: Introduction*, http://www.state.gov/g/drl/rls/hrrpt/2006/78717.htm. Accessed October 1, 2009.

U.S. Department of State (2007b) *2006 Country Reports on Human Rights Practices: Iran*, http://www.state.gov/g/drl/rls/hrrpt/2006/78852.htm. Accessed October 1, 2009.

U.S. Department of State (2007c) Bureau of Public Affairs 'United States Supports Press Freedom Worldwide' http://2001-2009.state.gov/r/pa/scp/84025.htm. Accessed September 14, 2010.

U.S. Department of State (2007d) *Private Sector Summit on Public Diplomacy: Models for Action*, http://www.instituteforpr.org/files/uploads/PrivSectorSummitPaper.pdf. Accessed April 22, 2010.

U.S. Department of State (2007e) Strategic Communications and Public Diplomacy Policy Coordinating Committee, *U.S. National Strategy for Public Diplomacy and Strategic Communications*, http://uscpublicdiplomacy.org/pdfs/stratcommo_plan_070531.pdf. Accessed August 30, 2010.

U.S. Department of State (2008) Bureau of Democracy, Human Rights and Labour. Request for Proposals: Promoting the Freedom of Expression and the Free Flow of Information through Technology, https://www.devex.com/en/projects/freedom-of-expression-and-information-through-technology-worldwide. Accessed November 30, 2013.

U.S. Department of State (2009) 'Funding Opportunity Title: New Empowerment Communication Technologies: Opportunities in the Middle East and North Africa' http://mepi.state.gov/opportunities/129624.htm. Accessed September 29, 2009.

U.S. Department of State (2011) 'Background Briefing by Senior State Department Officials on Internet Freedom Programs' June 15, 2011, http://www.state.gov/j/drl/rls/rm/2011/166295.htm. Accessed November 19, 2013.

U.S. Department of State (2012) Advisory Committee on International Communications and Information Policy Membership List, March 28, 2012, http://www.state.gov/e/eb/adcom/acicip/rls/120676.rtm. Accessed November 19, 2013.

U.S. General Accounting Office (2003a) *U.S. International Broadcasting: New Strategic Approach Focuses on Reaching Large Audience but Lacks Measurable Program Objectives*, http://www.gao.gov/cgi-bin/getpt?GAO-03-772. Accessed June 10, 2008.

U.S. General Accounting Office (2003b) *U.S. Public Diplomacy: State Department Expands Efforts but Faces Significant Challenges*, http://www.gao.gov/cgi-bin/getrpt?GAO-03-51. Accessed November 30, 2013.

U.S. Government Accountability Office (2005) *U.S. Public Diplomacy: Interagency Coordination Efforts Hampered by the Lack of a National Communication Strategy*, http://www.gao.gov/cgi-bin/getrpt?GAO-05-323. Accessed November 30, 2013.

U.S. Government Accountability Office (2006a) *Telecommunications: Broadband Deployment Is Extensive throughout the United States, but It Is Difficult to Assess the Extent of Deployment Gaps in Rural Areas*, http://www.gao.gov/new.items/d06426.pdf. Accessed June 20, 2009.

U.S. Government Accountability Office (2006b) *Intellectual Property: Strategy for Targeting Organized Piracy (STOP) Requires Changes for Long-term Success*, http://www.gao.gov/cgi-bin/getrpt?GAO-07-74. Accessed June 10, 2008.

U.S. Patent and Trademark Office (2007) *International Copyright Relations of the United States, 2007*, http://www.copyright.gov/circs/circ38a.pdf. Accessed September 3, 2010.

United States Trade Representative (2007) 'United States Files WTO Cases Against China Over Deficiencies in China's Intellectual Property Rights Laws and Market Access Barriers to Copyright-Based Industries' April 4, 2007, http://www.ustr.gov/Document_Library/Press_Releases/2007/April/United_States_Files_WTO_Cases_Against_China_Over_Deficiencies_in_Chinas_Intellectual_Property_Rights_Laws_Market_Access_Barr_printer.html. Accessed April 4, 2009.

United States Trade Representative (2008) *Results of the 2008 Section 1377 Review of Telecommunications Trade Agreements*, http://ustraderep.gov/assets/Trade_Sectors/Telecom-E-commerce/Section_1377/asset_upload_file386_14697.pdf. Accessed March 25, 2010.

United States Trade Representative (2008–2012) *Special 301 Report Priority Watch List*, http://www.ustr.gov/about-us/press-office/reports-and-publications/2013/2013-special-301-report (home page). Accessed November 30, 2013.

U.S. Trade Representative (2003) *USTR Special 301 Report 2003*, http://www.ustr.gov/assets/Document_Library/Reports_Publications/2003/2003_Special_301_Report/asset_upload_file665_6124.pdf. Accessed April 1, 2009.

U.S. Trade Representative (2005) *Out of Cycle Trade Review 2005*, http://www.ustr.gov/assets/Document_Library/Reports_Publications/2005/2005_Special_301/asset_upload_file835_7647.pdf. Accessed April 1, 2009.

U.S. Trade Representative (2007) 'United States Files WTO Cases Against China Over Deficiencies in China's Intellectual Property Rights Laws and Market Access Barriers to Copyright-Based Industries', http://www.ustr.gov/Document_Library/Press_Releases/2007/April/United_States_Files_WTO_Cases_Against_China_Over_Deficiencies_in_Chinas_Intellectual_Property_Rights_Laws_Market_Access_Barr_printer.html. Accessed April 4, 2009.

U.S. Trade Representative (2008) 'China to End Restrictions on Suppliers of Financial Information Services Challenged by United States in WTO Dispute', http://www.ustr.gov/about-us/press-office/press-releases/archives/2008/november/china-end-restrictions-suppliers-financi. Accessed November 30, 2013.

U.S. Trade Representative (2009) *Results of the 2008 Section 1377 Review of Telecommunications Trade Agreements*, http://ustraderep.gov/assets/Trade_Sectors/Telecom-E-commerce/Section_1377/asset_upload_file386_14697.pdf. Accessed March 25, 2010.

Wayne, E. Anthony (2002) Testimony before the House Appropriations Committee, Subcommittee on Commerce, Justice, State, the Judiciary and Related Agencies, http://2001-2009.state.gov/e/eeb/rls/rm/2002/9645.htm. Accessed September 10, 2010

White House Office of the U.S. Intellectual Property Rights Coordinator (2007) *Strategy for Targeting Organized Piracy: Accomplishments and Initiatives*.

White House Office of the U.S. Intellectual Property Enforcement Coordinator (2010) *2010 Joint Strategic Plan on Intellectual Property Enforcement*.

White House Office of Science and Technology Policy (1994) *Science in the National Interest*, August 1994, http://clinton1.nara.gov/White_House/EOP/OSTP/Science/html/Sitni_Home.html. Accessed September 10, 2010.

White House Office of Science and Technology Policy (2006) *American Competitiveness Initiative: Leading the World in Innovation*.

White House (1997) *Framework for Global Electronic Commerce, July 4, 1997*, http://clinton4.nara.gov/WH/New/Commerce/. Accessed August 30, 2010.

White House (2002) *The National Security Strategy 2002*, http://georgewbush-whitehouse.archives.gov/nsc/nss/2002/. Accessed April 18, 2010.

White House (2003a) 'Executive Order: Establishing the Office of Global Communications', http://www.whitehouse.gov/news/releases/2003/01/20030 121-3.html. Accessed June 10, 2008.

White House (2003b) *The Office of Global Communications* (home page) http://georgewbush-whitehouse.archives.gov/ogc/. Accessed April 18, 2009.

White House (2006) *The National Security Strategy 2006*, http://georgewbush-whitehouse.archives.gov/nsc/nss/2006/. Accessed April 18, 2010.

White House (2006) *National Strategy for Combating Terrorism 2006*, http://www.globalsecurity.org/security/library/policy/national/counter_terrorism_strategy.pdf. Accessed April 18, 2010.

White House (2011a) *A Strategy for American Innovation: Securing our Economic Growth and Prosperity*, http://www.whitehouse.gov/innovation/strategy. Accessed November 30, 2013.

White House (2011b) *International Strategy for Cyberspace*, http://www.whitehouse.gov/sites/default/files/rss_viewer/international_strategy_for_cyberspace.pdf. Accessed November 30, 2013.

Wiley Rein LLP (2013) http://www.wileyrein.com/index.cfm. Accessed May 18, 2014.

World Bank (2013) Global Information and Communications Technologies, Mission and Strategies, http://web.worldbank.org/WBSITE/EXTERNAL/TOPICS/EXTINFORMATIONANDCOMMUNICATIONANDTECHNOLOGIES/0,,contentMDK:20687829~menuPK:1785618~pagePK:210058~piPK:210062~theSitePK:282823,00.html (home page). Accessed November 30, 2013.

World Trade Organization (2009) WTO Issues Panel Report on US-China Dispute over Intellectual Property Rights, http://www.wto.org/english/news_e/news09_e/362r_e.htm. Accessed November 30, 2013.

Zoellick, R. (2004) Remarks, Electronic Industries Alliance Government Industry Dinner, http://www.eia.org/news/pressreleases//2004-05-26.159.phtml. Accessed March 25, 2010.

Interviews

David A. Gross, Former Ambassador for International Information and Communications Policy, George W. Bush Administration. Interview with Author, July 14, 2008.

Michael R. Nelson, Former Special Assistant for Information Technology at the White House Office of Science and Technology Policy, Clinton Administration. Interview with Author, July 3, 2008.

Richard A. Russell, Former Deputy Director of the White House Office for Science and Technology Policy, George W. Bush Administration. Interview with Author, September 12, 2008.

U.S. Department of Commerce Official *A*. Interview with Author, July 16, 2008.

U.S. Department of State Official *A*. Interviews with Author, July 24, 2008 and September 12, 2008.

U.S. Department of State Official *B*. Interview with Author, July 16, 2008.

U.S. Department of State Official *C*. Interview with Author, September 12, 2008.

Irene Wu, Director of Research, International Bureau, Federal Communications Commission. Interview with Author, July 31, 2008.

Index

Actor-Network Theory, 5, 51, 164n8
actors, design process, 38–9
Adorno, Theodor, 48
agents, technology, 68–9
Agricultural Age, 29
Amazon, 98, 125
American foreign policy, 163
  analysing policy rhetoric, 12–15
  Bush and Obama, 80–2
  free flow of information, 82–6
  Internet politics, 5, 9–11
  Open Door, 9–10, 16, 75–9, 110–11, 141–2
  pursuing net dividends, 86–8
Arab Spring, 68, 95, 112

Baer, Daniel, 103, 106
Barrett, Edward W., 82
BBG (Broadcasting Board of Governors), 12, 117–19
Beaird, Richard, 127, 128, 169n19
Beers, Charlotte, 84
Berman, Marshall, 32
Biden, Joe, 140
Bush administration, 12, 14, 108, 134
  American foreign policy, 74, 80–2
  communications policy, 83–4, 87

capitalism, 7, 20, 37, 170n7
  free-market, 131
  international politics, 62–4
  liberal democratic, 81–2, 84, 147, 161
  Marx critique of, 49
  momentum and, 36
  Open Door, 75
  production, 48
  social property relations, 57
  technology, 44–5, 59
  United States, 7, 78, 100, 169n4
censorship, 17, 32
  China, 143, 145

Internet, 64, 93–4, 96, 102, 105–9, 115–17, 118–20
China, 56, 76, 97, 99, 154
  censorship, 93–4, 115–16, 119–20, 143, 145
  denial of democracy, 115
  economic development, 126
  espionage, 11
  intellectual property rights, 143–5
  NSA leaks, 156
Clinton, Hillary, 85, 106, 112, 116, 171n7
Clinton administration, 84
Cohen, G. A., 46–7, 51, 151, 167n3
COINTELPRO surveillance, 155
Cold War, 2, 84, 109, 116, 159
consumer sovereignty, 172n11
Critical Discourse Analysis (CDA), 12, 15
culture, institutional power of material, 66–70, 167n10
cyber power, 68
cybersecurity, 11, 14, 65, 110, 112, 116, 136, 155, 173n15

DDoS (Distributed Denial of Service), 25, 119, 171n11
democracy promotion, Internet, 111–17
DeNardis, Laura, 34–6
Der Derian, James, 31–2
Dialectic of Enlightenment (Horkheimer and Adorno), 49, 151, 167n6
disconnection, Internet, 92–7
discourse analysis guide, 162–3
Domain Name Servers (DNS), 90
Domain Name System, 108, 134
domination
  capitalism, 48, 76–7
  Internet, 99
  of nature, 49, 50
  liberalism, 76
  power as, 30, 56

Eagleton, Terry, 69, 138
EEB (Bureau of Economic, Energy and Business Affairs), 13, 117
Enlightenment, 49, 151

Facebook, 34, 68, 86, 91, 98, 110, 112, 145, 155, 156
Feenberg, Andrew, 7, 16, 44, 50, 71, 151
filtering, Internet, 90–1, 93–6, 101–2, 115, 117–20, 135, 143, 145, 156
First World War, 1, 164n1, 170n7
foreign direct investment, 96, 140, 156
FOSS (free and open source), 124–6, 128, 172n9
Founding Fathers, 138–9
Frankfurt School, 30, 48, 49, 50, 71, 151, 160, 167n5
Freedom Online Coalition, 119
free flow of information, 9, 12, 16, 17, 25, 88, 136, 140, 153
  bias of network, 93
  cost of filtering, 94, 96, 99
  democracy, 111–17
  denial of, 102
  free markets and societies, 82–6
  future of, 154–6
  human rights and Internet openness, 102–11
  Internet, 39, 67, 69, 89–92, 101–2, 121
  responsibility of, 117–20
free software development model, 124–5

Gallagher, Michael, 133, 134
GIFT (Global Internet Task Force), 110, 171n7
Glassman, James K., 113
global economy, Internet as uneven, 97–9
Globalization Theory, 29
global politics, power of, 43–4
GNU–GPL (GNU–General Public License), 125, 172n4
Google, 91, 94, 98, 100, 141, 155, 156, 173n12
Gore, Al, 84

Gross, David A., 13, 84, 104, 112, 127, 140, 168n19

Habermas, Jurgen, 49, 50, 151, 167n7
hard power, 23–5, *see also* power
Hartz, Louis, 76
Hay, John, 76
Herrera, Geoffrey, 32–40, 165n2
historical materialism, 5, 43–73,151–4, 164n8, 166–9
  critical theory of technology, 50–5
  institutional power of material culture, 66–70
  international politics of technology, 62–6
  Marxist technological essentialism, 45–50
  Marxist technological instrumentalism, 44–5
  power, information technology and 'International', 55
  productive power, 59–62
  structural power, 56–9
Horkheimer, Max, 48
Hughes, Thomas, 33, 36, 53
human agency, 5, 20, 22, 26, 30, 32, 33, 36, 41, 45, 50, 114, 150, 166n16
human rights, Internet openness, 102–11

ICANN (Internet Corporation for Assigned Names and Numbers), 13, 40, 55, 122, 164n7, 169n21, 172n3
ICCPR (International Covenant on Civil and Political Rights), 104, 170n10
ICTs (information communications technologies), 5, 19–20, 41–2
  power, momentum and political economy of technology, 35–41
  social construction of, 32–5
  structuralist determinism, 30–2
  technological essentialism, 19, 28–9
  technological instrumentalism, 19, 21–8
  techno-optimists, 29–30
  techno-pessimists, 30–2

ideology, 5, 24, 44, 47, 59, 61, 69, 79, 113, 138, 151, 169n4
IGF (Internet Governance Forum), 39, 40, 55, 142, 173n20
Ikenberry, G. John, 78–9
India, 98, 126, 134
information, *see* free flow of information; ICT (information communications technologies)
Information Age, 29
information technology
  power and 'International," 55
  social construction of, 32–5
innovation, 163
  models of software, 124–7
  property, private sector and, 127–31
institutional power, material culture, 66–70, 165–6n9
Intellectual Property Rights (IPRs), 13, 17, 37, 102, 111, 143–4, 146, 153, 156
  innovation, 163
  innovation and, 127–31
  piracy threat, 136–42
  politics and piracy, 131–5
  software innovation, 124–7
International
  power, information technology and, 55
  technology, 63–4
International Political Economy, 66
International Relations (IR)
  future directions, 158–61
  power and technology, 151–2
  social construction of information technology, 32–5
  technology in, 1–6
International Relations Theory, 4, 54–5, 149
Internet
  analysing policy rhetoric, 12–15
  democracy promotion, 111–17
  disconnection costs, 92–7
  filtering, 90–1, 93–6, 101–2, 115, 117–20, 135, 143, 145, 156
  free flow of information, 82–6
  governance, 38–41, 173n12
  human rights and, openness, 102–11

  as a market, 97–9
  net neutrality, 22, 26, 90–1, 114, 142, 171–2n1
  Open Door policy, 9–13, 121, 123, 135, 147, 153
  politics, 9–11
  power of, 88–92
  rejecting values, 92–7
  representation of, 162
  technology, 5–6
  techno-optimism, 29–30
  techno-pessimism, 30–2
  threat of piracy, 135–42
  uneven global economy, 97–9
Internet policy, United States
  locating identity of private sector, 131–5
  models of software innovation, 124–7
  piracy, 131–5
  private sector and innovation, 127–31
  property rights, 124–7
  technological closure and structural power, 142–6
  threat of Internet piracy, 135–42
Internet Task Force Cybersecurity Green Paper of 2011, 39

Johnson, Lyndon, 82, 90

Kautsky, Karl, 45
Kennedy administration, 82
Keohane, Robert, 22–7, 56, 150
Keynesianism, 63, 78, 86

labour power, 46
Liberal Institutional approach, 63
Libya, 81

Marburger, John, 87
Marcuse, Herbert, 48
market, Internet as, 97–9
markets, 163
Marx, 97, 167n4
Marxism, 6, 16, 29, 43–73
  critical theory of technology, 50–5
  degenerating into barbarism, 47–50
  evolving towards socialism, 45–7

Marxism – *continued*
  institutional power of material culture, 66–70
  International Relations theory, 7
  pessimistic technological essentialism, 47–50
  position of labour, 58
  power, information technology, and 'the International,' 55
  productive power, 59–62
  state theory, 168*n*18
  states and capitals in international politics of technology, 62–6
  structural power, 56–9
  technological essentialism, 45–7
  technological instrumentalism, 44–5
May, Christopher, 130
Merkel, Angela, 154
Military–Industrial–Media–Entertainment network (MIME), 31
momentum, 53
  concept of, 54
  information technology, 35–7
Morgenthau, Hans, 2
Mueller, Milton, 11, 35, 40, 55, 65, 91, 172*n*5, 173*n*18, 178*n*20
multilateralism, Obama administration, 81–2

National Export Initiative, 87
natural security, 14, 77–9, 85, 124, 136–7, 141, 154–8, 160*n*1
National Security Agency (NSA), 15, 17, 85, 154–5
National Security Council, 68
neo–Trotskyism, 6
Niebhur, Reinhold, 2
NTIA (National Telecommunications and Information Administration), 65
Nye, Joseph, 22–7, 56, 150

Obama administration, 12–15
  American foreign policy, 80–2
  global information networks, 88
  international communications policy, 83–4
  Internet governance, 108–10, 132
  intervention government, 135
  multilateralism, 81–2
  Open Door policy, 74
  public diplomacy, 85–6
  Strategy for American Innovation, 138
  Strategy for Cyberspace, 128–9
  telecommunications policy, 65
Obama Doctrine, 82
Open Door
  American foreign policy, 9–10, 16, 75–9, 110–11, 141–2
  international communications, 86–8
  Internet policy, 9–13, 121, 123, 135, 147, 153
  national security, 79
  nature of policy, 74
  political ideas, 169–70*n*4
OSCE (Organization for Security and Cooperation in Europe), 106, 154

Peacefire.org, 118
piracy
  politics and, 131–5
  threat of Internet, 135–42
Political Marxism, 6, 59
Posner, Michael, 109, 111, 117
power, 3
  as domination, 30, 56
  faces of, 25
  form of causation, 27
  future of US, after Snowden, 154–8
  hard, 23–5
  information technology and 'International', 55
  institutional, 66–70
  institutional, of material culture, 66–70
  international relations, 6–9
  Internet, 88–92
  Internet governance, 38–41
  political economy of technology, 35–41
  productive, 46–7, 59–62, 122
  soft, 23–5, 26–7
  structural, 56–9, 142–6, 168*n*12
  technological essentialism, 28–9
  understanding technology and, 27–8

power of objects, 28–9, 41, 53
PRISM, NSA, 154, 155
privacy, 118, 140
private sector
  property and innovation, 127–31
  piracy, 131–5
productive power, 46–7, 59–62, 122
proprietary software model, 125–6
public speech, 64, 94

Radio Farda, 93, 117
Radio Sawa, 93, 117
Reagan, Ronald, 83
realism, 35, 81, 82
realist, 3, 10, 23, 63, 79, 82, 160, 165n2, 168n18
Rice, Condoleezza, 84, 112
Rosenau, James, 21–2
Rumsfeld, Donald, 84
Russia, 32, 99, 106, 154, 156

Science and Technology Studies (STS), 3–5, 7, 17, 33, 35–6, 71, 148
SCOT (Social Construction of Technology), 15, 37–8, 43–4, 50–1, 53, 150–1
  between essentialism and instrumentalism, 32–5
Second World War, 1, 78, 151, 155
securitization, 8, 14
Shultz, George, 83
Snowden, Edward, 15, 85, 154–8
socialism, 45–7
social media, 34, 86, 98, 112, 145
social-property relations, 57
soft power, 23–5
  generation of, 26–7
  see also power
software innovation, 124–7
sovereignty, 105–6
Soviet Union, 45, 83, 84, 109, 158
Special 301, 137, 142, 144, 173n19
Stallman, Richard, 125
states and capitals, international politics, 62–6
state theory, Marxist, 168n18
Strickling, Lawrence, 133
structuralist determinism, 30–2
structural power, 168n12

technological closure and, 142–6
and technological design, 56–9

technological closure, 52–3, 99–100
  democracy promotion, 111–17
  human rights and Internet openness, 102–11
  responsibility, 117–20
  structural power, 142–6
technological essentialism, 19, 28–9
  pessimistic, 47–50
  techno-pessimists, 30–2
technological instrumentalism, 19, 21–8, 44–5
technology
  closure, 52–3, 99–100
  critical theory of, 50–5
  design critique, 50–1
  international politics of, 62–6, 151–4
  International Relations and, 158–61
  Internet, 5–6
  path dependency of, 54
  physical construction of, 51–2
  place in International Relations, 1–6
  power, momentum and political economy of, 35–41
  power and international relations, 6–9
  productive power defining design of, 59–62
  structural power of design, 56–9
Thailand, 67, 70, 99
Transmission Control Protocol/ Internet Protocol (TCP/IP), 90–2
TRIPs (Trade Related Aspects of Intellectual Property Rights), 129, 142–4, 173n18, 173n20
Turner, Frederick Jackson, 75–6
Twitter, 34, 68, 86, 95, 98, 112, 145

UN Declaration of Human Rights (UDHR), 100, 103–5
UNESCO (United Nations Economic, Scientific and Cultural Organization), 81
uneven and combined development (U&CD), 8–9, 37, 44, 55, 64, 66, 159

United States
  capitalism in, 7, 78, 100, 169n4
  national security, 14, 77–9, 85, 124, 136–7, 141, 154–8, 160n1
  Thailand and, 67
  see also Internet policy, United States
USAID (United States Agency for International Development), 117–18

Voice of America, 93, 117, 119

War on Terror, 84, 85
Williams, Raymond, 27, 169n2
Williams, William A., 75–6, 169n3, 169–70n4, 170n7
World Bank, 87, 115, 129

World Conference on International Telecommunications, 65, 172n7
World Summit on the Information Society (WSIS), 103, 104, 127–9, 133–4, 172n5
World Telecommunications Standardization Assembly, 105
World War I, 76, *see also* First World War
World War II, *see* Second World War
Writson, Walter, 29
WTO (World Trade Organization), 28, 123, 129, 142–6, 159

Yahoo!, 98, 100, 141
YouTube, 86, 98, 145

Zoellick, Robert, 84

Printed and bound by CPI Group (UK) Ltd, Croydon, CR0 4YY